M000087302

The New Controller Guidebook

Fourth Edition

Steven M. Bragg

Published by AccountingTools, Inc., Centennial, Colorado.

For more information about AccountingTools® products, visit our Web site at www.accountingtools.com.

ISBN-13: 978-1-938910-87-6

Printed in the United States of America

Table of Contents

Preface

The controller position has many responsibilities, which can seem overwhelming to someone new to the job. *The New Controller Guidebook* eases the transition into the controller role by describing each responsibility, noting which ones are the most critical, and showing how to manage them properly.

In Chapters 1 through 10, we address the key management aspects of the job, including the management of cash, billings, collections, inventory, fixed assets, accounts payable, and payroll. We also cover management of the accounting department as a whole. In Chapters 11-15, we address all aspects of reporting, such as closing the books, the different formats available for the financial statements, the extra reports to be issued by a publicly-held company, and a variety of management reports and ratios. We then move to planning considerations in Chapters 16-17, with discussions of the entire system of budgets and capital budgeting. Finally, we cover how to select and install an accounting computer system.

You can find the answers to many questions about controllership in the following chapters, including:

- Which tasks should be handled by the chief financial officer?
- How do I construct a cash forecast?
- How do I manage the collection of overdue accounts receivable?
- How do I set up an inventory record keeping system?
- How can I improve the process flow of accounts payable?
- What methods are available for streamlining the payroll function?
- How do I use queue management to improve the accounting department?
- What steps should I follow to close the books?
- Which reports and ratios are of the most use for analysis purposes?
- How do I set up a system of budgets?
- How do I select and install an accounting computer system?

The New Controller Guidebook is designed for both professional accountants and students. Professionals can use it as a reference tool for improving the operation of their accounting departments, while it provides students with an overview of what to expect when they become controllers. Given its complete coverage of the controllership topic, *The New Controller Guidebook* may earn a permanent place on your book shelf.

Centennial, Colorado
April 2017

About the Author

Steven Bragg, CPA, has been the chief financial officer or controller of four companies, as well as a consulting manager at Ernst & Young. He received a master's degree in finance from Bentley College, an MBA from Babson College, and a Bachelor's degree in Economics from the University of Maine. He has been a two-time president of the Colorado Mountain Club, and is an avid alpine skier, mountain biker, and certified master diver. Mr. Bragg resides in Centennial, Colorado. He has written the following books and courses:

7 Habits of Effective CFOs
7 Habits of Effective Controllers
Accountant Ethics [for multiple states]
Accountants' Guidebook
Accounting Changes and Error Corrections
Accounting Controls Guidebook
Accounting for Casinos and Gaming
Accounting for Derivatives and Hedges
Accounting for Earnings per Share
Accounting for Inventory
Accounting for Investments
Accounting for Intangible Assets
Accounting for Leases
Accounting for Managers
Accounting for Stock-Based Compensation
Accounting Procedures Guidebook
Agricultural Accounting
Behavioral Ethics
Bookkeeping Guidebook
Budgeting
Business Combinations and Consolidations
Business Insurance Fundamentals
Business Ratios
Business Valuation
Capital Budgeting
CFO Guidebook
Change Management
Closing the Books
Coaching and Mentoring
Constraint Management
Construction Accounting
Corporate Cash Management
Corporate Finance
Cost Accounting (college textbook)
Cost Accounting Fundamentals
Fair Value Accounting
Financial Analysis
Financial Forecasting and Modeling
Fixed Asset Accounting
Foreign Currency Accounting
Fraud Examination
GAAP Guidebook
Governmental Accounting
Health Care Accounting
Hospitality Accounting
How to Run a Meeting
Human Resources Guidebook
IFRS Guidebook
Interpretation of Financial Statements
Inventory Management
Investor Relations Guidebook
Lean Accounting Guidebook
Mergers & Acquisitions
Negotiation
New Controller Guidebook
Nonprofit Accounting
Partnership Accounting
Payables Management
Payroll Management
Project Accounting
Project Management
Public Company Accounting
Purchasing Guidebook
Real Estate Accounting
Records Management
Recruiting and Hiring
Revenue Recognition
Sales and Use Tax Accounting
The MBA Guidebook
The Soft Close

(continued)

Cost Management Guidebook
Credit & Collection Guidebook
Developing and Managing Teams
Employee Onboarding
Enterprise Risk Management
The Statement of Cash Flows
The Year-End Close
Treasurer's Guidebook
Working Capital Management

On-Line Resources by Steven Bragg

Steven maintains the accountingtools.com web site, which contains continuing professional education courses, the Accounting Best Practices podcast, and hundreds of articles on accounting subjects.

The New Controller Guidebook is also available as a continuing professional education (CPE) course. You can purchase the course (and many other courses) and take an on-line exam at:

www.accountingtools.com/cpe

Chapter 1
The Controller Job Description

Introduction

You have just been hired or promoted into the controller position for the first time. It is necessary to appear like the consummate professional, but how to do so, what to do, and – above all – where to begin? In this chapter, we summarize the job descriptions of both the controller and the CFO. It is very helpful to know what the CFO does, so that the two of you do not end up in conflict over responsibilities. In addition, we walk through the most important activities to address during the first few days and weeks on the job, just to ensure that you pay attention to those areas most likely to cause problems.

Related Podcast Episodes: Episodes 87 and 123 of the Accounting Best Practices Podcast discuss the CFO and controller job positions, respectively. You can listen to them at: **accountingtools.com/podcasts** or **iTunes**

The Controller Job Description

The controller is responsible for all of the accounting operations within a business. This responsibility can be split into the following five general areas:

- *Management*. This involves overseeing the operations of the accounting staff, as well as of any outsourced activities. There should also be a management infrastructure in place, such as policies, procedures, and calendars of activities.
- *Transactions*. This involves the proper processing of all types of business transactions, which includes supplier invoices, billings to customers, payroll, and cash receipts and disbursements. It also requires the use of a system of controls to ensure that transactions are processed properly, and a record keeping system in which transactions are recorded and archived.
- *Reporting*. This involves the preparation of the standard set of monthly financial statements, as well as a variety of management reports.
- *Planning*. This involves coordinating the creation of the annual budget, as well as the investigation and reporting of any subsequent variances between it and actual results.
- *Compliance*. This involves compliance with a variety of tax reporting requirements, government reports, debt covenants, and accounting standards.

More specifically, the controller's job includes the following tasks:

Management

- Manage the operations of the accounting department.
- Oversee the activities of any supplier to which functions have been outsourced.
- Oversee the accounting operations of any subsidiaries of the parent company.
- Maintain a system of accounting policies and procedures.

Transactions

- Verify that supplier invoices should be paid, and pay them by the designated due date, taking early payment discounts where this is economical to do so.
- Issue invoices to customers as soon as goods have been sold or services delivered.
- Collect accounts receivable promptly.
- Process payroll information with minimal errors, and issue compensation payments to employees by scheduled pay dates.
- Record cash receipts in a timely manner and deposit them promptly.
- Complete bank reconciliations for all bank accounts at regular intervals.
- Make scheduled debt payments as needed.
- Operate an adequate accounting software package.
- Maintain a chart of accounts that fulfills the record keeping needs of the business.
- Maintain an orderly filing system for all paper-based accounting records, including a system of document archiving and destruction.
- Maintain a comprehensive system of controls over all accounting functions.

Reporting

- Compile and issue accurate financial statements on a timely basis.
- If the company is publicly-held, prepare reports for filing with the Securities and Exchange Commission.
- Measure the financial and operational performance of the business and report this information in ongoing reports to management.
- Prepare various financial analyses for management.
- Assist in the preparation of the company's annual report.
- Provide information needed by outside auditors to examine the company's financial statements and accounting system.

Planning

- Coordinate the creation of the annual budget, as well as testing it for achievability.
- Calculate variances between actual and budgeted results, and report the reasons for the variances to management.

Compliance

- Monitor the company's compliance with debt covenants and warn management of covenant breaches.
- Comply with any filing requirements imposed by local, state, or federal governing authorities.
- Comply with all tax reporting and payment requirements.

In short, most of the controller responsibilities involve detailed "nuts and bolts" transactions and their summarization into the financial statements. In essence, this is a middle management position that involves a large amount of staff and process monitoring. In addition, the controller reports to the chief financial officer, whose position is described in the next section.

The Chief Financial Officer Job Description

If there is a chief financial officer (CFO) as well as a controller, there can be some confusion about separating the responsibilities of the two positions. The job description noted in this section represents the normal set of responsibilities for a CFO, which encompasses the administrative, financial, and risk management aspects of a business. The job can be split into the following five general areas:

- *Planning.* This involves the formulation of the strategic direction of the business and the tactical plans, budgeting systems, and performance metrics required to achieve that direction.
- *Operations.* This involves the direct oversight of a number of departments, as well as coordinating the operations of those departments with other areas of the business. It can also include the selection, purchase, and subsequent integration of acquired businesses.
- *Financial information.* This involves the compilation of financial information into financial statements, and the presentation of this information to various internal and external recipients.
- *Risk management.* This involves understanding the current and potential risks to which the business is subjected and taking steps to mitigate those risks.
- *Financing.* This involves monitoring projected cash balances and arranging for either additional financing or investment options, depending on the amount of expected cash balances.

More specifically, the CFO's job includes the following tasks:

Planning

- Develop a strategic direction for the business, along with supporting tactics.
- Monitor the progress of the company in meeting its strategic goals.
- Oversee the formulation of the annual budget.
- Develop a system of performance metrics that support the company's strategic direction.

Operations

- Manage the accounting, treasury, tax, legal, human resources, and investor relations departments.
- Oversee the activities of any supplier to which functions have been outsourced.
- Participate in the functions and decisions of the executive management team.
- Implement operational best practices throughout his or her areas of responsibility.
- Engage in acquisition selection, purchase negotiations, and acquiree integration into the business.

Financial Information

- Oversee the compilation of financial information into financial statements, with accompanying disclosures.
- If the company is publicly-held, certify the financial statements filed with the Securities and Exchange Commission (SEC) as part of the Forms 10-Q and 10-K.
- Report financial results to management, the board of directors, and the investment community.

Risk Management

- Understand the current and potential risks to which the business is subjected.
- Take steps to mitigate risks, including the use of control systems, shifting risk to other parties, and insurance coverage.
- Report on risk issues to the board of directors.
- Ensure that the business complies with all regulatory and other legal requirements.
- Monitor known legal issues involving the company, as well as legal issues impacting the entire industry.
- Review and act upon the findings and recommendations of internal and external auditors.

Financing

- Monitor projected cash balances.
- Arrange for financing to meet future cash requirements.
- Invest excess funds based on projected cash balances.
- Invest funds on behalf of the company pension plan.
- Maintain relationships with banks, lenders, investors, investment bankers, and outside analysts.

Even the most cursory examination of the controller and CFO job descriptions reveals that the two positions are very different. The controller is responsible for the "nuts and bolts" daily operations of the accounting department, as well as for creating the financial statements and other reports. The CFO has a much broader and higher-level role, being responsible for planning, finances, risk management, and the management of a number of areas besides the accounting department.

In practice, the CFO is the supervisor of the controller, and so has the power to shift tasks between the two positions. Consequently, the controller may be placed in a more restricted or comprehensive role than what has been outlined here.

There is some duplication in the roles of the controller and CFO, as described in the preceding job descriptions. In particular:

- *Budgeting.* The controller is responsible for assembling the budget from input provided by planning participants. The CFO reviews the budget that the controller has assembled to see if it dovetails with the strategic direction of the business.
- *Financial statements.* The controller is responsible for assembling the financial statements. The CFO certifies to the SEC that the financial statements are correct, and also presents the statements to management and the investment community, along with relevant interpretations of the information.
- *Management.* The controller is directly responsible for the activities of the accounting department. The CFO supervises the controller, and so has indirect management responsibility over the accounting department.

In short, even when there appear to be duplicate responsibilities in some areas, the controller and CFO are engaged in different aspects of the same area.

The controller and CFO positions have inherently different educational and experience requirements. The controller needs a strong accounting education, and may have obtained an accounting certification. There is a much greater need for the CFO to have a strong ability to raise financing for the company, so this position is more likely to have an investment banking background, which does not necessarily call for accounting training or an accounting certification.

The New Controller Checklist

Anyone who has been hired into the controller position for the first time may feel overwhelmed, since the job description involves an enormous range of responsibilities. Where to begin?

The answer is simpler than you may think. Always focus on the ability of the business to survive. Thus, if there is not enough cash on hand to pay the short-term obligations of the business, all other controller responsibilities are insignificant, because the company will no longer be in business. Thus, the following issues should be addressed first, and in the order presented:

1. *Create a short-term cash forecast*. Develop a simple cash forecasting model on an electronic spreadsheet that reveals the expected cash balance at the end of each week for the next month. The initial results may not be that accurate, so compare actual to forecasted results, and adjust the forecast model to increase its accuracy over time. Cash forecasting is addressed in the Cash Management chapter.
2. *Understand receivables*. Review the accounts receivable aging report with the collections staff, to understand which customers pay on time (or not), and which receivables are likely to be delayed or uncollectible. Also, review all non-trade receivables to determine which ones are collectible, and when they are likely to be collected. Adjust the cash forecast based on this information. These issues are addressed in the Credit and Collections Management chapter.
3. *Understand payables*. Review the accounts payable aging report with the accounts payable staff, to learn about the payment terms associated with each supplier, the relations with each one, and which supplier invoices are likely to arrive during the cash forecasting period. Adjust the cash forecast based on this information. Refer to the Accounts Payable Management chapter for more information.
4. *Understand debt payments*. Review the schedule of debt payments. These payments are sometimes taken out of the company's bank account automatically by the bank (if it is the lender), so you can reliably estimate in the cash forecast when these cash deductions will occur.
5. *Reconcile accounts*. If no bank account reconciliations have been completed recently, do so now. This adjusts the company's recorded cash balance for any bank fees and other adjustments imposed by the bank. Adjust the cash forecast based on the revised current cash balance. The bank reconciliation is discussed in the Cash Management chapter.

The preceding steps allow you to generate a preliminary cash forecast almost immediately, and one that should rapidly increase in accuracy. Over the longer term, also consider reviewing any supplier contracts to see if there will be scheduled payments that should be included in the cash forecast. Also, talk to other departments to determine when they may want to purchase fixed assets, so that you can build these expenditures into the budget. Irrespective of these improvements, please note that the cash forecast will never be entirely accurate, even over a period of just a month, because cash inflows are subject to the whims of customers.

Now that there is a system in place for judging the short-term viability of the business, the next step should be to create a system of measurements, so that both you and the management team can monitor the condition of the organization. The initial measurements report is designed to report on the basic functions of the entity, such as:

- Days of receivables outstanding
- Days of inventory on hand
- Gross profit margin
- Net profit margin
- Return on equity
- Metrics required for loan covenants, such as the current ratio

Construct this report so that it reveals the metrics on a trend line. Doing so makes it easier for readers of the report to see if the most recent results are noticeably different from historical results.

When deciding upon which measurements to initially use, stick with those financial measurements that you can easily extract from the financial reporting system. Any other metrics, such as inventory accuracy or product quality, may be useful, but are too difficult to obtain for the first version of this report. You can add them later, once the basic reporting structure has been completed. The concept of metrics reporting is dealt with in more detail in the Management Reports chapter.

The cash forecast and metrics report should take very little time to construct; working models should be running within the controller's first day or two on the job. These reports reveal the essential operating information for the business. Next, spend time investigating the accounting department. Consider the following steps:

1. *Review collections.* The collections area is listed first, because the collections process and staff can have a major impact on the speed with which cash is brought into the department. Review the process flow, the timing of customer contacts, the collection tools available to the staff, and the performance of the collections personnel. Based on this review, itemize a list of changes involving staff training, new tools, employee changes, and alterations to the process flow. These concepts are described in the Credit and Collections Management chapter.
2. *Review billings.* Billings is listed next, because it also has an impact on incoming cash flows. Review the billing process with particular attention to billing errors and the speed with which billings are issued. Based on this review, it may be necessary to plan for alterations to the billing process. This topic is covered in the Billing Management chapter.
3. *Review cash management.* Cash management is listed next, since it still relates to cash inflows, and there may be opportunities to accelerate cash flow slightly. Examine the time required to process and deposit incoming

cash, as well as the controls governing the process. This topic is covered in the Cash Management chapter.

4. *Review payroll.* Payroll is listed immediately after the areas related to cash inflows, for two reasons. First, it can involve a larger cash outflow than accounts payable. Second, if there are errors in the payroll, it reflects badly upon the accounting department. For the second reason, install a payroll error tracking system and monitor it regularly. This issue and others are described in the Payroll Management chapter.
5. *Review accounts payable.* This review is listed last, because it does not involve cash inflows and it may involve less cash outflow than payroll. Nonetheless, there can be plenty of opportunities for streamlining this area and avoiding duplicate payments, so pay particular attention to payables errors and streamlining the process flow. A number of accounts payable improvement suggestions are revealed in the Accounts Payable Management chapter.

The preceding reviews should take about one week. At the end of that time, the process flows in each area should have been documented, an error tracking system should be in place (though probably not with too many results yet), and the controller should have a general idea of the capabilities of the accounting staff.

The next step is to spend a few days looking for holes in the accounting system that could cause problems. You can do this with an error tracking system, but it is quite possible that some issues have already been identified in the past. These problems can be found by reviewing the following documents:

- *Auditor management letter.* This is a letter that most auditors send to the president of the company following the annual audit, detailing either actual or potential control problems. Review these letters for the past three years, since these types of issues tend to linger for several years, if not addressed. Thus, an auditor comment from three years ago might still be valid. You might also consider scheduling a lunch with the audit manager to discuss any additional issues that were not included in the management letter.
- *Internal audit reports.* If the company is large enough, it may have its own audit staff. This group rotates through the company, examining a variety of areas and issuing reports containing their findings and recommendations. If there has not been an internal audit review of the accounting department in the recent past, ask the internal audit manager to schedule a review of selected areas.
- *Financial statement disclosures.* The company may have revealed accounting problems in the disclosures that accompany its financial statements. This is a weaker source of information, so do not spend too much time examining the financial statements for nuggets of information.

The review of these documents may yield clues that can be incorporated into the next step, which is to engage in a number of activities to improve the overall efficiency of the department. These concepts are addressed in the Department Management chapter, and may include:

- *Delegate*. Depending on the size of the department, the controller position may not be involved in *any* accounting transactions. This calls for an exceptional amount of delegating, leaving you free to plan activities, monitor results, and ensure that the company is in compliance with the latest accounting standards – in short, all of the things that a manager should be doing.
- *Schedule*. Create a schedule of activities for the department, and ensure that those activities are completed on time. This applies in particular to tax filings and remittances, as well as to closing the books.
- *Train*. Identify training opportunities for the staff, and monitor their progress toward training goals.
- *Review costs*. The accounting department is a cost center, which means that it is, to some extent, evaluated based on how little it can expend while completing a designated set of activities. The controller should always be tinkering with the cost structure of the department in order to arrive at the best mix of expenses and work products.
- *Review systems*. One of the last items to review is the state of the company's information technology. Existing systems can usually be stretched into an additional year, so you can delay a system overhaul until other aspects of the accounting department have been put in order. Generally speaking, it is less expensive and requires less time to improve the non-computer aspects of the department, so engage in those activities first. The Computer System Selection and Installation chapter addresses accounting technology issues.

This list of activities has not included some activities that only take place once a year, such as the budget. Instead, we have focused on repetitive events. If you are given the controller position in the midst of one of the annual events, then you will have to reshuffle the priorities noted here in order to achieve the completion date for the event.

Finally, do not think that a single pass through this list of activities will create the ideal accounting department. On the contrary, on the first pass, you will likely only create a list of future improvement activities and address a few of the easier issues. It will take several iterations of these activities to address the most critical improvements, and you will likely discover additional "to do" projects as you delve deeper into the innards of the department. Thus, consider these recommended activities to be only a first taste of the management activities that you will need to address over time.

Summary

This chapter has addressed a large number of activities for which the controller is responsible. If you are a new controller, this list may seem overwhelming. However, please note that being responsible for an activity does not necessarily mean personally performing it. Instead, the controller of a larger accounting department must display significant management skills to assign the appropriate amount of the time of *other* employees to each activity, and monitor those activities to ensure that they are completed on time. It is far more likely that you will spend time reviewing the results of others than wading through detailed accounting transactions alone. If it appears that you are doing most of the work, then it is likely that you are a bookkeeper, rather than a controller.

In the following chapters, we delve into each of the functions of the accounting department to show how to improve the efficiency and effectiveness of accounting operations, as well as issue meaningful information to the management team.

Chapter 2
Cash Management

Introduction

The basic cash management issues that every controller is responsible for are to complete a bank reconciliation at the end of each month and to maintain any petty cash funds within the company. In addition, it is difficult for a controller to manage accounts payable payments without having a good idea of short-term cash balances, so you should be able to construct a cash forecast. Finally, in the absence of a treasurer or CFO, the controller will probably be called upon to make short-term investments of excess cash. This chapter addresses all four issues – the bank reconciliation, petty cash, cash forecasting, and investments – in addition to other cash-related topics.

Related Podcast Episodes: Episodes 38, 137, and 187 of the Accounting Best Practices Podcast discuss automatic cash application, a lean system for cash receipts, and cash forecasting accuracy, respectively. You can listen to them at: **accountingtools.com/podcasts** or **iTunes**

Controller Responsibilities

Cash management is not an area generally considered to be a primary responsibility of the controller, especially if there is a finance person on the premises. However, a mistake in this area can lead to significant financing difficulties, and reflects poorly upon the controller. Thus, it is an area in which good performance is rarely noticed, but a mistake can be career-threatening. This risk makes controllers particularly risk-averse in regard to the following responsibilities:

- Conduct periodic bank reconciliations
- Administer the petty cash system
- Maintain a short-term cash forecast
- Invest short-term funds to balance the minimization of risk and maximization of return on investment
- Create and monitor an adequate system of controls over the cash asset

Overview of the Bank Reconciliation

A bank reconciliation is the process of matching the balances in an entity's accounting records for a cash account to the corresponding information on a bank statement, with the goal of ascertaining the differences between the two and booking changes to the accounting records as appropriate. The information on the bank statement is the bank's record of all transactions impacting the entity's bank account during the past month.

At a minimum, conduct a bank reconciliation shortly after the end of each month, when the bank sends the company a bank statement containing the bank's beginning cash balance, transactions during the month, and its ending cash balance. It is even better to conduct a bank reconciliation every day based on the bank's month-to-date information, which should be accessible on the bank's web site. By completing a daily bank reconciliation, one can spot and correct problems immediately.

It is extremely unlikely that a company's ending cash balance and the bank's ending cash balance will be identical, since there are probably multiple payments and deposits in transit at all times, as well as bank service fees, penalties, and not sufficient funds (NSF) deposits that the company has not yet recorded.

The essential process flow for a bank reconciliation is to start with the bank's ending cash balance, add to it any deposits in transit from the company to the bank, subtract any outstanding checks, and either add or deduct any other items. Then, go to the company's ending cash balance and deduct from it any bank service fees, NSF checks and penalties, and add to it any interest earned. At the end of this process, the adjusted bank balance should equal the company's ending adjusted cash balance.

The Bank Reconciliation Procedure

The following bank reconciliation procedure assumes that you are creating the bank reconciliation in an accounting software package, which makes the reconciliation process easier:

1. Enter the bank reconciliation software module. A listing of uncleared checks and uncleared deposits will appear.
2. Check off in the bank reconciliation module all checks that are listed on the bank statement as having cleared the bank.
3. Check off in the bank reconciliation module all deposits that are listed on the bank statement as having cleared the bank.
4. Enter as expenses all bank charges appearing on the bank statement, and which have not already been recorded in the company's records.
5. Enter the ending balance on the bank statement. If the book and bank balances match, then post all changes recorded in the bank reconciliation, and close the module. If the balances do not match, then continue reviewing the bank reconciliation for additional reconciling items. Look for the following issues:

    - Checks recorded in the bank records at a different amount from what is recorded in the company's records.
    - Deposits recorded in the bank records at a different amount from what is recorded in the company's records.
    - Checks recorded in the bank records that are not recorded at all in the company's records.

- Deposits recorded in the bank records that are not recorded at all in the company's records.
- Inbound wire transfers from which a lifting fee has been extracted. A lifting fee is the transaction fee charged to the recipient of a wire transfer, which the recipient's bank imposes for handling the transaction. The term also applies to foreign bank processing fees, which may be applied to a variety of other financial transactions besides a wire transfer.

EXAMPLE

Milagro Corporation is closing its books for the month ended April 30. Milagro's controller must prepare a bank reconciliation based on the following issues:

1. The bank statement contains an ending bank balance of $320,000.
2. The bank statement contains a $200 check printing charge for new checks that the company ordered.
3. The bank statement contains a $150 service charge for operating the bank account.
4. The bank rejects a deposit of $500, due to not sufficient funds, and charges the company a $10 fee associated with the rejection.
5. The bank statement contains interest income of $30.
6. Milagro issued $80,000 of checks that have not yet cleared the bank.
7. Milagro deposited $25,000 of checks at month-end that were not deposited in time to appear on the bank statement.

Based on this information, the controller creates the following reconciliation:

	$	Item No.	Adjustment to Books
Bank balance	$320,000	1	
- Check printing charge	-200	2	Debit expense, credit cash
- Service charge	-150	3	Debit expense, credit cash
- NSF fee	-10	4	Debit expense, credit cash
- NSF deposit rejected	-500	4	Debit receivable, credit cash
+ Interest income	+30	5	Debit cash, credit interest income
- Uncleared checks	-80,000	6	None
+ Deposits in transit	+25,000	7	None
Book balance	$264,170		

Bank Reconciliation Problems

There are several problems that continually arise as part of the bank reconciliation, and which the controller should be aware of. They are:

- *Uncleared checks that continue to not be presented.* There will be a residual number of checks that either are not presented to the bank for payment for a long time, or which are never presented for payment. In the short term, treat them in the same manner as any other uncleared checks – just keep them in the uncleared checks listing in the accounting software, so they will be an ongoing reconciling item. In the long term, contact the payee to see if they ever received the check; you will likely need to void the old check and issue them a new one.
- *Checks clear the bank after having been voided.* As just noted, if a check remains uncleared for a long time, you will probably void the old check and issue a replacement check. But what if the payee then cashes the original check? If you voided it with the bank, the bank should reject the check when it is presented. If you did not void it with the bank, then you must record the check with a credit to the cash account and a debit to indicate the reason for the payment. If the payee has not yet cashed the replacement check, void it with the bank at once to avoid a double payment. Otherwise, you will need to pursue repayment of the second check with the payee.
- *Deposited checks are returned.* There are cases where the bank will refuse to deposit a check, usually because it is drawn on a bank account located in another country. In this case, reverse the original entry related to that deposit, which will be a credit to the cash account to reduce the cash balance, with a corresponding debit (increase) in the accounts receivable account.

The three items noted here are relatively common, and you will likely have to deal with each one at least once a year.

The Bank Reconciliation Statement

When the bank reconciliation process is complete, print a report through the accounting software that shows the bank and book balances, the identified differences between the two (mostly uncleared checks), and any remaining unreconciled difference. Retain a copy of this report for each month. The auditors will want to see it as part of their year-end audit. The format of the report will vary by software package; a simplistic layout is:

Sample Bank Reconciliation Statement

For the month ended March 31, 20X3:	$	Notes
Bank balance	$850,000	
Less: Checks outstanding	-225,000	See detail
Add: deposits in transit	+100,000	See detail
+/- Other adjustments	0	
Book balance	$725,000	

Accounting for Petty Cash

Petty cash is a small amount of cash kept on hand in a business to pay for incidental expenses. As the controller, you are responsible for the proper accounting for petty cash. This is an unusual area in modern accounting, since petty cash records are initially recorded on paper, and then transferred in aggregate to the accounting system. Thus, it is perhaps the most primitive of all accounting systems.

Petty cash is usually maintained in a petty cash box. Within the petty cash box is the current amount of petty cash, as well as all receipts exchanged by employees for cash withdrawn from the petty cash box. These receipts may be in the form of a petty cash voucher, which is a preprinted form used as a receipt. Petty cash vouchers are available at office supply stores.

At any time, the total of cash on hand and petty cash vouchers should equal the total amount of designated funding for a petty cash box. Thus, if the petty cash fund is designated as $300, and there is $100 of cash in the box, then there should also be $200 of petty cash vouchers representing cash that was withdrawn for various expenditures.

The person responsible for petty cash disburses funds from the petty cash box and ensures that petty cash vouchers are exchanged for the disbursed cash. Each petty cash voucher should include the purchase date, expenditure amount, and the name of the supplier. If there is a supplier receipt, this should be stapled to the petty cash voucher. It is also helpful to record the general ledger account to which the expense should be charged.

The person responsible for petty cash should also record petty cash expenditures in a petty cash book. This is usually a spreadsheet, on which are listed the types of expenses for which cash was expended. One petty cash book format is to record all debits and credits in a single column, with a running cash balance in the column furthest to the right, as shown in the following example. This format is an excellent way to monitor the current amount of petty cash remaining on hand.

Sample Petty Cash Book (Running Balance)

Date	Purchase/Receipt	Amount	Balance
4/01/xx	Opening balance	$250.00	$250.00
4/05/xx	Kitchen supplies	-52.80	197.20
4/08/xx	Birthday cake	-24.15	173.05
4/11/xx	Pizza lunch	-81.62	91.43
4/14/xx	Taxi fare	-25.00	66.43
4/23/xx	Kitchen supplies	-42.00	24.43

Another variation on the petty cash book is to maintain it as a spreadsheet, where each item is recorded in a specific column that is designated for a particular type of receipt or expense. This format makes it easier to record petty cash activity in the general ledger. An example of this format, using the same information as the preceding example, follows:

Sample Petty Cash Book (Columnar)

Date	Description	Meals	Supplies	Travel
4/05/xx	Kitchen supplies		$52.80	
4/08/xx	Birthday cake	$24.15		
4/11/xx	Pizza lunch	81.62		
4/14/xx	Taxi fare			$25.00
4/23/xx	Kitchen supplies		42.00	
	Totals	$105.77	$94.80	$25.00

The information in the petty cash book is then used to record the expenses in the general ledger. For example, the journal entry to record the information shown in the preceding sample petty cash book would be:

	Debit	Credit
Meals expense	105.77	
Supplies expense	94.80	
Travel expense	25.00	
Petty cash		225.57

Tip: There will be a small amount of missing petty cash from time to time, likely caused by someone not substituting a petty cash voucher for withdrawn cash. This is not a large issue, since the total amount of petty cash on hand is so small. You can record the shortage in the Other Expenses account, or in any other account to which petty cash charges are usually made.

When the amount of petty cash on hand declines to near zero, as is caused by withdrawals for various expenditures, the petty cash custodian requests a replenishment of the petty cash fund, which is a transfer of cash from the normal bank account to the petty cash account. The usual entry to record a replenishment is:

	Debit	Credit
Petty cash	xxx	
Cash		xxx

We do not recommend that you have a petty cash box, since it is possible for someone to steal cash from the box relatively easily. Instead, either require employees to pay for expenditures themselves and request reimbursement, or use company procurement cards.

The Cash Forecast

The controller needs to know the amount of cash that will probably be on hand in the near future, in order to decide which supplier invoices to pay and to ensure that the cash needed for the company's payroll is available.

Some accounting software packages include a feature that estimates cash balances in the near future, but these packages make assumptions about when cash will arrive from customers, and those assumptions can be substantially incorrect. Over the short term, when you need to know if there will be enough cash on hand to cover the obligations of the business, it is wiser to manually maintain the cash forecast.

From the perspective of the controller, the cash forecast only needs to address the next month, since that period covers the scheduled cash inflows and outflows of the business. Beyond that period, cash forecasting is based largely on estimates of revenues that have not yet occurred and supplier invoices that have not yet arrived, and so yields increasingly tenuous results after much more than a month has passed. Thus, we will address cash forecasting only for a one-month period.

The cash forecast needs to be sufficiently detailed to create an accurate cash forecast, but not so detailed that it requires an inordinate amount of labor to update. Consequently, include a detailed analysis of only the largest receipts and expenditures, and aggregate all other items. The detailed analysis involves the manual prediction of selected cash receipts and expenditures, while the aggregated results are scheduled based on average dates of receipt and payment.

The following table notes the treatment of the key line items in a cash forecast, including the level of detailed forecasting required.

+/-	Line Item	Discussion
+	Beginning cash	This is the current cash balance as of the creation date of the cash forecast, or, for subsequent weeks, it is the ending cash balance from the preceding week. Do not include restricted cash in this number, since you may not be able to use it to pay for expenditures.
+	Accounts receivable	Do not attempt to duplicate the detail of the aged accounts receivable report in this section of the forecast. However, you should itemize the largest receivables, stating the period in which cash receipt is most likely to occur. All other receivables can be listed in aggregate.
+	Other receivables	Only include this line item if there are significant amounts of other receivables (such as customer advances) for which you expect to receive cash within the forecast period.
-	Employee compensation	This is possibly the largest expense item, so be especially careful in estimating the amount. It is easiest to base the compensation expense on the amount paid in the preceding period, adjusted for any expected changes.
-	Payroll taxes	List this expense separately, since it is common to forget to include it when aggregated into the employee compensation line item.
-	Contractor compensation	If there are large payments to subcontractors, list them in one or more line items.
-	Key supplier payments	If there are large payments due to specific suppliers, itemize them separately. You may need to change the dates of these payments in the forecast in response to estimated cash positions.
-	Large recurring payments	There are usually large ongoing payments, such as rent and medical insurance, which you can itemize on separate lines of the forecast.
-	Debt payments	If you know there are significant principal or interest payments coming due, itemize them in the report.
-	Dividend payments	If dividend payments are scheduled, itemize them in the forecast; this tends to be a large expenditure.
-	Expense reports	If there are a large number of expense reports in each month, they are probably clustered near month-end. You can usually estimate the amount likely to be submitted.
=	Net cash position	This is the total of all the preceding line items.
+/-	Financing activities	Add any new debt, which increases cash flow, or the reduction of debt, which decreases cash flow.
	Ending cash	This is the sum of the net cash position line item and the financing activities line item.

The following example illustrates a cash forecast, using the line items described in the preceding table.

EXAMPLE

The controller of Milagro Corporation constructs the following cash forecast for each week in the month of September.

+/-	Line Item	Sept. 1-7	Sept. 8-14	Sept. 15-22	Sept. 23-30
+	Beginning cash	$50,000	$30,000	$2,000	$0
+	Accounts receivable				
+	Alpha Coffee Roasters	120,000		60,000	
+	Third Degree Coffee		85,000		52,000
+	Major League Coffee	29,000		109,000	
+	Other receivables	160,000	25,000	48,000	60,000
+	Other receivables	10,000		5,000	
-	Employee compensation	140,000		145,000	
-	Payroll taxes	10,000		11,000	
-	Contractor compensation				
-	Bryce Contractors	8,000		8,000	
-	Johnson Contractors	14,000		12,000	
-	Key supplier payments				
-	Ethiopian Coffee Co-op	100,000		35,000	
-	Kona Coffee Beans	20,000	80,000	29,000	14,000
-	Other suppliers	35,000	40,000	30,000	48,000
-	Large recurring payments				
-	Medical insurance				43,000
-	Rent				49,000
-	Debt payments		18,000		
-	Dividend payments			20,000	
-	Expense reports	12,000	0	0	21,000
=	Net cash position	$30,000	$2,000	-$66,000	-$63,000
+/-	Financing activities			66,000	63,000
=	Ending cash	$30,000	$2,000	$0	$0

The forecast reveals a cash shortfall beginning in the third week, which will require a cumulative total of $129,000 of additional financing if the company wants to meet its scheduled payment obligations.

The model we have outlined in this section requires a weekly update. It only covers a one-month period, so its contents become outdated very quickly. Ideally, block out time in the schedule of department activities to complete the forecast at the same time, every week.

Tip: Do not schedule an update of the cash forecast on a Monday or Friday, since too many of these days involve holidays. Instead, schedule the forecast update on any other business day, thereby increasing the odds of completing a new forecast every week.

Cash Investments

The controller may be asked to engage in the short-term investment of excess cash, if there is no treasurer or chief financial officer to handle this task. If so, keep the investment strategy as simple as possible, using two guidelines:

- *Minimize risk.* Do not attempt to earn an unusually high return by placing funds in a risky investment. Even a quite modest return is acceptable, as long as the investment is safe.
- *Maximize liquidity.* Be able to move all invested funds back into the company's cash accounts on extremely short notice.

With the preceding two guidelines in mind, we recommend only the following two investments:

- *Money market funds.* You can shift funds into and out of a money market fund with little notice, and the investment is considered very safe. However, the return on investment is low. A manual transfer of funds is usually needed.
- *Repurchase agreement.* Your bank may offer an overnight repurchase agreement, under which it automatically shifts funds out of your bank accounts and into an interest-earning overnight investment, after which it moves the funds back into your account the next morning. This approach earns a very low interest rate, and the bank charges a minimum fixed fee to move funds every day, so this approach may generate only a small net return.

These two investments are simple and safe, but yield low returns. Nonetheless, they give almost immediate access to funds, and so are preferred for excess cash in the short term.

An additional consideration is the use of cash sweeping, which is offered by many banks. In essence, this is a system for automatically shifting cash from a company's checking accounts into a central account, from which the funds can be more easily invested. This approach keeps you from having to manage the funds in a variety of checking accounts, which makes it an attractive alternative if there are a number of company locations, each with its own checking account. You may need to keep track of where the swept cash came from; if so, you can record an inter-company loan from each subsidiary to the parent company that matches the amount of cash swept into the central account. You may need this information for reporting cash balances at the subsidiary level, as well as for allocating interest income to the subsidiaries.

Investment is not a key responsibility of the controller, so do not try to get fancy. The investment steps noted here are of the simplest kind, and should be sufficient for the day-to-day movement of cash in and out of highly liquid investments.

Negative Cash on the Balance Sheet

It is possible for a negative cash balance to appear on the month-end balance sheet if you have issued checks for more funds than you have in the cash account. If so, it is customary to use a journal entry to move the amount of the overdrawn checks into a liability account, and set up the entry to automatically reverse at the beginning of the next reporting period.

There are two options for which liability account to use to store the overdrawn amount, which are:

1. *Separate account.* The more theoretically correct approach is to segregate the overdrawn amount in its own account, such as "Overdrawn Checks" or "Checks Paid Exceeding Cash." However, since this is likely to be a small account balance, it clutters the balance sheet with an extra line. Or, if you are aggregating smaller accounts together on the balance sheet, it will not appear by itself on the balance sheet, and so conveys no real information to the user. If so, try the next option.
2. *Accounts payable account.* Enter the amount into the "Accounts Payable" account. If you do, then the accounts payable detail report will no longer exactly match the total account balance. However, as long as the entry automatically reverses, the overdrawn amount should not clutter up the account for long. This approach is especially appealing if overdrawn checks are a rarity.

Based on this discussion, it is reasonable to assume that any time you see a company's balance sheet with a zero cash balance, it probably has an overdrawn bank account; this brings up questions about its liquidity, and therefore its ability to continue as a going concern. To allay such concerns for anyone reading the financial statements, try to avoid being in a situation where there is a zero cash balance.

Cash Controls

Given the nature of cash, it requires considerably more controls than are usually considered necessary for other assets. However, the exact number and type of controls can vary, depending upon the nature of the business. For example, a casino handles so much cash that its entire control system is focused on this asset, nearly to the exclusion of all other assets. Conversely, a business that has little cash on-site may be able to function with a small fraction of the controls needed for a casino.

Consequently, we will list the more common cash controls below, from which you can select those most applicable to your situation:

- *Stamp checks.* Someone should stamp "For deposit only," with the company's account number, on all checks as soon as they are received. This makes it more difficult for someone to deposit the checks elsewhere.
- *Create list of checks at point of receipt.* Have someone record a summary of all checks received at the point when they are removed from envelopes, and forward a copy of this list to someone not involved with cash recordation. This control is used as part of the following control.
- *Match list of checks.* Have someone not involved with the handling of cash match the initial list of checks to the checks recorded in the cash receipts journal for that day, as well as to the deposit sent to the bank that day. This control is used to detect checks that were removed subsequent to receipt.
- *Conduct bank reconciliation.* Someone not involved in cash handling or cash recordation should complete the monthly bank reconciliation, which makes it more difficult to abscond with funds.
- *Separate duties.* Have one person receive cash, another person record cash in the accounting system, and yet another person conduct the monthly bank reconciliation. Under this approach, more than one person would have to collude to steal cash without detection.
- *Move cash receipts to lockbox.* If cash is being received in a bank lockbox located outside of the company, then far fewer controls are needed to keep anyone from absconding with the funds.
- *Require daily deposits.* If cash is removed from the premises every day, there is no need for elaborate controls to safeguard cash held on-site.
- *Audit petty cash.* Conduct audits of petty cash with no warning. The intent is to spot situations where someone has "temporarily" removed cash from the petty cash box, with the intent of replacing it later.
- *Eliminate petty cash.* The greatest risk of cash theft is probably from petty cash, since it is not well guarded, so consider eliminating petty cash.
- *Impose ACH debit blocks on all bank accounts.* Require the bank to block all attempts to remove funds from the company's bank accounts by imposing debit blocks.
- *Lock up check stock.* Keep all unused check stock in a locked location, and track the ranges of check numbers that have been used. If the company uses a signature stamp or plate to sign checks, then store it in a different locked location.

In a smaller organization, it may be difficult to separate all of the cash-related functions among different personnel. If so, you will have to accept some risk of loss by concentrating cash activities with too few people. In this situation, at least have someone else prepare the bank reconciliation, shift incoming cash to a lockbox that is maintained by the company's bank, and deposit cash at the bank every day. These steps mitigate the risks associated with cash to some extent.

Cash Record Keeping

The records to maintain for cash correspond closely to the documentation requirements that an auditor would request for the year-end audit. The documents that an auditor would want to peruse include:

- Bank reconciliations for every month of the period being audited
- List of all checks and deposits outstanding as of the end of each month
- Bank statements for every month of the period being audited
- Cash receipts journal for the audit period
- Cash disbursements journal for the audit period

You usually do not have to print the cash receipts journal and cash disbursements journal for each month, since this information is stored within the accounting system, and can be printed at any time for the auditors.

Summary

At a minimum, any controller must have a good system of controls over cash, as well as conduct a detailed monthly bank reconciliation for all open bank accounts. Also, in the absence of a treasury department, maintain a short-term cash forecast and update it every week; this gives you sufficient information to determine if there is enough cash for the daily expenditures required of the department. Where possible, consider eliminating petty cash, thereby sidestepping the time-consuming monitoring of this minor asset. Finally, if there is no one else tasked with investments, have a sufficient knowledge of investments to know how to shift funds into short-term investments that can be readily converted back into cash.

Chapter 3
Credit and Collections Management

Introduction

One of the first areas in which the new controller should become actively involved (or at least knowledgeable) is credit and collections. These functions have a major impact on the amount of cash received, and the speed with which it arrives. Consequently, if a company is facing a difficult cash flow situation, the controller should be spending a large amount of time in the credit and collections area. This chapter addresses the best ways to measure and manage credit and collections, and also covers the cost of early payment discounts, accounting for bad debts, and key controls.

Related Podcast Episode: Episode 55 of the Accounting Best Practices Podcast discusses targeted collections. You can listen to it at: **accountingtools.com/podcasts** or **iTunes**

Controller Responsibilities

The collection of overdue accounts receivable is nearly always assigned to the accounting department, and therefore is a responsibility of the controller. The effectiveness of the collection function is partially based on the proper assignment of credit to customers, so this area may also fall under the jurisdiction of the controller. Key responsibilities in these areas include:

- Assign credit to customers based on a standard credit policy.
- Use alternative methods to obtain sales while mitigating credit risk.
- Use prudent early payment discount terms to obtain early customer payment, if cost-effective.
- Direct a collections staff that engages in the collection of overdue accounts receivable in a cost-effective manner.
- Alter the billing and payment system to accelerate the collection of cash from customers.
- Estimate and properly account for the allowance for doubtful accounts.
- Maintain a system of controls to mitigate bad debt losses.

Receivables Measurement

Before you delve into specific problems in the accounts receivable area, spend a few minutes creating the measurement system you need to track progress in the department.

The classic measurement for accounts receivable is days sales outstanding (DSO), which is the average number of days that an invoice is outstanding before being collected. You can calculate it with the following three-step process:

1. *Determine sales per day.* You need to calculate sales per day for the company. To do so, divide total credit sales for the past year by 365 days. Or, if sales have changed from the long-term average in the past few months, consider dividing total sales for the past quarter by 91 days.
2. *Determine average accounts receivable.* The amount of accounts receivable fluctuates throughout the month, so find the average amount outstanding. The easiest method is to add together the beginning and ending accounts receivable balances and divide by two. If there has been little change in receivables recently, you can just use the ending receivables number.
3. *Calculate DSO.* Divide average accounts receivable by sales per day.

Thus, the formula for DSO is:

$$\frac{(\text{Beginning receivables} + \text{Ending receivables}) \div 2}{\text{Annual credit sales} \div 365 \text{ days}}$$

EXAMPLE

The new controller of Milagro Corporation wants to calculate the days sales outstanding for the company as of the end of May. The ending April receivables balance was $1,800,000, and the ending May receivables balance was $2,200,000. The company's total credit sales over the past 12 months were $20,000,000. Therefore, the DSO calculation is:

$$\frac{(\$1{,}800{,}000 \text{ Beginning receivables} + \$2{,}200{,}000 \text{ Ending receivables}) \div 2}{\$20{,}000{,}000 \text{ Annual credit sales} \div 365 \text{ days}}$$

$$=$$

$$\frac{\$2{,}000{,}000 \text{ Average accounts receivable}}{\$54{,}795 \text{ Credit sales per day}}$$

$$= \underline{\underline{36.5}} \text{ Days sales outstanding}$$

You will find that the company likely has settled into a certain DSO amount, and does not vary much from it over time. This DSO figure is indicative of the mix of customers, the amount of credit granted to them, and their propensity to pay within a certain number of days of the payment date specified on each invoice. Thus, you will need to alter one or more of these issues to improve DSO, such as dropping late-paying customers.

Tip: Always track DSO on a trend line. Since DSO tends to be about the same from month to month, a sudden surge in DSO is a major warning flag that a large proportion of receivables are being collected later than normal.

You may conclude that the DSO measurement is the only one you need for the credit and collections function. If you have room for an additional measurement, consider using the collection effectiveness index (CEI). This measurement compares the amount of receivables available for collection to the amount actually collected, where a CEI score close to 100% is excellent. You can calculate CEI with the following steps:

1. *Calculate receivables collected.* Add together the receivable balance at the beginning of the period and credit sales during the period, and subtract the ending receivable balance.
2. *Calculate receivables available for collection.* Add together the receivable balance at the beginning of the period and credit sales during the period, and subtract the ending amount of current receivables (i.e., those receivables not yet due for payment).
3. *Calculate CEI.* Divide receivables collected by the receivables available for collection.

Thus, the formula for CEI is:

$$\frac{\text{Beginning receivables + Credit sales - Ending total receivables}}{\text{Beginning receivables + Credit sales - Ending current receivables}} \times 100$$

EXAMPLE

The controller of Milagro Corporation accumulates the following information to calculate the collection effectiveness index:

Beginning total accounts receivable	$1,800,000
Ending total accounts receivable	2,200,000
Ending current accounts receivable	1,350,000
Credit sales in the period	1,750,000

He uses this information to derive the CEI, as follows:

$$\frac{\text{\$1,800,000 Beginning receivables + \$1,750,000 Credit sales - \$2,200,000 Ending total receivables}}{\text{\$1,800,000 Beginning receivables + \$1,750,000 Credit sales - \$1,350,000 Ending current receivables}} \times 100$$

$$= \frac{\$1{,}350{,}000 \text{ Receivables collected}}{\$2{,}200{,}000 \text{ Receivables available for collection}} \times 100$$

$$= \underline{61\%} \text{ CEI}$$

> **Tip:** If you assign customers to specific collections employees, you can run the CEI measure for each individual. However, some customers are more difficult to collect from than others, so the mix of customers assigned to each collections person can influence their CEI numbers.

By using either the DSO or CEI measurements, or both, you can get an immediate feel for the state of the company's credit and collection activities. Better yet, compare these measurements to the same calculations for the same months in each of the preceding two years. By doing so, you gain a long-term perspective on the company's collection activities, while also avoiding the impact of seasonality by comparing current results to the results in the same months in the other years.

Credit Management

The measurement of receivables may reveal that it is taking too long to collect cash from customers. If so, the issue may be in the company's process for granting credit to customers. However, before installing or expanding a credit department, consider the extent of credit risk to which the company is subjected. Credit risk is the risk of loss by a business that has extended credit to another party, if that other party does not pay the specified amount within the appointed time period.

If the company sells goods at a large profit, its credit risk is confined to the cost of the items it is selling, which may not be that large. If so, it may be more cost-effective to maintain a minimal credit analysis function and accept a fair amount of bad debt losses. This is a particularly common approach when customer orders are so small that there is no way to justify the cost of the associated credit report or review work by a credit analyst. Conversely, if profit margins are slim and order sizes are large, it may be more cost-effective to maintain a significant credit function. In short, consider the circumstances of the business before automatically assuming that the company must have a credit department.

As the controller, you may be responsible for the credit function (otherwise, credit may be handled by the treasury department, if there is one). If you are responsible for the function, it is quite likely that you will field complaints from the sales staff that they have worked inordinately hard to obtain an order from a new customer, only to find that the credit department rejects the order as being too risky. You may be on the receiving end of intense pressure from the sales staff to approve credit on these orders. What is to be done?

The problem is that the sales staff did not warn the credit department in advance. Reverse the process flow, so that the sales department presents its list of customer prospects to the credit department before they engage in detailed sales efforts. This immediately steers the sales staff away from those customers who are poor credit risks, and also eliminates any subsequent conflict with the credit department.

> **Tip:** How are you supposed to evaluate a sales prospect in advance, before the customer has filled out a credit application? An advance analysis is best accomplished with a credit report purchased from a third-party credit analysis firm. The information in the report should be sufficient to give you a general idea of the financial condition of the prospective customer.

The basic process flow for credit management is to require all new customers with orders above a certain minimum limit to fill out a credit application form, if they want to be invoiced and pay the company at a later date. You can obtain adequate credit application forms at any office supply store, or set up an on-line application form on the company website that helps to speed up the application process.

The credit staff then uses the completed credit application as the basis for its determination of the amount of credit that customers are entitled to. This determination should be based on a specific set of rules, which can vary based on the circumstances of the business. For example:

1. If the customer order is for obsolete items and the order is for less than $5,000, or if the order is for less than $1,500, automatically approve the order.
2. If the customer order is for more than $1,500 but less than $10,000, require that a credit application be submitted, and allow a credit limit of [possible choices]:
   - __% of cash on hand
   - __% of net working capital
   - __% of net worth
   - $____ fixed credit limit until first order is paid for, followed by re-evaluation
3. If the customer has at least a one-year history of paying the company, grant it an automatic credit increase of __%.
4. If the customer order is for more than $10,000 or there is a recent history of payment problems, forward it to the credit manager for review.
5. Are any invoices currently at least 60 days overdue for payment and for more than $____? If so, cancel all further credit and issue instructions to the shipping department to halt any further orders until the situation is examined by the credit manager.

Again, the exact set of rules that work best for a business depend upon its specific circumstances. Ideally, re-examine the credit granting rules regularly, in light of recent bad debt losses, and adjust the rules to reduce credit risk.

Tip: It is a mistake to require a credit application only at the beginning of a relationship with a customer. Instead, request periodic updates, possibly with financial statements attached, for those customers placing large orders with the company. Otherwise, changes in the financial circumstances of customers may lead to large bad debts at some point in the future.

It is also possible to develop a detailed in-house credit analysis software package, or subscribe to one maintained by a third party. These systems are only economical if there are many customers placing significant orders, and there is credit risk. Most smaller companies can operate with the rules-based system just described, rather than investing in a more substantial system.

Tip: Once the credit staff has decided upon a credit limit for a customer, contact the customer and explain the amount of credit granted, as well as the payment terms associated with it. You might also consider mailing the customer a procedure describing where payments should be sent, the company's bank information (in case of a wire transfer), early payment discounts, and so forth. This level of proactive contact can avoid payment problems with some customers.

What if the credit manager concludes that a customer is not a good credit risk? This does not necessarily mean that the company should abandon the order. Instead, consider the following options:

- *Credit insurance*. It may be possible to obtain credit insurance, which shifts some or all of the credit risk to the insurer. This will require the payment of an insurance fee to the insurer, which you may be able to pass through to the customer.
- *Outside financing*. Arrange with a third-party lender to extend a loan or lease to the customer. By doing so, the lender takes on the credit risk.
- *Distributor*. If there are distributors of the company's products, refer the customer to one of the distributors. It is possible that the distributor has different credit standards, and will accept the order.
- *Restrict credit*. Extending a smaller amount of credit may be an acceptable risk, and may still provide sufficient credit if the payment term is shortened. For example, a customer may request $10,000 of credit with 30-day payment terms; the company may instead allow $5,000 of credit with 15-day payment terms, which is effectively the same amount of credit over a 30-day period, but at less risk to the company.
- *Personal guarantee*. Require someone with substantial personal resources to guarantee payment of the invoice. It can be difficult to collect on personal guarantees, so it is better to treat this approach as a backup to another more robust form of risk mitigation.

Tip: If a customer with a relatively poor credit history wants to buy goods from you that are nearing obsolescence, it may be worthwhile to approve the sale. The reason is that the goods will soon be dispositioned at a vastly reduced price, so even a higher risk of customer default may still make the deal look reasonable.

In short, the role of the credit department is not necessarily to be a gatekeeper that denies credit to customers; instead, the role is to identify those customers who represent an unacceptable credit risk, and find alternative ways to do business with them that still generates revenue without the offsetting credit risk. This will undoubtedly result in the loss of some revenues in cases where there is no way to come to an alternative arrangement, but that is likely to be for only those customers at the highest risk of default.

Credit Terms and the Cost of Credit

A key question for the controller is whether to offer early payment terms to customers in order to accelerate the flow of inbound cash. This is a common ploy if the company is cash-strapped, or where there is no backup line of credit with the local bank to absorb any cash shortfalls.

The early payment terms that you offer to customers need to be sufficiently lucrative for them to want to pay their invoices early, but not have such egregious terms that the company is effectively paying an inordinately high interest rate for access to the funds that it is receiving early.

The term structure used for credit terms is to first state the number of days you are giving customers from the invoice date in which to take advantage of the early payment credit terms. For example, if a customer is supposed to pay within 10 days without a discount, the terms are "net 10 days," whereas if the customer must pay within 10 days to qualify for a 2% discount, the terms are "2/10." Or, if the customer must pay within 10 days to obtain a 2% discount or can make a normal payment in 30 days, then the terms are stated as "2/10 net 30."

The table below shows some of the more common credit terms, explains what they mean, and also notes the effective interest rate that you are offering customers with each one.

Credit Terms	Explanation	Effective Interest
Net 10	Pay in 10 days	None
Net 30	Pay in 30 days	None
Net EOM 10	Pay within 10 days of month-end	None
1/10 net 30	Take a 1% discount if pay in 10 days, otherwise pay in 30 days	18.2%
2/10 net 30	Take a 2% discount if pay in 10 days, otherwise pay in 30 days	36.7%
1/10 net 60	Take a 1% discount if pay in 10 days, otherwise pay in 60 days	7.3%
2/10 net 60	Take a 2% discount if pay in 10 days, otherwise pay in 60 days	14.7%

In case you are dealing with terms different from those shown in the preceding table, be aware of the formula for calculating the effective interest rate associated with early payment discount terms. The calculation steps are:

1. Calculate the difference between the payment date for those taking the early payment discount and the date when payment is normally due, and divide it into 360 days. For example, under "2/10 net 30" terms, you would divide 20 days into 360 to arrive at 18. Use this number to annualize the interest rate calculated in the next step.
2. Subtract the discount percentage from 100% and divide the result into the discount percentage. For example, under "2/10 net 30" terms, you would divide 2% by 98% to arrive at 0.0204. This is the interest rate being offered through the credit terms.
3. Multiply the result of both calculations together to obtain the annualized interest rate. To conclude the example, multiply 18 by 0.0204 to arrive at an effective annualized interest rate of 36.72%.

Thus, the full calculation for the cost of credit is:

(Discount % ÷ (1 – Discount %)) × (360 ÷ (Allowed payment days – Discount days))

Tip: It usually takes a large discount to persuade customers to pay early. Consequently, unless the company has a desperate need for cash, it is generally not worthwhile to offer a temptingly-high discount. However, consider offering a discount with a low effective interest rate on an ongoing basis; this might trigger a few early payments at little cost to the company.

Collections Management

If there are a number of overdue customer payments or deductions to be resolved, you may need a substantial and effective collections department to ensure that these issues do not overwhelm the accounting department. Several characteristics of a well-run collections department are:

- *Management.* Depending upon the size of the group, it may require a collections manager to monitor the progress of the collections team and ensure that the knottier collection problems are addressed.
- *Bad debt handling.* There should be a system in place for deciding which overdue invoices are to be written off, which are to be pursued with more aggressive collection techniques, and which are to be handed off to a third-party collection agency.
- *Customer assignments.* It is usually best to assign certain customers to specific collections staff on an ongoing basis, so that the collections staff gains familiarity with the payment foibles of individual customers.
- *Deduction management.* Certain customers may take a number of deductions of various types from their payments. If so, have deduction specialists

who are experts in the handling of certain types of deductions. Otherwise, there could be an intractable backlog of unresolved deductions.

- *Collections software*. If there is a larger collections staff, you can improve their productivity substantially by obtaining collections software. This software ties into the accounting software, usually with a custom interface, and provides all of the following functionality and more:

    - *Promises*. Maintains a history of payment promises made by customers.
    - *Contacts*. Maintains a database of customer contact information.
    - *Auto-dial*. Automatically calls the appropriate customer contact for a collection call.
    - *Information presentation*. Pulls up relevant information pertaining to a call on the collection person's computer screen.
    - *Information forwarding*. Issues information pertaining to a collection issue to customers by e-mail, such as invoices and receipt information.
    - *Dunning contacts*. Automatically issues e-mailed dunning notices to customers for overdue amounts.

There should be a system in place for economically collecting payment on overdue invoices. The exact sequence and timing of events will depend upon the industry, but the following is a reasonable sequence of events to consider:

1. *Administrative call*. Contact customers in advance of payment dates for the larger invoices, to verify that payment will be made on the expected date and in full. If not, making the administrative call gives you time to rectify the situation before the payment due date arrives.
2. *Dunning message*. If payments are slightly overdue and the amounts are not large, issue a dunning letter or e-mail message, politely reminding customers of their obligations to pay.
3. *Telephone call*. After it becomes clear that an invoice will not be paid on time, the collections staff should call the customer, ascertain the reason for the payment delay, and either obtain a promise to pay as of a specific date or begin the process of resolving the underlying issue. Resolving the issue may involve a number of approaches, such as:

    - Return the purchased goods
    - Adopt a payment plan
    - Place a credit hold on the customer
    - Accept payment in kind
    - Accept a reduced payment
    - Replace the purchased goods

4. *Attorney letter*. If the customer is still not responsive, consider contracting with a local attorney to issue an attorney letter. This approach relies upon

the involvement of an attorney and a mildly threatening letter to convince a customer that paying is less expensive than a lawsuit in the near future.

5. *Small claims complaint.* Fill out a small claims court form and send a copy to the customer. This does not mean that you have filed the form with the court, only that you have filled out the paperwork. The receipt of such official-looking paperwork might convince the customer that you are serious. Small claims courts allow only smaller claims, so this approach is only available for unpaid invoices usually under $10,000.
6. *Collection agency.* If all of the preceding approaches have not worked, consider shifting the claim to a collection agency, which may engage in more vigorous collection techniques. These agencies may charge up to one-third of the total amount of each invoice as their fee (if they achieve a collection), so use the preceding techniques first, and use the collection agency only as a last resort.

Of the collection techniques noted here, the first three are typical ones that are an expected part of business between long-term business partners, and the exchanges are expected to be polite and professional. However, once you progress to attorney letters, small claims complaints, and collection agencies, the assumption is that the company will no longer be doing business with the customer, since these actions are considerably more aggressive. Consequently, warn the sales manager before engaging in the more aggressive collection techniques, since these actions will effectively terminate relations with the customer.

We generally do not recommend a full-blown lawsuit to collect against a customer, since the expense is substantial, and those customers forced into a lawsuit may not have enough cash to pay off a judgment against them.

Other Cash Acceleration Techniques

As the controller, a key responsibility is to accelerate the payment of cash from customers to the company – but this does not just involve proper credit and collection management. You can also accelerate cash flow by changing the underlying system. One or more of the following four methods may be of assistance:

- *ACH debit.* If you always bill customers for the same amount, every month, then ask the customers if you can debit the funds directly from their bank accounts on a specific day each month. By doing so, you gain an extremely reliable and predictable source of funds. It can take some effort to persuade customers to allow these payments. You might consider requiring it for all new customers, or point out that it saves them the cost of printing and mailing a check, or offer a small early payment discount.

> **Tip:** Have each customer sign a document stating that they approve of the ACH debit. This protects the company in case the customer later complains that the deductions were taken from its account without permission.

- *Remote deposit capture.* If you cannot always convey customer payments to the bank in a timely manner, or if the bank takes extra time to process these payments into its system, you do not have use of the cash for a period of time. A solution is to see if your bank offers a remote deposit capture option. This is a portable check scanner that you can connect to a computer in the accounting department. Just run the checks through it, and a software application on the computer transmits the check information into the bank's computer. The bank then posts the cash to the company's bank account. Not only does this approach give faster access to cash, but it also saves a trip to the bank each day.
- *Cash application sequencing.* The cash application procedure may state that someone must first apply all customer payments to unpaid accounts receivable, and *then* deposit the payments at the bank. If there is a delay in applying cash, then there is no deposit at the bank, and the company does not have use of the funds. To avoid this delay, photocopy all checks and have the cash application staff use the copies; you can then deposit the funds at once. Or, if you use remote deposit capture (as just described), then deposit the checks immediately through the check scanner, and turn over the original checks to the cash application staff.
- *Lockbox.* An alternative to remote deposit capture is the lockbox. Under this approach, the company determines where customers are located around the country, and positions lockboxes in each geographic cluster of customers. The customers are then instructed to send their payments to the lockbox closest to them. The bank operating the lockboxes deposits all checks immediately. The bank also makes electronic copies of the checks that the accounting staff can access online, and uses them to apply payments to unpaid invoices. This approach eliminates one or two days of mail float, but there are offsetting bank fees, so run a cost-benefit analysis to see if lockboxes will save any money.

Of the cash acceleration techniques described here, remote deposit capture is the most universally applicable. The only reason against it is if the bank charges an outrageous monthly fee for it. ACH debits are only applicable in a minority of situations, while lockboxes are not economical unless a significant amount of cash is made available sooner, thereby offsetting the bank's lockbox fees.

The Allowance for Doubtful Accounts

The allowance for doubtful accounts is a reduction of the total amount of accounts receivable appearing on a company's balance sheet. It is listed as a deduction immediately below the accounts receivable line item. This allowance reflects your best estimate of the amount of accounts receivable that the company will never be paid by its customers.

There are several possible ways to estimate the allowance for doubtful accounts, which are:

- *Risk classification.* Assign a risk score to each customer, and assume a higher risk of default for those having a higher risk score. Here are the steps to follow to create a risk-based bad debt forecast:

  a. Periodically obtain new risk scores for all current customers, excluding those with minimal sales.
  b. Load the scores for each customer into an open field in the customer master file.
  c. Print a custom report that sorts current customers in declining order by risk score.
  d. Divide the sorted list into fourths (low risk through high risk), and determine the bad debt percentage for the previous year for each category. The result is shown in the following sample report:

Sample Bad Debt Analysis Based on Customer Risk

Risk Category	Current Receivable Balance	Historical Bad Debt Percentage	Estimated Bad Debt by Risk Category
Low risk	$1,100,000	0.8%	$8,800
Medium low	606,000	1.6%	9,696
Medium high	384,000	3.9%	14,976
High risk	110,000	7.1%	7,810
Totals	$2,200,000		$41,282

  The risk classification approach can be expensive to update, since you may need to buy credit risk reports for all major customers. To avoid this expense, consider using the next approach, which can be developed entirely with internally-available information.

- *Time bucket percentage.* If a certain percentage of accounts receivable became bad debts in the past, then expect the same percentage in the future. This method works best for large numbers of small account balances. Here are the steps to follow to create a bad debt expense based on historical percentages:

  a. Print the accounts receivable aging report.
  b. Assign the historical bad debt percentage applicable to each 30-day time bucket.
  c. Multiply the ending receivable balances in each 30-day time bucket by the applicable bad debt percentage to arrive at the total amount of the allowance for doubtful accounts. The result is shown in the following sample report.

Sample Bad Debt Analysis Based on Time Buckets

	0-30 Days	31-60 Days	61-90 Days	90+ Days
Ending balance	$1,500,000	$562,000	$108,000	$30,000
Estimated bad debt percentage	1.0%	2.5%	6.2%	30.0%
Estimated bad debt amount	$15,000	$14,050	$6,696	$9,000

At a less precise level, you can also calculate the allowance based on a simple percentage of the entire amount of outstanding accounts receivable, but that can be notably imprecise, especially if the proportion of older receivables to total receivables varies constantly.

- *80/20 analysis*. Review the largest accounts receivable that make up 80% of the total receivable balance, and estimate which specific customers are most likely to default. Then use the preceding historical percentage method for the remaining smaller accounts. This method works best if there are a small number of large account balances.

You can also evaluate the reasonableness of an allowance for doubtful accounts by comparing it to the total amount of seriously overdue accounts receivable, which are presumably not going to be collected. If the allowance is less than the amount of these overdue receivables, the allowance is probably insufficient.

The balance in the allowance for doubtful accounts should be reviewed as part of the month-end closing process, to ensure that the balance is reasonable in comparison to the latest bad debt forecast. For companies with minimal bad debt activity, a quarterly update may be sufficient.

If the company is using the accrual basis of accounting, record an allowance for doubtful accounts, since it provides an estimate of future bad debts that improves the accuracy of the company's financial statements. Also, by recording the allowance at the same time that you record a sale, the company is properly matching the projected bad debt expense against the related sale in the same period, which provides an accurate view of the true profitability of a sale.

EXAMPLE

Milagro Corporation records $2,000,000 of sales to several hundred customers, and projects (based on historical experience) that it will incur 1% of this amount as bad debts, though it does not know exactly which customers will default. The controller records the 1% of projected bad debts as a $20,000 debit to the Bad Debt Expense account and a $20,000 credit to the Allowance for Doubtful Accounts. The bad debt expense is charged to expense right away, and the allowance for doubtful accounts becomes a reserve account that offsets the account receivable of $2,000,000 (for a net receivable outstanding of $1,980,000). The entry is:

	Debit	Credit
Bad debt expense	20,000	
Allowance for doubtful accounts		20,000

Later, several customers default on payments totaling $4,000. Accordingly, the controller credits the accounts receivable account by $4,000 to reduce the amount of outstanding accounts receivable, and debits the allowance for doubtful accounts by the same amount. This entry reduces the balance in the allowance account to $16,000. The entry does not impact earnings in the current period. The entry is:

	Debit	Credit
Allowance for doubtful accounts	4,000	
Accounts receivable		4,000

A few months later, a collection agency succeeds in collecting $1,500 of the funds that the controller had already written off. He can now reverse part of the previous entry, thereby increasing the balance in the allowance account. The entry is:

	Debit	Credit
Accounts receivable	1,500	
Allowance for doubtful accounts		1,500

Finally, the controller records the receipt of cash from the collection agency for the $1,500 receivable, net of a collection fee of $500. The entry is:

	Debit	Credit
Cash	1,000	
Collection expense	500	
Accounts receivable		1,500

The only impact that the allowance for doubtful accounts has on the income statement is the initial charge to bad debt expense when the allowance is initially funded. Any subsequent write-offs of accounts receivable against the allowance for doubtful accounts only impact the balance sheet.

The Direct Write-off Method

The direct write-off method is the practice of charging bad debts to expense in the period when individual invoices have been clearly identified as bad debts. The specific activity needed to write off an account receivable under this method is to create a credit memo for the customer in question, which exactly offsets the amount of the bad debt. Creating the credit memo requires a debit to the bad debt expense account and a credit to the accounts receivable account.

This method delays the recognition of expenses related to a revenue-generating transaction, and so is considered an excessively aggressive accounting method, since it delays some expense recognition, making a business look more profitable than it really is. For example, a company may recognize $1 million in sales in one period, and then wait three or four months to collect all of the related accounts receivable, before finally charging some items off to expense. This creates a lengthy delay between revenue recognition and the recognition of expenses that are directly related to that revenue. Thus, the profit in the initial month is overstated, while profit is understated in the month when the bad debts are charged to expense.

The direct write-off method can be considered a reasonable accounting method if the amount written off is an immaterial amount, since doing so has minimal impact on the financial results of the business. However, given the reasons just noted, there are few instances when the direct write off method should be used. Instead, use the allowance for doubtful accounts that was described in the preceding section; it more closely matches revenues with any associated bad debt expenses.

Credit and Collection Controls

There are a few key controls to consider for the credit and collections area. Fraud prevention is the foundation for some controls, but other controls are needed simply to head off errors in the processing of customer orders. The following controls are worth considering:

- *Review credit memos*. The primary area in which fraud can be perpetrated is when an accounting clerk intercepts incoming cash from a customer and writes a credit memo to hide the missing funds. The credit memo may be represented to you as clearing out an overdue invoice that is a bad debt. You can generally detect the presence of this type of fraud by seeing if one clerk submits more credit memos than other clerks. A clever clerk may only use this approach with a few smaller customer invoices in order to evade detection, though doing so also decreases the potential *amount* of fraud.
- *Segregate tasks*. To keep the last item from occurring, separate the tasks of handling incoming cash and processing credit memos. This control is not possible in smaller accounting departments where most tasks are shared.
- *Require credit approval*. The shipping staff should be prohibited from shipping goods to a customer if there is no formal approval from the credit department on the shipping documents. Better yet, arrange the flow of documents to the shipping department so that the paperwork never arrives until the credit department approves a customer order. This is not a fraud prevention step, but rather the avoidance of shipments to customers who may never pay the company.
- *Review suspense account*. Customers sometimes pay partial amounts or do not specify how payments are to be applied to open invoices. The account-

ing staff typically records these amounts in a suspense account, with the intent of resolving them later. A suspense account is an account in the general ledger that is used to temporarily store any transactions for which there is some uncertainty about the account in which they should be recorded. The trouble is that some payments are never researched, and so will linger in the suspense account for an inordinate amount of time. Have a standard work step in place to investigate the suspense account regularly and resolve any remaining items.

Of the controls noted here, none are critical. For example, if there is no history of significant credit memo issuances, you can probably institute a required approval for larger credit memos and ignore all others. Also, if customer orders are small and there are established credit histories with most customers, you may be able to restrict credit approval to only the largest orders. Further, there may be no suspense account if customer invoices are simple and therefore not subject to confusion in the cash application process. In short, the circumstances may allow you to avoid most controls in the areas of credit and collections.

Summary

This chapter has addressed a number of action items for credit and collections. Which ones should you address immediately? The first item is to calculate days sales outstanding, both for the past month and for the same month one year ago, to gain a perspective on collection trends. If these measures reveal a problem, then examine the credit granting and collection systems to see if adjustments must be made. Only after you have addressed the issues directly impacting incoming cash flow should you move to the less critical accounting task of devising an allowance for doubtful accounts, and adjusting the system of controls.

Chapter 4
Billing Management

Introduction

Creating customer invoices is not as simple as it may at first appear. One should be aware of the different process flows that lead up to the generation of an invoice, as well as how to alter the structure of invoices to accelerate cash collections. It is also important to understand how invoices, accrued revenue, and sales taxes are handled in the accounting records. We address all of these topics and more in the following sections.

Related Podcast Episodes: Episodes 73 and 229 of the Accounting Best Practices Podcast discuss billing best practices and sales taxes, respectively. You can listen to them at: **accountingtools.com/podcasts** or **iTunes**

Controller Responsibilities

The controller is completely responsible for customer billings. A proper billing process is required to reliably arrive at the monthly revenue figure, which is perhaps the number most closely followed by senior management. Consequently, to generate irrefutable revenue information, the controller should have considerable interest in a billing process that functions near-perfectly. This involves the following responsibilities:

- Maintain a reliable billing process that generates error-free invoices.
- Properly distribute billed amounts to the correct revenue and other accounts.
- Accrue revenue when revenue recognition rules and company policies allow it.
- Bill sales taxes to customers when required, and properly remit the receipts to the applicable government authorities in a timely manner.
- Maintain a system of controls to ensure that all shipments and services are billed in the correct amounts and to the correct customers.

Billing Management

When you sell goods or services to a customer and allow them to pay you at a later date, this is known as selling on credit, and it creates a liability for the customer to pay your business. Conversely, this creates an asset for your company, which is called accounts receivable, or trade accounts receivable. This is considered a short-term asset, since you are normally paid in less than one year.

An account receivable is documented through an invoice, which you are responsible for issuing to the customer. The invoice describes the goods or services sold to the customer, the amount it owes you, and when it is supposed to pay. The structure of the invoice is described in the next section.

There are several management areas to focus on when dealing with customer billings. The first is the billing notification process, which is different for products and services. These processes are:

1. *Product billings*. The shipping department ships a product to a customer, and enters the shipment in a shipping log that is maintained in the shipping department. Someone from the department delivers a shipping notification to the accounting department, which uses this information to construct a customer billing. This billing may also include a freight charge, which is based on the delivery information also forwarded from the shipping department. The key weakness in this process is that the accounting department may never be notified of a shipment, so no billing is issued.
2. *Service billings, event based*. The company provides a specific service, and bills the customer for time and materials used during the event. In this case, the person engaged in the service completes a form that details the hours worked and materials used, and forwards it to the accounting department for billing. Again, the weakness in this process is the possible lack of notification of the accounting staff.
3. *Service billings, time based*. The company issues a month-end billing to the customer, based on the hours worked by employees during the month. The information needed for the billing is derived from employee timesheets, which are accumulated during the month by the accounting staff. The weakness in this process is more likely to be incorrect time recording by an employee that shifts billable hours to the wrong customer, or which incorrectly designates hours worked as billable. It is also possible that employees worked on a contract for which there is not sufficient remaining authorized contract funding.

Tip: Use accounting software that includes a shipping module. This means that a shipment is automatically flagged for billing in the accounting software as soon as it is shipped. This eliminates the risk of not being notified of a shipment, though there is still a risk that a shipping person never logs a shipment into the system.

Once the accounting department has received notification for billing, there are several issues to consider regarding the timing and summarization level of invoices. The issues are:

- *Separation of line items*. Customers typically hold payment on an entire invoice if they are questioning just one line item on the invoice. Therefore, if you have customers with a tendency to delay payments for this reason, consider shifting the largest line item to a separate invoice, and clustering all other line items on a second invoice. This may improve the speed of payment for the largest-dollar items.

- *Summarization of deliveries.* If there are multiple low-priced deliveries, consider aggregating them into a single periodic invoice. Only use this approach if the cost of creating additional invoices is large enough to offset the payment delay associated with having fewer invoices.
- *Issue invoices early.* If the company bills its customers a predictable amount every month (such as for a recurring rent payment), consider issuing the invoices a few days early. This can accelerate payments from customers.
- *Match to customer payment cycle.* If the customer regularly pays its invoices on the same day of the month, be sure to issue invoices well in advance of this date, and consider using overnight delivery to meet the deadline for payment. Otherwise, payments could be significantly delayed.
- *Multiple invoices per period.* If the company is under a long-term services contract where billings are usually made at the end of each month, consider more frequent billings to improve cash flow, such as once a week or twice a month.

Another issue is where to send each invoice. This is not as simple a task as it may appear, since some organizations prefer to route invoices directly to the accounting department, while others prefer a routing to the person who placed the order. An additional issue arises when customer addresses change. Here are some ways to ensure that invoices are sent to the correct location on the first try:

- *Ask.* Contact the customer's accounting department and clarify where invoices are to be sent.
- *Route updates to accounting department.* A well-organized customer sends change of address notifications to all of its business partners. Instruct the mailroom staff to forward these notifications to the accounting department, where they are used as the basis for an update to the customer file in the accounting software.
- *Request review by sales staff.* If the company has long-standing relationships with its customers, have the sales staff review the customer list from time to time and note any address changes.
- *Request address correction.* Stamp the words "Address Correction Requested" on each envelope mailed to a customer and handled by the United States Postal Service. If there has been a customer address change, the Postal Service will notify the sender of the change. There is a small fee for this notification service.

A final issue is the invoice delivery method. Some approaches result in more immediate payment, and so should be used if they are cost-effective. Here are several methods to consider:

- *Certified mail.* In cases where customers repeatedly complain that they are not receiving invoices, send the invoices by certified mail. This provides you with evidence of receipt, and takes away the customer's excuse that it never received the invoice. If the customer is using this complaint as an excuse for not paying, it may shift to a different excuse, resulting in no net improvement in the speed of collection.

- *E-mail.* Many accounting systems allow you to convert an invoice to PDF format, or you can use a scanner to convert a printed invoice to this format. Then attach the PDF to an e-mail to the customer's accounts payable department. This approach involves no mailing cost and strips away the mail float. However, it is common for customers to lose invoices delivered in this manner.
- *Mail.* This is the traditional method of invoice delivery, and still works fine when payment terms are longer than a few days. The Postal Service is reliable, and the accounts payable systems of customers are specifically designed to handle invoices delivered through the mail.
- *Overnight delivery service.* Though expensive, overnight delivery is the fastest way to send a hard copy of an invoice, along with any attachments. If you are only using this method for proof of receipt, consider using certified mail instead, which provides the same service at a lower cost with a delivery delay of a few days.
- *Website entry.* Larger companies have secure websites in which you can enter invoices. These transactions typically involve the manual re-entry of each invoice. However, they also ensure that invoices are entered in the customer's computer system. These systems commonly allow you to enter bank account information, so that the customer can issue ACH payments directly into the company's bank account.

Of the invoice delivery methods described here, mail delivery still works very well. E-mail delivery is not recommended, except as a follow-up to a late payment, since invoices delivered by this means are more likely to be lost. Website entry will eventually supplant mail delivery, and is recommended where available, despite the labor cost of entering invoice information into these sites.

Structure of the Invoice

The accounting software always contains a standard invoice template, which most businesses use with only minor adjustments. You may want to make several modifications to the template to reduce the time required to receive payments from customers, as well as to reduce the number of customer payment errors. Consider implementing the adjustments in the following table:

Invoice Format Changes

Credit card contact information	If customers want to pay with a credit card, include a telephone number to call to pay by this means.
Early payment discount	State the exact amount of the early payment discount and the exact date by which the customer must pay in order to qualify for the discount.
General contact information	If customers have a question about the invoice, there should be a contact information block that states the telephone number and e-mail address they should contact.
Payment due date	Rather than entering payment terms on the invoice (such as "net 30"), state the exact date on which payment is due. This should be stated prominently.

The goal in creating an invoice format is to present the minimum amount of information to the customer in order to prevent confusion, while presenting the required information as clearly as possible. The following sample invoice template incorporates the invoice format changes that we just addressed.

In the sample invoice template, note the addition of the three blocks of information at the bottom of the invoice, each designed to clearly state either contact or payment information.

Accounting for Billings

When you sell services to a customer, you normally create an invoice in the billing module of the accounting software, which automatically creates an entry to credit the revenue account and debit the accounts receivable account. When the customer later pays the invoice, you debit the cash account and credit the accounts receivable account. For example, if a business invoices a customer for $10,000 in services, the entry generated by the billing module would be:

	Debit	Credit
Accounts receivable	10,000	
Revenue - services		10,000

If you were to sell goods to a customer on credit, then not only would you have to record the sale and related account receivable, but you would also record the reduction in inventory that was sold to the customer, which then appears in the cost of goods sold expense. For example, if a business were to conclude a sale transaction for $15,000 in which it sold merchandise having an inventory cost of $12,000, the entry would be as shown on the next page.

Sample Enhanced Invoice Template

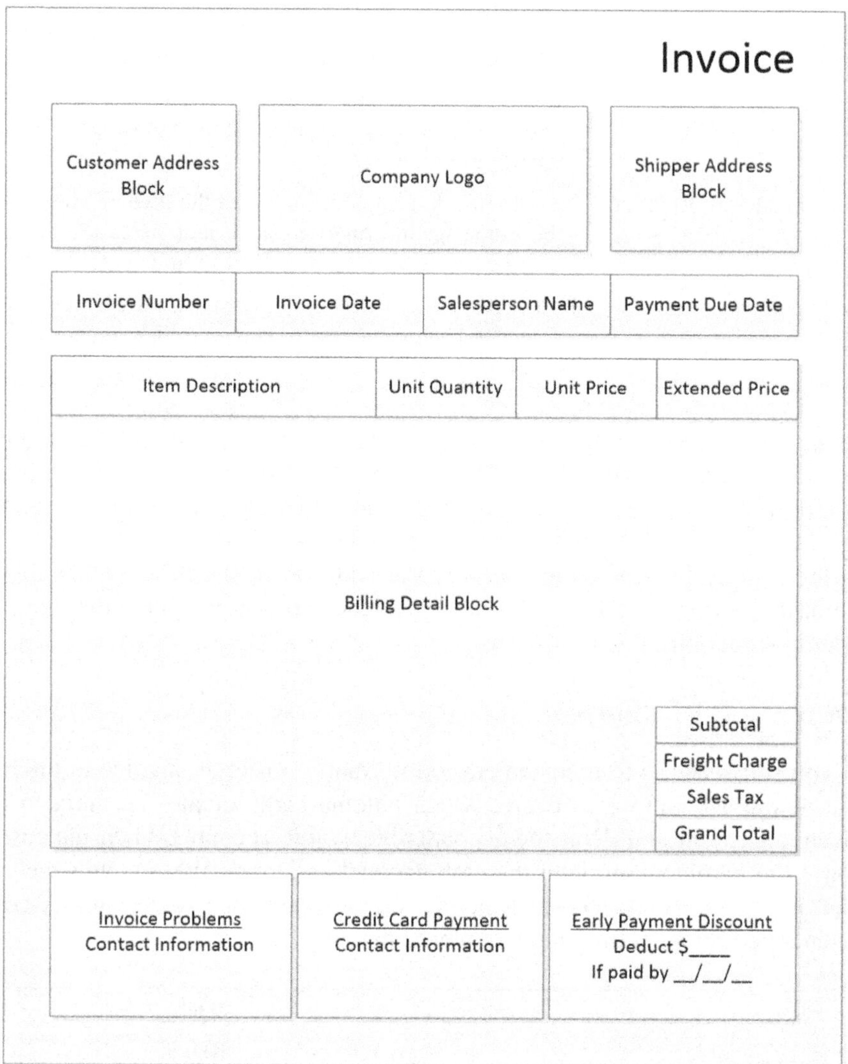

	Debit	Credit
Accounts receivable	15,000	
Revenue - products		15,000
Cost of goods sold	12,000	
Inventory		12,000

There is an issue with the timing of the preceding sale transaction. If the sale is made under *FOB shipping point* terms(where the buyer takes delivery of goods being shipped to it by a supplier once the goods leave the supplier's shipping dock), the seller is supposed to record both the sale transaction and related charge to the cost of goods sold at the time when the shipment leaves its shipping dock. From that point onward, the delivery is technically the responsibility of either a third-party shipper or the buyer.

If a sale is made under *FOB destination* terms (where the buyer takes delivery of goods being shipped to it by a supplier once the goods arrive at the buyer's receiving dock), then the seller is supposed to record these transactions when the shipment arrives at the customer; this is because the delivery is still the responsibility of the seller until it reaches the customer's location.

From a practical perspective, most companies record their sale transactions as though the delivery terms were FOB shipping point, because it is easiest to initiate a sale transaction in the accounting system as soon as the goods are shipped.

If you offer customers a discount when they pay early and they take advantage of the offer, they will pay an amount less than the invoice total. You need to eliminate this residual balance by charging it to the sales discounts account, which can be treated as either a reduction of sales or an expense. For example, if a customer takes advantage of a $100 early payment discount on a $2,000 invoice, the following entry would be used to record the payment:

	Debit	Credit
Cash	1,900	
Sales discounts	100	
Accounts receivable		2,000

Accrued Revenue

There may be situations where you have not issued an invoice to a customer, but still want to recognize the revenue. This typically occurs under one of the following scenarios:

- *Milestone*. A milestone has been reached in a contract with a customer, where the company is clearly entitled to a specific, pre-defined amount, but the contract does not yet allow you to issue an invoice; or
- *Services*. The contract with the customer states that the customer will pay for hours worked, rather than for a specific work product. For example, there may be 10 hours of work that will eventually be billed at a rate of $80 per hour, so you accrue the receivable for $800.

The journal entry to create an accrued receivable is a debit to an accounts receivable account and a credit to a revenue account. It may be useful to create a unique general ledger account for accrued receivables, rather than using the main trade receivables account, in order to clearly show these transactions. In addition, set these journal entries to automatically reverse themselves in the next accounting period; you would then replace the accrual in the next period with the actual invoice (assuming that there is a billing event in the next period). If you are unable to create an invoice in the next period, then continue to accrue and reverse the revenue and receivable in every period on a cumulative basis until you can eventually issue an invoice.

EXAMPLE

Milagro Corporation has completed a milestone in a project to install a coffee roasting facility for a customer, though it is not allowed under the contract to issue an invoice more frequently than once a quarter. It therefore accrues revenue and a receivable of $50,000 at the end of February with the following entry:

	Debit	Credit
Accounts receivable - accrued	50,000	
Revenue		50,000

The accounting software automatically reverses the entry at the beginning of March with the following entry:

	Debit	Credit
Revenue	50,000	
Accounts receivable - accrued		50,000

Milagro then earns another $70,000 on the next project milestone in March. The company is allowed to issue a quarterly invoice at the end of March, so it issues an invoice for $120,000. By using accruals, Milagro has recognized $50,000 of revenue and receivables in February and another $70,000 in March, rather than recognizing all $120,000 in March, when it issued the invoice.

Do not use accrued receivables if you cannot justify to an auditor that there is a clear obligation by the customer to pay the company for the amount of the accrued receivable. Otherwise, there is a presumption that the business has not yet reached the point where the customer has a clear obligation to pay. For example, do not accrue revenue in a case where a business is providing services under a fixed fee contract, and it earns revenue only when the entire project is complete and approved by the customer. Revenue has not really been earned prior to completion, so there should be no accrual prior to that point.

Tip: Consider setting a minimum dollar threshold below which it is standard procedure to *never* accrue revenue. By doing so, you can avoid the supporting documentation typically demanded by auditors.

Accounting for Sales Taxes

You are required to charge customers a sales tax on certain types of sales transactions if you have nexus in the territory of the government entity that charges the sales tax. Nexus is the concept that you are doing business in an area if you have a place of business there, use your own vehicles to transport goods to customers there, or (in some cases) have employees situated or living there.

If the company does not have nexus where a customer is located, then the company does not have to charge a sales tax to the customer; instead, the customer is supposed to self-report a use tax to its local government. Use tax is the same as sales tax, except that the party remitting the tax to the applicable government entity is the buyer of taxable goods or services, rather than the seller.

All accounting software includes a billing feature that allows you to include the sales tax at the bottom of each invoice, after the subtotal of line items billed. When you charge customers the sales tax, you eventually collect it and then remit it to the state government, which in turn pays it out to the various local governments.

When you bill a customer for sales taxes, the journal entry is a debit to the accounts receivable account for the entire amount of the invoice, a credit to the revenue account for that portion of the invoice attributable to goods or services billed, and a credit to the sales tax liability account for the amount of sales taxes billed.

At the end of the month (or longer, depending on your remittance arrangement), fill out a sales tax remittance form that itemizes sales and sales taxes, and send the applicable government the amount of the sales tax recorded in the sales tax liability account. This remittance may take place before the customer has paid for the sales tax.

What if the customer does not pay the sales tax portion of the invoice? In that case, issue a credit memo that reverses the amount of the sales tax liability and eliminates the unpaid taxes from the accounts receivable account. It is quite likely that you will have already remitted this sales tax to the government, so the customer's non-payment becomes a reduction in your next sales tax remittance to the government.

EXAMPLE

Milagro Corporation issues an invoice to The Cupertino Beanery for $1,000 of goods delivered, on which there is a seven percent sales tax. The entry is:

	Debit	Credit
Accounts receivable	1,070	
Revenue		1,000
Sales tax liability		70

Following the end of the month, Milagro remits the sales taxes withheld to the state government. The entry is:

	Debit	Credit
Sales tax liability	70	
Cash		70

Later in the following month, the customer pays the full amount of the invoice. The entry is:

	Debit	Credit
Cash	1,070	
Accounts receivable		1,070

When a company bills its customers for sales taxes, those taxes are not an expense to the company; they are an expense only to customers. From the company's perspective, these sales tax billings are liabilities to the local government until remitted.

Tip: Consider setting up a separate sales tax liability account for each government entity. If the company has nexus in multiple jurisdictions, this makes it much easier to reconcile the accounts, and is essentially mandatory if there is a sales tax audit.

Sales Tax Exemption Certificates

A business may not be required to pay sales taxes under either of two scenarios, which are as follows:

- *Usage basis.* The state government has declared that, as long as a product is used in a certain way, no sales tax will be charged. For example, fuel purchased for industrial use may be considered tax-exempt, but if the fuel is then taken by an employee for personal use, the designated usage exemption is being avoided, and use tax should be paid. The most common usage basis for a sales tax exemption is when the buyer of goods intends to include them in the production of its own products, which will then be sold to another party. In this case, only the final customer is required to pay sales tax.
- *Entity exemption.* The state government has declared that certain types of organizations do not have to pay sales taxes. The most common of these entities are religious, government, and non-profit organizations. The government may issue a separate type of exemption certificate to these entities, such as a non-profit certificate of exemption. There are also industry-specific exemptions, such as an agricultural exemption, where a farmer is exempt from purchases used in the conduct of his business.

The manner in which an exemption is administratively handled will vary by state. For example, one state might issue certificates of exemption that prevent applicable sales taxes from being charged at the point of sale. Or, another state might require that sales tax be paid at the point of sale, after which organizations may apply to the Department of Revenue for an annual refund. The latter approach carries a higher administrative burden for all parties, but gives the government use of the remitted funds for up to a year.

A seller should only skip a sales tax billing to a customer when the customer produces a sales tax exemption form (sometimes called a resale certificate) that has been issued by the local state government. By signing an exemption form, a business is committing to only use purchased goods in the manner claimed on the certificate; if the business uses the goods in some other way, it acknowledges responsibility for then submitting the applicable use tax to the government.

Sales Tax Audits

The state government may periodically send a sales tax audit team to a business to examine its records and see if the government has been shortchanged on the amount of sales tax remittances that it should have received. If so, the audit team can charge the company for the amount of the sales tax shortfall, plus penalties and interest. This amount can be substantial, and is especially galling for management, since the presumption in a sales tax audit is that the business is presumed guilty unless it can prove otherwise.

A business will find that the likelihood of a sales and use tax audit will increase as its sales grow. The reason is that audit teams are expensive, and so must generate a return for the employing government. Thus, a small organization is much less likely to be subjected to an audit, simply because even quite a large adverse finding would still represent a relatively small return for the government. Conversely, a proportionally small sales and use tax issue at a large firm might still represent a major cash inflow for the state government.

The audits can be conducted by any government that believes a company owes it sales taxes, so the number of these audits to which a business can be subjected is nearly unlimited.

There are some variations on how an audit can be conducted, but the basic steps are as follows:

1. The auditor sends a notice of audit to the targeted business and arranges for a range of dates during which the audit will take place.
2. The auditor defines the audit objective, which is usually to locate mistakes in a company's tax compliance. Based on this objective, the auditor decides which areas are most likely to contain errors, and focuses the audit work on those areas.
3. The auditor requests that a specific date range of customer and supplier invoices be made available by the target company.
4. The auditor selects a sample of the total population of customer invoices that is considered to be representative of the entire population, so that a con-

clusion regarding error rates can be drawn with a high degree of confidence for the entire population. Or, if the business is quite a small one, the auditor reviews the entire population of invoices.

5. The auditor examines the invoices to determine whether sales tax was charged on all taxable items and that the tax was properly remitted to the government.
6. For those items for which sales tax was not charged, the auditor investigates whether there is a valid sales tax exemption certificate that supports the transaction. Also, the auditor examines the products purchased by the customer to see if they qualified for the exemption.
7. The auditor verifies that all funds collected from customers were remitted to the government, and in a timely manner.
8. The auditor compiles a list of exceptions found and forwards them to the company's accountant for review.

When an audit team conducts a sales and use tax audit, some exceptions will likely be found. A common approach is for the audit team to then use *error rate extrapolation*, where they multiply the rate at which errors occurred within their sampling work to the total number of company transactions. For example, if the team finds that $100 of sales tax was not collected in a sample that comprises ½% of a company's total sales volume, it will extrapolate this finding to the rest of the company's sales – which in this case results in a total charge for uncollected sales taxes of $20,000, which is calculated as follows:

$100 Error ÷ .005 = $20,000 Total extrapolated amount

Further, the auditors will then add a penalty and interest charge to the total extrapolated amount. This extrapolated amount can turn into quite a large assessment. The size of this potential assessment can be a significant inducement for a firm to create a detailed set of procedures for dealing with sales and use taxes, thereby driving down its error rate.

Errors in Compliance

An audit team may judge a number of events to be errors in compliance. The accountant should understand the nature of each of these error types in order to keep them from occurring. Here are several examples of compliance errors:

- Applying the wrong sales tax rate to a transaction
- Exempting a transaction from sales tax without a certificate of exemption
- Failing to determine whether the organization has nexus in another state
- Incorrectly reporting the total amount of sales taxes due for a reporting period
- Incorrectly reporting the total amount of sales generated in a reporting period

Audit Best Practices

There are a number of techniques that an accountant can use to reduce the impact of a sales tax audit on the organization. They are noted within the following headings for planning and prevention:

Planning Topics

The work associated with a sales tax audit begins well before the government's audit team walks in the door. The accountant should have spent time in advance negotiating certain aspects of the audit, while also reviewing the documents that the auditors plan to examine. More specifically:

- *Schedule appropriately.* Within reasonable limits, an auditor is usually willing to schedule an audit around the schedule of a company's accounting department. This means shifting the audit away from the closing period and any seasonal activities that might leave little time to assist the auditor.
- *Negotiate the audit period.* It may be possible to negotiate the date range over which the auditor wants to examine records. There are several reasons for doing so, one of which is to reduce the number of invoice records that must be pulled from the archives. Another reason is to point the auditor at those periods when it is most likely that the company was in compliance with all sales tax requirements, such as slow periods or when the most reliable staff person was in charge of billings.
- *Use electronic access.* It may be possible for the auditors to conduct a review of the company's electronic records. This is advantageous for the company, since there is no need for the accounting staff to pull printed records from the archives, and the auditor may be able to conduct some of the work from an off-site location – which reduces the on-site disruption. Further, electronic access eliminates the risk of being unable to locate an invoice in the archives. This situation is most likely when a company has a large volume of transactions stored in an electronic format and especially when the auditors would otherwise need to access documents from multiple company locations.
- *Review certificates.* Conduct a detailed examination of every sales tax exemption certificate on file to ensure that it is complete and has not expired. If there are any issues, correct them before the arrival of the auditors.
- *Flag special sales.* The sales records may contain a few isolated cases where a sale was unusual, such as an order for a custom product or a large one-time order. Consider requesting that the related invoices be pulled from the samples being reviewed by the audit team, since they are not representative of the entire population of invoices.
- *Reconcile reports.* Verify that the gross sales figure stated on the company's federal income tax return and financial statements matches the aggregate amount of gross sales figures stated on the state sales tax reports for the same period. Prepare a reconciliation statement if there are any differences.

- *Organize documents.* Do not hand the audit team a disorganized sheaf of invoices and other documents for their review. Doing so only prolongs their visit, since they have to spend extra time sorting through the documents. Instead, organize the documents in the order in which they were requested, or at least in an order that would make logical sense from the perspective of someone reviewing them.
- *Allocate work space.* Reserve space for the auditors in a room that is sufficiently far away from other business activities that they will not overhear conversations, which they might otherwise misconstrue. Always provide a workspace that has ample room; providing cramped quarters makes the auditors less efficient, which may prolong the duration of their audit.

Prevention Topics

Certain best practices should be engaged in on an ongoing basis, and irrespective of the presence of sales tax auditors. The following practices are intended to improve the level of an organization's compliance with sales and use tax regulations:

- *Conduct internal audits.* Conduct the company's own sales tax audit at regular intervals, using the same analysis techniques that a government audit team would use. Whenever an error is found, examine the underlying policies and procedures to determine how it occurred, and fix the system to ensure that it does not happen again.
- *Examine exemption certificates.* Trace a selection of un-taxed sales to exemption certificates. Note all exceptions, where an exemption certificate cannot be found or the certificate is out-of-date. Examine the exceptions to see if the system for handling sales tax exemptions should be altered.
- *Identify contractors.* In most states, the rule is that a contractor charging a lump sum for a construction contract is responsible for paying sales tax, rather than the client of the contractor. When this is the case, clearly identify the contractor as such in the accounting records, so that the auditors will not count these invoices as an exception. It can be helpful to prepare a list of all lump-sum contractors in advance and give it to the auditors when they arrive.
- *Maintain excellent records.* One way to keep an audit team from finding any compliance errors is to maintain well-organized records that detail the sales taxes paid, along with the invoices on which they were paid.
- *Verify taxable items.* Routinely review the applicable Department of Revenue's listing of transactions subject to sales tax and verify that the company is paying use tax on these items when sales tax is not billed by suppliers. Pay particular attention to taxable business purchases, such as furniture and office supplies.

Once an audit has been completed, ask the auditors if they found any issues that the business can correct by altering its policies and procedures. The auditors see many accounting systems as part of their work, and so can be considered experts on what constitutes inadequate systems.

A final note regarding sales tax audits is that a large assessment will likely trigger an ongoing series of periodic audits. Once the Department of Revenue has found a large new source of revenue, it can be expected to keep returning in later years in hopes of finding yet more revenue. Further, later audit teams will use the work papers written by the initial audit team to pinpoint the best places to locate sales tax issues, and will zero in on these areas again. Conversely, if there is only a small assessment or (better yet) no assessment at all, the manager in charge of the audit will conclude that the company is not a good source of additional revenue, and so may avoid scheduling additional audits for a long time.

Billing Controls

Controls over accounts receivable are largely involved with the initial creation of the invoice. Key controls to consider are:

- *Verify contract terms*. If there is a large invoice with unusual payment terms, verify them before creating the invoice. Otherwise, customers may refuse to pay until you issue a replacement invoice. This control usually only applies when there is a contractual arrangement underlying the billing.
- *Verify funding*. If an invoice is based on a contract with a customer, verify that there is sufficient funding left on the contract before issuing the invoice. A more comprehensive version of this control is to monitor available funding throughout the month and stop any additional work on a contract once the funding limit has been reached.
- *Proofread invoices*. If an invoice for a large-dollar amount contains an error, the customer may hold up payment until you send a revised invoice. Consider requiring the proofreading of larger invoices to mitigate this problem.
- *Audit invoice packets*. After invoices are completed, there should be a document packet on file that contains the customer order, credit authorization, bill of lading and an invoice copy. The internal audit staff should review a selection of these packets to verify that the billing clerk properly compiled the information in the supporting paperwork into an invoice.
- *Review journal entries*. Accounts receivable transactions almost always go through a billing module in the accounting software that generates its own accounting entries. Therefore, there should almost never be a manual journal entry in the accounts receivable account. Investigate any such entries.
- *Match billings to shipping log*. There may be a disconnect between the shipping and accounting departments where the accounting staff is not notified of a shipment, and so an invoice is never issued. To detect these situations, compare billings to the shipping log, and investigate any differences.

The most important billing issue requiring a control is the risk that a shipment will be sent without a corresponding invoice being produced. Accordingly, be sure to have a robust system for forwarding shipping documentation from the shipping department to the billing clerk. The other controls noted here may occasionally highlight an issue, but are less critical.

Summary

Customer billings should be considered a high-volume activity. This means that the controller should set up invoicing as a production process, with a highly-regimented procedure that is closely followed by a well-trained billing staff. Also, as you uncover billing errors, address the underlying problems and incorporate your changes into the main billing procedure. Only by rigorously pursuing a high level of standardization can you achieve the level of efficiency needed for one of the primary accounting activities.

Chapter 5
Inventory Management

Introduction

The value of a company's inventory is a key component of its reported cost of goods sold, which is a key driver of its profitability. This should give the controller a keen level of interest in the accuracy of inventory records. Unfortunately, those records are usually maintained by the warehouse staff, so the controller does not have direct control over them. Nonetheless, the controller can exert pressure to maintain accurate inventory records, and so should be aware of the systems available for doing so. It is also essential to know how costs are assigned to inventory. We address both inventory record keeping and valuation in this chapter.

Related Podcast Episodes: Episodes 56, 66, 192, and 225 of the Accounting Best Practices Podcast discuss inventory record accuracy, obsolete inventory, cycle counting, and the reserve for obsolete inventory, respectively. You can listen to them at: **accountingtools.com/podcasts** or **iTunes**

Controller Responsibilities

The warehouse manager is responsible for inventory records, so the controller's responsibilities related to inventory are somewhat limited. They are:

- Conduct physical inventory counts as needed.
- Develop and maintain inventory costing systems.
- Monitor obsolete inventory designations and adjust inventory valuations based on this information.

The controller may also take responsibility for maintaining an ongoing system of inventory audits, though this task could be handled by the warehouse manager or the internal audit staff.

The Periodic Inventory System

The periodic inventory system only updates the ending inventory balance when you conduct a physical inventory count. Since physical inventory counts are time-consuming, few companies do them more than once a quarter or year. In the meantime, the inventory account continues to show the cost of the inventory that was recorded as of the last physical inventory count.

Under the periodic inventory system, all purchases made between physical inventory counts are recorded in a purchases account. When a physical inventory count is done, you then shift the balance in the purchases account into the inventory account, which in turn is adjusted to match the cost of the ending inventory.

The calculation of the cost of goods sold under the periodic inventory system is:

Beginning inventory + Purchases = Cost of goods available for sale

Cost of goods available for sale – Ending inventory = Cost of goods sold

---

EXAMPLE

Milagro Corporation has beginning inventory of $100,000, has paid $170,000 for purchases, and its physical inventory count reveals an ending inventory cost of $80,000. The calculation of its cost of goods sold is:

$100,000 Beginning inventory + $170,000 Purchases - $80,000 Ending inventory

= $190,000 Cost of goods sold

The periodic inventory system is most useful for smaller businesses that maintain minimal amounts of inventory. For them, a physical inventory count is easy to complete, and they can estimate cost of goods sold figures for interim periods. However, there are several problems with the system:

- It does not yield any information about the cost of goods sold or ending inventory balances during interim periods when there has been no physical inventory count.
- You must estimate the cost of goods sold during interim periods, which will likely result in a significant adjustment to the actual cost of goods whenever you eventually complete a physical inventory count.
- There is no way to adjust for obsolete inventory or scrap losses during interim periods, so there tends to be a significant (and expensive) adjustment for these issues when a physical inventory count is eventually completed.

A more up-to-date and accurate alternative to the periodic inventory system is the perpetual inventory system, which is described in the next section.

The Perpetual Inventory System

Under the perpetual inventory system, an entity continually updates its inventory records to account for additions to and subtractions from inventory for such activities as received inventory items, goods sold from stock, and items picked from inventory for use in the production process. Thus, a perpetual inventory system has the advantages of both providing up-to-date inventory balance information and requiring a reduced level of physical inventory counts. However, the calculated inventory levels derived by a perpetual inventory system may gradually diverge from actual inventory levels, due to unrecorded transactions or theft, so periodically compare book balances to actual on-hand quantities with cycle counting (as explained later in the Cycle Counting section).

EXAMPLE

This example contains several journal entries used to account for transactions in a perpetual inventory system. Milagro Corporation records a purchase of $1,000 of widgets that are stored in inventory:

	Debit	Credit
Inventory	1,000	
Accounts payable		1,000

Milagro records $250 of inbound freight cost associated with the delivery of widgets:

	Debit	Credit
Inventory	250	
Accounts payable		250

Milagro records the sale of widgets from inventory for $2,000, for which the associated inventory cost is $1,200:

	Debit	Credit
Accounts receivable	2,000	
Revenue		2,000
Cost of goods sold	1,200	
Inventory		1,200

Milagro records a downward inventory adjustment of $500, caused by inventory theft, and detected during a cycle count:

	Debit	Credit
Inventory shrinkage expense	500	
Inventory		500

How to Set Up Inventory Record Keeping

If you are going to use a perpetual inventory system to track inventory levels, there must be an organizational and record keeping structure in place to support it. Otherwise, the inventory records will be hopelessly inaccurate. The following steps are of considerable use in setting up a warehouse structure that can support a perpetual inventory system:

1. *Identify inventory.* Create a part numbering system, and ensure that every item in inventory has been properly labeled with a part number. There should also be a procedure for identifying and labeling all new inventory as it is received or manufactured.
2. *Consolidate inventory.* If the same inventory items are stored in multiple locations, try to consolidate them into one place. This makes the counting process easier.
3. *Package inventory.* Where possible, put loose inventory items in boxes or bags, seal the containers, and mark the quantity on the sealing tape. This greatly reduces the counting effort.
4. *Create locations.* Create a system of inventory locations throughout the warehouse, which state the aisle, rack, and bin number in a logical manner. Verify that all locations in the warehouse have a prominently displayed location tag.
5. *Segregate the warehouse.* Install a fence around the warehouse, so that inventory can only pass through a central gate. You can then count and record inventory as it passes through the central gate.
6. *Count inventory.* After all of the preceding steps have been completed, conduct a physical inventory count (see the Physical Inventory Count section later in this chapter).
7. *Record information.* Record the inventory quantities and locations in the inventory database.

Once you have an inventory record keeping system in place, work on upgrading the accuracy of the inventory records. You can do this by installing a daily cycle counting program, which is discussed in the next section.

Cycle Counting

Cycle counting is the process of counting a small proportion of the total inventory on a daily basis, and not only correcting any errors found, but also investigating the underlying reasons why the errors occurred. An active cycle counting program should result in a gradual increase in the level of inventory record accuracy.

> **Tip:** Only the more experienced warehouse staff should engage in cycle counting, since they have the most experience with the inventory. Anyone else would probably make so many mistakes that they would *decrease* the level of inventory record accuracy.

There are three methods most commonly used for selecting the inventory items to be counted each day for a cycle counting program. They are:

- *By location.* Simply work your way through the warehouse, section by section. This approach ensures that all inventory items will be counted, and is a simple way to coordinate the daily counts.

- *By usage*. The materials management department places a higher emphasis on the inventory record accuracy of those items used most frequently in the production process, since an unexpected shortage on one of these items could stop production. Consequently, you would count the high-usage items more frequently.
- *By valuation*. The accounting department is most concerned with the record accuracy of those inventory items having the largest aggregate cost, since an error here would impact reported profits. Consequently, you would count the high-valuation items more frequently.

Some inventory items may move so slowly that there is little need to subject them to cycle counts. In these situations, create a single annual cycle count for them, and exclude them from all other counts during the year.

Once a cycle counting methodology is in place, use the following steps to conduct daily cycle counts:

1. *Complete transactions*. Verify that all prior inventory transactions have been recorded in the inventory database. If you allow cycle counts when there are still some unrecorded transactions, counters will find differences between their counts and the cycle counting report and make adjustments, after which the original transactions are also recorded, resulting in reduced inventory record accuracy.
2. *Print reports*. Print cycle counting reports for the cycle counters, which itemize the counts to be made based on the cycle counting methodology (e.g., by location, usage, or valuation).
3. *Count*. Each cycle counter traces the items listed on his or her cycle counting report to their locations, counts the units in the storage bin, and marks any corrections on the report. Further, the counters should also trace items from the bin back to the report, to see if there are any items in stock that are not in the inventory database.
4. *Reconcile errors*. Investigate any differences between the inventory record and the amounts counted. This process is discussed in the following Inventory Reconciliation section.
5. *Correct errors*. The warehouse staff adjusts the inventory database for any errors found. These adjustments should be clearly designated as cycle counting adjustments.
6. *Take preventive action*. If certain errors are appearing on a repetitive basis, the warehouse manager should adjust the warehouse procedures to keep them from arising in the future.

Tip: You can reinforce the importance of cycle counting by having an accounting or internal audit person conduct a weekly audit of the inventory, and calculate an overall inventory accuracy percentage that is posted for the warehouse staff to see. In addition, consider paying bonuses to the warehouse staff for continuing improvements in inventory record accuracy.

The following section addresses how to investigate the errors found during cycle counts.

Inventory Reconciliation

Inventory is reconciled when you compare the inventory counts in your records to the actual amounts on the warehouse shelves, figure out why there are differences between the two amounts, and make adjustments to your records to reflect this analysis. This is the job of the warehouse manager, but the controller should push for reconciliations to be made.

Inventory reconciliation is an extremely important part of cycle counting, since the warehouse staff uses it to continually update the accuracy of its inventory records. Inventory reconciliation is not as simple as adjusting the book balance to match the physical count. There may be other reasons why there is a difference between the two numbers that cannot be corrected with such an adjustment. In particular, consider following any or all of these steps:

- *Recount the inventory.* It is entirely possible that someone incorrectly counted the inventory. If so, have a different person count it again (since the first counter could make the same counting mistake a second time). Further, if the physical count appears to be significantly lower than the book balance, it is quite possible that there is more inventory in a second location - so look around for a second cache of inventory. Recounting is the most likely reason for a variance, so consider this step first.
- *Match the units of measure.* Are the units of measure used for the count and the book balance the same? One might be in individual units (known as "eaches"), while the other might be in dozens, or boxes, or pounds, or kilograms. If you have already conducted a recount and there is still a difference that is orders of magnitude apart, it is quite likely that the units of measure are the problem.
- *Verify the part number.* It is possible that you are misreading the part number of the item on the shelf, or guessing at its identification because there is no part number at all. If so, get a second opinion from an experienced warehouse staff person, or compare the item to the descriptions in the item master records. Another option is to look for some other item for which there is a unit count variance in the opposite direction - that could be the part number that you are looking for.
- *Look for missing paperwork.* This is an unfortunately large source of inventory reconciliation issues. The unit count in the inventory records may be incorrect because a transaction has occurred, but no one has yet logged it. This is a massive issue for cycle counters, who may have to root around for unentered paperwork of this sort before they feel comfortable in making an adjusting entry to the inventory records. Other examples of this problem are receipts that have not yet been entered (so the inventory record is too low)

or issuances from the warehouse to the production area that have not been entered (so the inventory record is too high).

- *Examine scrap.* Scrap can arise anywhere in a company (especially production), and the staff may easily overlook its proper recordation in the accounting records. If you see a modest variance where the inventory records are always just a small amount higher than the physical count, this is a likely cause.
- *Investigate possible customer ownership.* If you have no record of an inventory item at all in the accounting records, there may be a very good reason for it, which is that the company does not own it – a customer does. This is especially common when the company remodels or enhances products for its customers.
- *Investigate possible supplier ownership.* To follow up on the last item, it is also possible that you have items in stock that are on consignment from a supplier, and which are therefore owned by the supplier. This is most common in a retail environment and highly unlikely anywhere else.
- *Investigate backflushing records.* If your company uses backflushing to alter inventory records (where you relieve inventory based on the number of finished goods produced), then the bill of materials and the finished goods production numbers had better both be in excellent condition, or the reconciliation process will be painful. Backflushing is not recommended unless manufacturing record keeping is superb.
- *Accept the variance.* If all forms of investigation fail, then you really have no choice but to alter the inventory record to match the physical count. It is possible that some other error will eventually be found that explains the discrepancy, but for now you cannot leave a variance; when in doubt, the physical count is correct.

The preceding points give the controller a solid grounding in the reasons why there are errors in inventory records, but they are not the only reasons; other errors may be caused by unique record keeping systems or in particular industries, so compile a list of errors that have been discovered in the past, and use it when conducting an inventory reconciliation.

The Physical Inventory Count

If the company uses a periodic inventory system, or if the inventory records are inaccurate, then the controller will likely be in charge of a physical inventory count at the end of an accounting period. This count provides the unit totals that form the basis for the ending inventory valuation. Follow these steps when administering a physical inventory count:

Prior to the count:

1. *Tags*. Order a sufficient number of sequentially numbered count tags for the count. These should be two-part tags, and include line items for the product name, product identification number, quantity, and location. Also consider adding space for the counter's initials.
2. *Part numbers*. Identify all inventory items that do not have a legible part number, and have the warehouse staff properly identify them prior to the count.
3. *Pre-counts*. Where possible, count items in advance, seal them in containers, and mark the quantities on the outside of the containers.
4. *Segregation*. Move all items not to be counted out of the counting area, or identify them with "Do not count" tags.
5. *Cutoff*. Segregate all received goods if they arrive after the cutoff date for the physical inventory count.
6. *Outside locations*. Notify all outside locations to count their inventory and send in their count totals.

Counting activities:

1. *Train teams*. Instruct the counting teams regarding counting procedures, and issue them count tags that are numerically sequential. Keep track of which team has been issued a set of tags.
2. *Count inventory*. Each counting team must count the inventory in the area assigned to it, fill out the count information on an inventory tag, and tape a tag to each inventory item, retaining the copy of each tag. One person should count inventory, while a second person writes down the information on tags. When a count team is done, it turns in its copies of the tags, as well as any unused tags.
3. *Track tags*. A person responsible for tags verifies that all used and unused tags have been received, and accounts for any missing tags.
4. *Data entry*. Enter all tags into a database, and summarize the quantities by part number and location.
5. *Comparison*. If the company uses a perpetual inventory system, compare the count totals to the inventory records. Investigate any variances by recounting the inventory.
6. *Reporting*. Print a final report that summarizes the unit quantities of all counted inventory items.

Once you have reliable inventory unit quantities, it is time to assign a cost to the inventory. That subject is dealt with in the next section.

Inventory Costing

Five methods for calculating the cost of inventory are shown in the following sections. Of the methods presented, only the first in, first out method and the weighted average method have gained worldwide recognition. The last in, first out method cannot realistically be justified based on the actual flow of inventory, and is only used in the United States under the sanction of the Internal Revenue Service; it is specifically banned under International Financial Reporting Standards. Standard costing is an acceptable alternative to cost layering, as long as any associated variances are properly accounted for. Finally, the retail inventory method should be used only to derive an approximation of the ending inventory cost, and so should be used only in interim reporting periods where a company does not intend to issue any financial results to outside parties.

The First In, First Out Method

The first in, first out (FIFO) method of inventory valuation operates under the assumption that the first goods purchased are also the first goods sold. In most companies, this accounting assumption closely matches the actual flow of goods, and so is considered the most theoretically correct inventory valuation method.

Under the FIFO method, the earliest goods purchased are the first ones removed from the inventory account. This results in the remaining items in inventory being accounted for at the most recently incurred costs, so that the inventory asset recorded on the balance sheet contains costs quite close to the most recent costs that could be obtained in the marketplace. Conversely, this method also results in older historical costs being matched against current revenues and recorded in the cost of goods sold, so the gross margin does not necessarily reflect a proper matching of revenues and costs.

EXAMPLE

Milagro Corporation decides to use the FIFO method for the month of January. During that month, it records the following transactions:

	Quantity Change	Actual Unit Cost	Actual Total Cost
Beginning inventory (layer 1)	+100	$210	$21,000
Sale	-75		
Purchase (layer 2)	+150	280	42,000
Sale	-100		
Purchase (layer 3)	+50	300	15,000
Ending inventory	= 125		

The cost of goods sold in units is calculated as:

100 Beginning inventory + 200 Purchased – 125 Ending inventory = 175 Units

Milagro's controller uses the information in the preceding table to calculate the cost of goods sold for January, as well as the cost of the inventory balance as of the end of January.

	Units	Unit Cost	Total Cost
Cost of goods sold			
FIFO layer 1	100	$210	$21,000
FIFO layer 2	75	280	21,000
Total cost of goods sold	175		$42,000
Ending inventory			
FIFO layer 2	75	280	$21,000
FIFO layer 3	50	300	15,000
Total ending inventory	125		$36,000

Thus, the first FIFO layer, which was the beginning inventory layer, is completely used up during the month, as well as half of Layer 2, leaving half of Layer 2 and all of Layer 3 to be the sole components of the ending inventory.

Note that the $42,000 cost of goods sold and $36,000 ending inventory equals the $78,000 combined total of beginning inventory and purchases during the month.

The Last In, First Out Method

The last in, first out (LIFO) method operates under the assumption that the last item of inventory purchased is the first one sold. Picture a store shelf where a clerk adds items from the front, and customers also take their selections from the front; the remaining items of inventory that are located further from the front of the shelf are rarely picked, and so remain on the shelf – that is a LIFO scenario.

The trouble with the LIFO scenario is that it is rarely encountered in practice. If a company were to use the process flow embodied by LIFO, a significant part of its inventory would be very old, and likely obsolete. Nonetheless, a company does not actually have to experience the LIFO process flow in order to use the method to calculate its inventory valuation.

The reason why companies use LIFO is the assumption that the cost of inventory increases over time, which is a reasonable assumption in times of inflating prices. If you were to use LIFO in such a situation, the cost of the most recently acquired inventory will always be higher than the cost of earlier purchases, so the ending inventory balance will be valued at earlier costs, while the most recent costs appear in the cost of goods sold. By shifting high-cost inventory into the cost of goods sold, a company can reduce its reported level of profitability, and thereby defer its recognition of income taxes. Since income tax deferral is the only justification for LIFO in most situations, it is banned under International Financial Reporting Standards (though it is still allowed in the United States under the approval of the Internal Revenue Service).

EXAMPLE

Milagro Corporation decides to use the LIFO method for the month of March. The following table shows the various purchasing transactions for the company's Elite Roasters product. The quantity purchased on March 1 actually reflects the inventory beginning balance.

Date Purchased	Quantity Purchased	Cost per Unit	Units Sold	Cost of Layer #1	Cost of Layer #2	Total Cost
March 1	150	$210	95	(55 x $210)		$11,550
March 7	100	235	110	(45 x $210)		9,450
March 11	200	250	180	(45 x $210)	(20 x $250)	14,450
March 17	125	240	125	(45 x $210)	(20 x $250)	14,450
March 25	80	260	120	(25 x $210)		5,250

The following bullet points describe the transactions noted in the preceding table:

- *March 1.* Milagro has a beginning inventory balance of 150 units, and sells 95 of these units between March 1 and March 7. This leaves one inventory layer of 55 units at a cost of $210 each.
- *March 7.* Milagro buys 100 additional units on March 7, and sells 110 units between March 7 and March 11. Under LIFO, we assume that the latest purchase was sold first, so there is still just one inventory layer, which has now been reduced to 45 units.
- *March 11.* Milagro buys 200 additional units on March 11, and sells 180 units between March 11 and March 17, which creates a new inventory layer that is comprised of 20 units at a cost of $250. This new layer appears in the table in the "Cost of Layer #2" column.
- *March 17.* Milagro buys 125 additional units on March 17, and sells 125 units between March 17 and March 25, so there is no change in the inventory layers.
- *March 25.* Milagro buys 80 additional units on March 25, and sells 120 units between March 25 and the end of the month. Sales exceed purchases during this period, so the second inventory layer is eliminated, as well as part of the first layer. The result is an ending inventory balance of $5,250, which is derived from 25 units of ending inventory, multiplied by the $210 cost in the first layer that existed at the beginning of the month.

Before implementing the LIFO system, consider the following points:

- *Consistent usage.* The Internal Revenue Service states that a company using LIFO for its tax reporting must also use it for its financial reporting. Thus, a company wanting to defer tax recognition through early expense recognition must show those same low profit numbers to the outside users of its financial statements.
- *Layering.* Since the LIFO system is intended to use the most recent layers of inventory, you may never access earlier layers, which can result in an administrative problem if there are many layers to document.

- *Profit fluctuations*. If early layers contain inventory costs that depart substantially from current market prices, a company could experience sharp changes in its profitability if those layers are ever used.

In summary, LIFO is only useful for deferring income tax payments in periods of cost inflation. It does not reflect the actual flow of inventory in most situations, and may even yield unusual financial results that differ markedly from reality.

The Weighted Average Method

When using the weighted average method, divide the cost of goods available for sale by the number of units available for sale, which yields the weighted-average cost per unit. In this calculation, the cost of goods available for sale is the sum of beginning inventory and net purchases. You then use this weighted-average figure to assign a cost to both ending inventory and the cost of goods sold.

The singular advantage of the weighted average method is the complete absence of any inventory layers, which avoids the record keeping problems that you would encounter with either the FIFO or LIFO methods that were described earlier.

EXAMPLE

Milagro Corporation elects to use the weighted-average method for the month of May. During that month, it records the following transactions:

	Quantity Change	Actual Unit Cost	Actual Total Cost
Beginning inventory	+150	$220	$33,000
Sale	-125		
Purchase	+200	270	54,000
Sale	-150		
Purchase	+100	290	29,000
Ending inventory	= 175		

The actual total cost of all purchased or beginning inventory units in the preceding table is $116,000 ($33,000 + $54,000 + $29,000). The total of all purchased or beginning inventory units is 450 (150 beginning inventory + 300 purchased). The weighted average cost per unit is therefore $257.78 ($116,000 ÷ 450 units.)

The ending inventory valuation is $45,112 (175 units × $257.78 weighted average cost), while the cost of goods sold valuation is $70,890 (275 units × $257.78 weighted average cost). The sum of these two amounts (less a rounding error) equals the $116,000 total actual cost of all purchases and beginning inventory.

In the preceding example, if Milagro used a perpetual inventory system to record its inventory transactions, it would have to recompute the weighted average after every purchase. The following table uses the same information in the preceding example to show the recomputations.

	Units on Hand	Purchases	Cost of Sales	Inventory Total Cost	Inventory Moving Average Unit Cost
Beginning inventory	150	$--	$--	$33,000	$220.00
Sale (125 units @ $220.00)	25	--	27,500	5,500	220.00
Purchase (200 units @ $270.00)	225	54,000	--	59,500	264.44
Sale (150 units @ $264.44)	75	--	39,666	19,834	264.44
Purchase (100 units @ $290.00)	175	29,000	--	48,834	279.05
Total			$67,166		

Note that the cost of goods sold of $67,166 and the ending inventory balance of $48,834 equal $116,000, which matches the total of the costs in the original example. Thus, the totals are the same, but the moving weighted average calculation results in slight differences in the apportionment of costs between the cost of goods sold and ending inventory.

Standard Costing

The preceding methods (FIFO, LIFO, and weighted average) have all operated under the assumption that some sort of cost layering is used, even if that layering results in nothing more than a single weighted-average layer. The standard costing methodology arrives at inventory valuation from an entirely different direction, which is to set a standard cost for each item and to then value those items at the standard cost – not the actual cost at which the items were purchased.

Standard costing is clearly more efficient than any cost layering system, simply because there are no layers to keep track of. However, its primary failing is that the resulting inventory valuation may not equate to the actual cost. The difference is handled through several types of variance calculations, which may be charged to the cost of goods sold (if minor) or allocated between inventory and the cost of goods sold (if material).

At the most basic level, you can create a standard cost simply by calculating the average of the most recent actual cost for the past few months. An additional factor to consider when deriving a standard cost is whether to set it at a historical actual cost level that has been proven to be attainable, or at a rate that should be attainable, or one that can only be reached if all operations work perfectly. Here are some considerations:

- *Historical basis*. This is an average of the costs that a company has already experienced in the recent past, possibly weighted towards just the past few months. Though clearly an attainable cost, a standard based on historical results contains all of the operational inefficiencies of the existing production operation.

- *Attainable basis*. This is a cost that is more difficult to reach than a historical cost. This basis assumes some improvement in operating and purchasing efficiencies, which employees have a good chance of achieving in the short term.
- *Theoretical basis*. This is the ultimate, lowest cost that the facility can attain if it functions perfectly, with no scrap, highly efficient employees, and machines that never break down. This can be a frustrating basis to use for a standard cost, because the production facility can never attain it, and so always produces unfavorable variances.

Of the three types of standards noted here, use the attainable basis, because it gives employees a reasonable cost target to pursue. If you continually update standards on this basis, a production facility will have an incentive to continually drive down its costs over the long term.

Standard costs are stored separately from all other accounting records, usually in a bill of materials for finished goods, and in the item master file for raw materials. An item master is a record that lists the name, description, unit of measure, weight, dimensions, ordering quantity, and other key information for a component part.

At the end of a reporting period, the following steps show how to integrate standard costs into the accounting system (assuming the use of a periodic inventory system):

1. *Cost verification*. Review the standard cost database for errors and correct it as necessary. Also, if it is time to do so, update the standard costs to more accurately reflect actual costs.
2. *Inventory valuation*. Multiply the number of units in ending inventory by their standard costs to derive the ending inventory valuation.
3. *Calculate the cost of goods sold*. Add purchases during the month to the beginning inventory and subtract the ending inventory to determine the cost of goods sold.
4. *Enter updated balances*. Create a journal entry that reduces the purchases account to zero and which also adjusts the inventory asset account balance to the ending total standard cost, with the offset to the cost of goods sold account.

EXAMPLE

A division of the Milagro Corporation is using a standard costing system to calculate its inventory balances and cost of goods sold. The company conducts a month-end physical inventory count that results in a reasonably accurate set of unit quantities for all inventory items. The controller multiplies each of these unit quantities by their standard costs to derive the ending inventory valuation. This ending balance is $2,500,000.

The beginning balance in the inventory account is $2,750,000 and purchases during the month were $1,000,000, so the calculation of the cost of goods sold is:

Beginning inventory	$2,750,000
+ Purchases	1,000,000
- Ending inventory	(2,500,000)
= Cost of goods sold	$1,250,000

To record the correct ending inventory balance and cost of goods sold, the controller records the following entry, which clears out the purchases asset account and adjusts the ending inventory balance to $2,500,000:

	Debit	Credit
Cost of goods sold	1,250,000	
Purchases		1,000,000
Inventory		250,000

The calculation and reporting of the variances between standard and actual costs is addressed in the Management Reports chapter.

The Retail Inventory Method

The retail inventory method is sometimes used by retailers that resell merchandise to estimate their ending inventory balances. This method is based on the relationship between the cost of merchandise and its retail price. To calculate the cost of ending inventory using the retail inventory method, follow these steps:

1. Calculate the cost-to-retail percentage, for which the formula is (Cost ÷ Retail price).
2. Calculate the cost of goods available for sale, for which the formula is (Cost of beginning inventory + Cost of purchases).
3. Calculate the cost of sales during the period, for which the formula is (Sales × cost-to-retail percentage).
4. Calculate ending inventory, for which the formula is (Cost of goods available for sale - Cost of sales during the period).

EXAMPLE

Milagro Corporation sells home coffee roasters for an average of $200, and which cost it $140. This is a cost-to-retail percentage of 70%. Milagro's beginning inventory has a cost of $1,000,000, it paid $1,800,000 for purchases during the month, and it had sales of $2,400,000. The calculation of its ending inventory is:

Beginning inventory	$1,000,000	(at cost)
Purchases	+ 1,800,000	(at cost)
Goods available for sale	= 2,800,000	
Sales	- 1,680,000	(sales of $2,400,000 × 70%)
Ending inventory	= $1,120,000	

The retail inventory method is a quick and easy way to determine an approximate ending inventory balance. However, there are also several issues with it:

- The retail inventory method is only an estimate. Do not rely upon it too heavily to yield results that will compare with those of a physical inventory count.
- The retail inventory method only works if you have a consistent mark-up across all products sold. If not, the actual ending inventory cost may vary wildly from what you derived using this method.
- The method assumes that the historical basis for the mark-up percentage continues into the current period. If the mark-up was different (as may be caused by an after-holidays sale), then the results of the calculation will be incorrect.

Accounting for Obsolete Inventory

Obsolete inventory is a major problem for the controller, because it tends to build up over time until discovered by the auditors at the end of the year, resulting in a large (and unexpected) write-off. The controller then presents management with the unexpected loss, and is frequently blamed for it.

You can reduce the risk of having a large amount of obsolete inventory by creating a materials review board. This group is drawn from members of the production, engineering, purchasing, and accounting departments, and is tasked with rooting out and selling off obsolete inventory. The group should meet once a month, and either reviews inventory usage reports or physically examines the inventory to determine which items should be disposed of.

You then review the findings of the materials review board to determine the most likely disposition price of the obsolete items, subtract this projected amount from the book value of the obsolete items, and set aside the difference as a reserve. As the company later disposes of the items, or the estimated amounts to be received from disposition change, adjust the reserve account to reflect these events.

EXAMPLE

Milagro Corporation has $100,000 of excess home coffee roasters it cannot sell. However, it believes there is a market for the roasters through a reseller in China, but only at a sale price of $20,000. Accordingly, the controller recognizes a reserve of $80,000 with the following journal entry:

	Debit	Credit
Cost of goods sold	80,000	
Reserve for obsolete inventory		80,000

After finalizing the arrangement with the Chinese reseller, the actual sale price is only $19,000, so the controller completes the transaction with the following entry, recognizing an additional $1,000 of expense:

	Debit	Credit
Reserve for obsolete inventory	80,000	
Cost of goods sold	1,000	
Inventory		81,000

The example makes inventory obsolescence accounting look simple enough, but it is not. The issues are:

- *Timing.* You can improperly alter a company's reported financial results by altering the timing of the actual dispositions. As an example, if a supervisor knows that he can receive a higher-than-estimated price on the disposition of obsolete inventory, then he can either accelerate or delay the sale in order to shift gains into whichever reporting period needs the extra profit.
- *Expense recognition.* Management may be reluctant to suddenly drop a large expense reserve into the financial statements, preferring instead to recognize small incremental amounts which make inventory obsolescence appear to be a minor problem. Since Generally Accepted Accounting Principles mandate immediate recognition of any obsolescence as soon as it is detected, the controller may have a struggle forcing immediate recognition through the objections of management.
- *Timely reviews.* Inventory obsolescence is a minor issue as long as management reviews inventory on a regular basis, so that the incremental amount of obsolescence detected is small in any given period. However, if management does not conduct a review for a long time, this allows obsolete inventory to build up to quite impressive proportions, along with an equally impressive amount of expense recognition. To avoid this issue, conduct frequent obsolescence reviews, and maintain a reserve based on historical or expected obsolescence, even if the specific inventory items have not yet been identified. Also, encourage the warehouse manager to make full use of the reserve, which he should treat as an opportunity to eliminate ancient items from stock.
- *Management resistance.* Senior managers may not believe the controller when he presents them with a massive inventory write down, and so will reject any attempt to recognize an obsolescence reserve. If so, hire outside consultants who will independently review the inventory and present their

own obsolescence report to management. This second opinion may bring sufficient professional weight to bear that management will grudgingly allow you to create the reserve.

EXAMPLE

Milagro Corporation sets aside an obsolescence reserve of $25,000 for obsolete roasters. However, in January the purchasing manager knows that the resale price for obsolete roasters has plummeted, so the real reserve should be closer to $35,000, which would call for the immediate recognition of an additional $10,000 of expense. Since this would result in an overall reported loss in Milagro's financial results in January, he waits until April, when Milagro has a very profitable month, and completes the sale at that time, thereby incorrectly delaying the additional obsolescence loss until the point of sale.

Summary

When selecting systems for the tracking and costing of inventory, the key issue is to achieve very high levels of inventory record accuracy. This gives the accounting department very reliable cost information. Consequently, push for the use of a perpetual inventory system and a robust cycle counting program.

Inventory management is an area of particular concern to the controller, for it is usually supervised by someone outside of the accounting department. Thus, it is entirely possible that inventory record accuracy will reflect poorly upon the controller, despite having little control over it. You can eliminate this problem by obtaining direct supervisory control over the warehouse. This allows for much better record accuracy, and therefore more reliable financial statements.

Not all subjects related to inventory have been addressed in this chapter. You can also find discussions of month-end overhead allocations and the application of the lower of cost or market rule in the Closing the Books chapter. For an in-depth discussion of all accounting concepts related to inventory, see the author's *Accounting for Inventory* book, which is available at accountingtools.com.

Chapter 6
Fixed Assets Management

Introduction

The controller is responsible for managing the accounting records related to fixed assets, as well as the system of fixed asset controls. This chapter addresses both topics, as well as the basic entries required to account for fixed assets, and the range of systems available for tracking them.

Related Podcast Episodes: Episodes 122, 139, and 196 of the Accounting Best Practices Podcast discuss fixed asset disposals, a lean system for fixed assets, and fixed asset counting, respectively. You can listen to them at: **accountingtools.com/podcasts** or **iTunes**

Controller Responsibilities

The controller is not usually responsible for authorizing the purchase of fixed assets, but is responsible for all record keeping once they have been acquired. This involves the following responsibilities:

- Create a fixed asset tracking system.
- Record the acquisition of and changes to fixed assets, either through their purchase or exchange.
- Properly calculate depreciation and amortization on all fixed assets having a useful life.
- Record the disposal of fixed assets, including their removal from the records of the business.
- Establish a system of controls over the purchase, disposal, existence, and recordation of fixed assets.
- Maintain adequate property records for all fixed assets regarding their cost, depreciation, and other information.

Fixed Asset Tracking

The controller may be held responsible for fixed assets, or at least for the tracking system used to monitor where they are located. There are a number of methods for tracking fixed assets, which are outlined in this section.

Tag Tracking

The traditional approach to tracking assets is to epoxy a metal tag onto each fixed asset. The tag has an asset number engraved on it; the asset number corresponds to a record number in a computer database or a manual record that itemizes the name, description, location, and other key information about a fixed asset.

The advantage of the metal tag is that it is almost indestructible and provides a unique identifier. However, a determined thief can remove the tag, and it may be considered a detriment to the resale value of an asset.

Some variations on the tag tracking concept that have differing advantages and disadvantages are:

- *Etching.* You can etch the asset number directly onto the surface of a fixed asset. This makes it nearly impossible to remove the asset number, but also defaces the asset, and may reduce its resale value.
- *Paper tags.* If you intend to resell a fixed asset at a later date and do not want to deface it with a metal tag, affix a plastic-laminated paper tag instead (or a paper tag that has been covered with tape). The lamination tends to reduce the amount of damage to the tag. The problem with this approach is that the tags may fall off.
- *Serial numbers.* If most fixed assets already have a manufacturer's serial number attached to them, you can use this information instead. Serial numbers are generally affixed quite securely, and so are a good alternative. However, they may be located in out-of-the-way places, and they may involve such long character strings that they do not fit in the tag number field in the company's tag tracking software.

Some companies do not bother with asset tagging, if their assets are few or so immovable that they are easily tracked without any identification method at all. Also, companies dealing with large numbers of low-cost fixed assets may view them as essentially office supplies that will be replaced every few years (such as laptop computers), and which are therefore not worth the effort of such a formalized tracking system.

Bar Code Tracking

Some asset tags can contain quite a long string of digits, especially if you use the manufacturer's serial number as a substitute for an asset tag. It is easy to transpose these numbers when copying them down, which leads to identification errors. It is also a slow process to write down tag numbers. A faster, more efficient, and less error-prone technique is to instead track fixed assets using bar coded labels.

Bar code tracking involves printing a bar code that contains the tag number (and sometimes additional information), laminating the label to prevent tearing, affixing it to a fixed asset, and using a portable scanner to read the label. The person performing the scans may also punch in a location code, and perhaps an asset condition code, and then uploads the record to the fixed assets database, where it is matched to the fixed asset record using the tag number.

Tip: Do not apply too many lamination layers to a bar code label, or else the bar code scanner will not be able to read it.

It is possible for bar code labels to fall off an asset and be lost, and they can easily be removed by a thief. Thus, they do not necessarily provide a permanent tag. However, they present an extremely efficient method for quickly recording asset locations, as you may do during an annual fixed asset audit.

> **Tip:** If you use bar code tracking, put the bar code in an easily accessible part of the asset, so that you can access it with a portable bar code scanner. In addition, securely affix a metal asset tag in a less accessible part of the asset, where a thief is less likely to see it.

Bar coding is especially useful when you are dealing with large numbers of fixed assets that are not easily differentiated from each other, such as cubicle walls.

RFID Tracking – Active Transmission

The trouble with the bar coding solution just described is that someone needs to locate the asset, then locate the bar code on the asset, then scan it with a portable scanner, and then upload the contents of the scanner to the computer system in order to log the asset into the system. This means that you have to go to the asset in order to track it, which can be fairly labor-intensive. An alternative that eliminates these problems to a great extent is radio frequency identification (RFID).

In an RFID system, you affix an RFID tag to each asset, which periodically transmits its location through RFID receiving stations to a central database for viewing. The system determines the locations of assets based on their relative signal strengths as received by the RFID receiving stations located throughout the facility. The RFID tags have their own batteries, which can last as long as five years before requiring replacement. A variation on the RFID concept is the transmission of ultrasound signals. Ultrasound does not penetrate room walls, and so does not create the false-location signals that may sometimes arise in an RFID system.

If most of your fixed assets are bolted down or so heavy as to be essentially immovable, then there is clearly no need to install an RFID tracking system. Instead, only use it to track those assets that will probably be moved from time to time, and for which there is an absolute need to know their locations (such as medical equipment in a critical care facility). In this latter case, the RFID system may actually *reduce* the investment in fixed assets, since you will be able to avoid purchasing additional fixed assets that might otherwise have been held in reserve to cover for assets that could not be located. An RFID system also makes it easier for the maintenance staff to locate equipment that is scheduled for maintenance, eliminates the time spent searching for equipment, speeds up the auditing of fixed assets, and prevents managers from hoarding equipment.

RFID Tracking – Passive Transmission

The RFID tracking system just noted incorporates battery-powered RFID tags that transmit their own signals to RFID receivers, so that a signal is being generated at regular intervals. An alternative system employs RFID tags that contain no batteries at all. Instead, these tags use the power from a nearby RFID transceiver to transmit a signal. These tags are less expensive, and also can potentially last for many years without replacement. This passive transmission system is ideal for monitoring the movement of fixed assets past a fixed point, such as an exit from a building. If you place an RFID transceiver at that point, it can trigger an alarm when a fixed asset is moved past it, or can activate a camera that photographs both the person moving the asset and the asset itself, along with a time and date stamp on any images taken.

Use passive RFID tags on those fixed assets that are easily movable and which have a high resale value (such as laptop computers and other office equipment).

Accounting for Fixed Assets

This section does not address the multitude of accounting standards related to fixed assets, but does contain the most common accounting entries that you are likely to deal with. For a detailed examination of the accounting standards related to fixed assets, see the author's *Fixed Asset Accounting* book. The following journal entries show the format to use for most accounting transactions related to fixed assets. They are sorted in alphabetical order by type of activity.

Amortization. To record the amortization of intangible assets for a reporting period.

	Debit	Credit
Amortization expense	xxx	
Accumulated amortization		xxx

Asset exchange. To record the exchange of dissimilar assets. This entry also eliminates the accumulated depreciation on the asset being relinquished. There are line items in the entry for the recognition of either a gain or a loss on the exchange. You may need to add either a debit or a credit to this entry if cash is being paid or accepted.

	Debit	Credit
Asset acquired [state the account]	xxx	
Accumulated depreciation	xxx	
Loss on asset exchange [if any]	xxx	
Gain on asset exchange [if any]		xxx
Asset relinquished [state the account]		xxx

Asset impairment. To record the reduction in an asset's book value to its fair value when the fair value is less than its book value.

	Debit	Credit
Impairment loss	xxx	
Accumulated impairment		xxx

Component replacement. To record the replacement of a component. This entry eliminates the original asset and any accumulated depreciation, while a second entry records the replacement component. There is a loss on asset derecognition stated in the entry, on the assumption that the asset being replaced has not yet been fully depreciated as of the replacement date.

	Debit	Credit
Loss on asset derecognition [if any]	xxx	
Accumulated depreciation	xxx	
Asset [being replaced, state the account]		xxx

	Debit	Credit
Asset [state the account]	xxx	
Cash or Accounts payable		xxx

Depreciation. To record the depreciation expense incurred for a reporting period. Many line items are presented for the depreciation for different departments.

	Debit	Credit
Depreciation expense – Administration	xxx	
Depreciation – Engineering		
Depreciation – Materials management		
Depreciation – Production		
Depreciation – Purchasing		
Depreciation – Sales and marketing		
Accumulated depreciation		xxx

Derecognition (sale). To eliminate a fixed asset from the accounting records upon its disposal through a sale to a third party. The entry provides for recognition of either a gain or loss on the transaction.

	Debit	Credit
Cash	xxx	
Accumulated depreciation	xxx	
Loss on asset sale [if any]	xxx	
Gain on asset sale [if any]		xxx
Asset [state the account]		xxx

Interest capitalization. To capitalize the interest cost associated with the construction of a fixed asset.

	Debit	Credit
Asset [state the account]	xxx	
Interest expense		xxx

Fixed Asset Controls

There can be a large amount of cash tied up in fixed assets, so it is imperative to have a system of controls over them. The key issues are ensuring that investments are made in only those fixed assets that the business actually needs, making it difficult for them to be stolen, and ensuring that they are disposed of properly. We address these controls below.

Controls for Fixed Asset Acquisition

The key focus of controls for the acquisition of fixed assets is to ensure that the company needs the assets. This means that controls are designed to require an evaluation of how a proposed acquisition will fit into the company's operations, and what kind of return on investment it will generate. Consider using the following controls:

- *Require an approval form.* There should be an approval form that requires an applicant to describe the asset, how it is to be used, and the return on investment that will be generated (if any). This standardizes the information about each fixed asset, and also provides a handy signature form for various approvals.
- *Require independent analysis of the approval form.* Someone who is skilled in asset analysis should review each submitted approval form. This analysis should include a verification that all supporting documents are attached to the form, that all assumptions are reasonable, and that the conclusions reached appear to be valid. The person conducting this analysis does not necessarily render an opinion on whether to acquire the asset, but should point out any flaws in the proposal.
- *Reconcile fixed asset additions to approval forms.* If asset purchases are allowed without an authorizing purchase order, then compare all additions

listed in the fixed asset general ledger accounts to the signed approval forms, to see if any assets were bought without approval.

A final control that is quite useful for judging the accuracy of asset purchase requests is to conduct a post-completion project analysis. This analysis highlights variations between the projections that managers inserted into their original asset purchase proposals and what eventually transpired. There will always be differences between these two sets of information, since no one can forecast results perfectly. However, it is useful to look for patterns of unbridled optimism in the original purchase proposals to determine which managers are continually overstating their projections in order to have their proposals approved.

The controls noted here will absolutely slow down the fixed asset acquisition process, and with good reason – part of their intent is to encourage more deliberation of why an asset is being acquired. Nonetheless, these controls will appear onerous to those people trying to obtain assets that are relatively inexpensive, so it is acceptable to adopt a reduced set of controls for such assets, perhaps simply treating them as accounts payable that require a single approval signature on a purchase order.

Controls for Fixed Asset Theft

Fixed assets may have a notable resale value, which makes the more portable ones subject to theft. Here are several controls that can be of assistance in preventing or at least mitigating asset losses due to theft:

- *Segregate fixed asset responsibilities.* You are making it much easier for an employee to steal an asset if you give that person complete responsibility over all aspects of asset purchasing, recordation, and disposal, since they can alter documents at will. Consequently, the person who receives a fixed asset should not be the same person who records the transaction, while the person who disposes of an asset cannot also record the sale. Further, the person who audits fixed assets should not be involved with fixed assets in any other way.
- *Restrict access to assets.* If some assets are especially valuable and can be easily removed from the premises, restrict access to them with a variety of security card access systems, gates, security guards, and so forth.
- *Assign assets to employees.* Assign responsibility for specific assets to employees, and tie some portion of their annual performance appraisals to the presence and condition of those assets. This control works best at the department level, where department managers are assigned responsibility for the assets in their areas. Create a system that issues a periodic report to each responsible person, detailing the assets under their control, and reminding them to notify a senior manager if any assets are missing. Also, if you shift responsibility for assets from one person to another, you need a process for doing so, where the newly-responsible person formally evaluates the condition of each asset and takes responsibility for it.

- *Conduct a fixed asset audit.* Have an internal auditor conduct an annual audit of all fixed assets to verify where they are located, the condition they are in, and whether they are still being used.
- *Link RFID tags to alarm system.* Install an RFID scanner next to every point of exit, which will trigger an alarm if anyone attempts to remove an asset that has an RFID tag attached to it.

Controls for Fixed Asset Disposal

There tends to be a certain amount of fixed asset "leakage" out of a company, especially for smaller and more mobile assets, such as computers. In many cases, the resale value of these items near the end of their useful lives is so small that a company may very well be justified in giving them away to employees or simply dropping them into the scrap bin. However, there may be some residual value remaining in these assets, so consider using the following controls to recapture some of that value:

- *Conduct asset disposition reviews.* The goals of this review are to decide whether a company no longer needs a fixed asset, and if so, how to obtain the highest price for it. If you do not use this control, assets tend to remain on the premises long after they are no longer useful, and lose value during that time. The best group for conducting this analysis is the industrial engineering staff, since they are responsible for the production layout, and most fixed assets are located in this area.
- *Require signed approval of asset dispositions.* Create a form that describes the asset to be disposed of, the method of disposition, and the cash to be received (if any). The person whose authorization is required could be a specialist in asset disposition, or perhaps the purchasing manager, who might have some knowledge of asset values. The point of this control is to require a last look by someone who might know of a better way to gain more value from a disposal.
- *Monitor cash receipts from asset sales.* Most fixed assets are sold for cash. Given the amount of funds involved, it can be quite a temptation for employees to find ways to either not record asset sales or falsify sale documents to record smaller sales, and then pocket the undocumented cash. You can monitor this by requiring that a bill of sale from the purchasing entity accompany the documentation for each asset sale.

Fixed Asset Record Keeping

At a minimum, maintain a fixed asset record keeping system where copies of the purchase records for all fixed assets are stored in a well-organized binder. This is extremely useful for auditors, who reference the binder when auditing the fixed asset records. In addition, it may be useful to maintain more detailed records for each fixed asset, in order to address such issues as locations, serial numbers, responsible parties, and so forth. The level of detail will depend on the situation and the usefulness of the resulting information. As an example of more thorough record keeping, you could track some or all of the following information:

- *Description*. This is a description of the equipment that is sufficient to identify it.
- *Tag number*. This is the identification number of the asset tag that the company affixes to its assets.
- *Serial number*. If no tag numbers are used, instead list the serial number of the asset, as assigned by the manufacturer.
- *Location*. Note the location where the asset resides.
- *Responsible party*. This is the name or position of the person who is responsible for the equipment.
- *In service date*. This is the date on which the equipment is ready for its intended use, and is the traditional trigger date for the start of depreciation.
- *Cost*. The cost may simply be the original purchase price, or it may be a more extensive record of additions to the equipment over time as high-cost items are replaced.
- *Useful life*. This can be the manufacturer's recommended equipment life, or you can supplement it over time if management concludes that the useful life should be changed, with notations regarding the impact on the depreciation rate.
- *Asset class*. Note the class of assets in which the equipment is categorized. Since a standard depreciation method is typically assigned to an asset class, you do not also have to specify the depreciation method. If you use a standard useful life for an asset class, then you do not have to separately record an asset's useful life.
- *Warranty period*. This is the period during which the manufacturer will pay for repairs to the equipment. If there is a cost-effective warranty extension option, note it here.
- *Supplier contact information*. This may include several addresses for the supplier, such as for its field servicing, customer service, warranty, and sales departments.
- *Impairment circumstances*. If there has been a write down in the value of the equipment due to impairment, note the circumstances of the impairment and when it occurred. This may require extensive documentation if there have been several impairments.

It is useful to consolidate this information in one place with any manufacturer's warranty documents, as well as a copy of key maintenance records.

How long should you retain documents related to fixed assets? The exact requirements will vary, depending upon the rules imposed by any taxing authority that wishes to audit them. Given that the retention period may be quite long, consider the following two policies:

- *Do not keep title records on site.* Title records are too valuable to keep on site, where they may be stolen, lost, or destroyed. Instead, keep copies on site for audit purposes, and keep the originals in a secure place, such as a lock box in a bank.
- *Exclude fixed asset records from archiving.* An efficient company likely has an archiving process for shifting its less necessary documents off-site into lower-cost storage areas, and then destroying them at pre-planned intervals. Exclude *all* fixed asset records from the archiving process, to avoid any risk of destroying the paperwork associated with a fixed asset that may still be on the premises. Instead, have a separate procedure for eliminating these documents only when the related assets have been disposed of and there is no government requirement for further document retention.

Audit Requirements

If a company has a large investment in its fixed assets, expect the outside auditors to demand a detailed accounting of all transactions as part of the annual audit. If there is a significant amount of activity in the fixed asset accounts, it can be difficult to maintain proper records. To ensure that the records are in adequate condition for the auditors, construct a fixed asset roll forward report, and update it as part of every month-end close. By doing so, this key report will be ready for submission to the auditors without any missing documentation or accounting errors.

Sample Fixed Asset Roll Forward Report

Account Number	Description	Beginning Balance 12/31/20x1	Additions/ Deletions	Ending Balance 12/31/x2
Asset Categories				
1510	Computer equipment	$4,200,000	$380,000	$4,580,000
1520	Furniture and fixtures	350,000	(20,000)	330,000
1535	Land improvements	150,000	--	150,000
1545	Machinery	3,100,000	600,000	3,700,000
1550	Office equipment	200,000	40,000	240,000
	Asset totals	$8,000,000	$1,000,000	$9,000,000
Accumulated Depreciation Categories				
1610	Computer equipment	$(1,050,000)	$(500,000)	$(1,550,000)
1620	Furniture and fixtures	(160,000)	(50,000)	(210,000)
1635	Land improvements	(10,000)	(10,000)	(20,000)
1645	Machinery	(900,000)	(320,000)	(1,220,000)
1650	Office equipment	(30,000)	(20,000)	(50,000)
	Accumulated depreciation totals	$(2,150,000)	$(900,000)	$(3,050,000)
	Grand total fixed assets	$5,850,000	$100,000	$5,950,000

The fixed asset roll forward is a summary table that begins with the totals for each fixed asset account at the beginning of the audit period, adds to it any changes during the period that related to asset additions and deletions, and then concludes with the ending balances for all of these accounts. The auditors trace the beginning balances in this table to their audited financial statements from the preceding year, as well as the ending balances listed in their trial balance for this year, and all of the changes listed for the current period. This is a significant document for the auditors, so one should ensure that the information in it is correct and ties to all general ledger balances before submitting it to them.

Summary

This chapter described the day-to-day management issues related to fixed assets. The controller should be primarily concerned with the detailed accounting and record keeping required for fixed assets. Given the amount of money involved, this is an area in which auditors expect to see accurate record keeping that incorporates proper depreciation calculations. If these records have not been properly maintained, it reflects poorly upon the performance of the controller.

In addition, it is possible that the accounting staff may become involved in capital budgeting, which is the analysis of proposals to acquire additional fixed assets. We address this topic separately in the Capital Budgeting chapter.

Chapter 7
Accounts Payable Management

Introduction

The accounts payable function can be a snarled mass of unresolved paperwork, because a traditional payables system calls for the verification of all supplier invoices prior to payment, as well as the detailed review of all employee expense reports. The result can be late payments, angry suppliers, and unreimbursed employees. This chapter describes a number of methods for improving the accounts payable process flow, as well as a discussion of the controls needed for this process.

Related Podcast Episodes: Episodes 81, 82, and 138 of the Accounting Best Practices Podcast discuss accounts payable best practices, accounts payable matching, and a lean system for accounts payable, respectively. You can listen to them at: **accountingtools.com/podcasts** or **iTunes**

Controller Responsibilities

In general, the controller is responsible for the timely payment of suppliers, so there are no issues with the ongoing functions of the business. More specifically, the controller is responsible for the following:

- Maintain a reliable payables processing system that generates the correct payments by scheduled payment due dates.
- Properly distribute payments to the correct general ledger accounts.
- Accrue supplier expenses as needed.
- Calculate and remit use taxes.
- Maintain a system of controls to ensure that only valid payments are made to suppliers.
- Make use of early payment discounts offered by suppliers, if doing so is economical for the company.

This chapter addresses all of the preceding responsibilities.

Accounts Payable Management

A poorly-managed accounts payable function can be extremely inefficient, primarily because of the underlying flow of paperwork and authorizations. The following management topics address a variety of ways to streamline the accounts payable function, making it easier to issue payments on time while using fewer staff resources. The improvement concepts are:

Paper Flow

- *Delivery of invoices.* Supplier invoices may be delivered to all parts of a business – to the sales staff, the receiving department, the purchasing department, and so on. When this happens, it may take weeks for the invoice recipients to forward them to the accounting department. The accounting staff must then make rush payments, and is probably unable to take advantage of any early payment discounts. To avoid this problem, contact all new suppliers and inform them that invoices are to be sent straight to the accounts payable department.
- *On-line data entry.* If the company's accounts payable system is sufficiently sophisticated, consider linking it to a web-based invoice data entry system, and having suppliers enter their invoices directly into the on-line system. Doing so eliminates all data entry by the accounts payable staff.
- *Streamline approvals.* A major problem is sending invoices out for approval, and either receiving them back late or not at all. Some managers consider invoice approvals to be of minimal importance, and so they persistently let invoices pile up on their desks. There are several ways to avoid this problem. The best is the concept of *negative approval*, where the accounting department records each incoming supplier invoice in the accounting system for payment, and then sends a copy of the invoice to the relevant person for approval; the department assumes that the invoice is approved, unless it hears otherwise from the approver. Thus, the approver can simply throw away his or her copy of an invoice if there is no problem with it, and the accounting department processes the original document for approval. We highly recommend this approach, since it greatly streamlines the payment process. However, if some invoices are so large that approval is mandatory, then the best approach is to manually walk the invoice to the approver, and wait while the approver examines it; if the person is not available, walk it to the backup approver. This approach is very labor-intensive, but ensures that larger invoices are approved at once. Another option is to exempt from approval all recurring or small-dollar items, though it may be worthwhile to conduct an occasional review of them.

Systems

- *Automate expense reporting.* There are several third-party providers of automated expense reporting that allow employees to enter their expense reports through a web site. The site uses a decision engine to automatically examine submissions for compliance with the company's expense reporting policies, and accepts or rejects expense line items based on that review. The results are then sent to the company's accounting system through an interface. This approach allows for the detailed examination of expense reports, but is too expensive for smaller organizations.
- *Create a payment factory.* If the company has a number of dispersed accounts payable operations in different subsidiaries, consider centralizing

them into a single operation, known as a payment factory. By doing so, you can concentrate on installing the most efficient process flow, similar to what might be found in a well-engineered production operation. This typically involves scanning supplier invoices into the accounting software and using a workflow management system to ensure that payment approvals are obtained in a timely manner. A key procedural issue with the payment factory concept is ensuring that supplier invoices are forwarded from the subsidiaries as quickly as possible, to ensure that payments are made by the required due dates.

Data

- *Scrub accounts payable.* This is the periodic cleanup of the vendor master file in the accounting software. When you scrub accounts payable, you are eliminating duplicate entries in the file, so there are no duplicate records for the same supplier. It also means that you delete inactive suppliers from the file. Scrubbing reduces the risk of having different records for the same supplier, each with potentially different payment terms, addresses, and so forth. Also, by concentrating purchases under a single record, you can more easily approach suppliers about volume discounts. Consider scheduling an accounts payable scrubbing at least once a year.
- *Invoice number assignment.* Some invoices arrive without an invoice number, so you run a risk of paying them twice because they are not uniquely identified. This is a common problem with utility bills and employee expense reports. If they are uniquely and consistently identified, the accounts payable software should flag duplicate invoices. To correct the problem, create a procedure for uniquely identifying each invoice based on information within the invoice. For example, you can create an invoice number based on the date of the invoice. Thus, a December 15, 2014 invoice could be assigned an invoice number of 12152014. Or, if an employee submits several expense reports on the same day, you could assign an invoice number based on the beginning and last expenditure dates listed on each expense report. Thus, if the first expenditure was on December 7, 2014 and the last expenditure was on December 14, 2014, then the invoice number could be 12072014-12142014. The key issue is to be consistent, so that if a copy of an invoice is submitted, the accounting staff will use the procedure to derive exactly the same invoice number that it created for the original invoice, which the accounting software will then flag as a duplicate and reject for payment.

Efficiencies

- *Issue procurement cards.* Each purchase made by a company generates an inordinate amount of paperwork, and most of that paperwork finds its way into the accounts payable area. To reduce this paperwork, roll out company procurement cards (i.e., credit cards) to those people within the company who buy large amounts of lower-cost items on a recurring basis. By making these purchases with procurement cards, there is a greatly reduced need for purchase orders, while the number of supplier invoices reaching the accounting department is similarly reduced. There are risks involving unauthorized purchases, so procurement cards should only be issued to those employees capable of handling the purchasing responsibility.

- *Highlight early payment discounts.* When a supplier offers early payment discounts, it is normally an ongoing offer, which can therefore be flagged in the vendor master file, along with the discount percentage and the date by which payment must be made. Use the report writer in the accounting software to generate a daily report that only shows the unpaid invoices of those suppliers offering early payment discounts, as well as the amount of the discounts to be earned. You can then monitor these invoices to ensure that they are approved and paid by the date required to earn the early payment discount.
- *Withhold payments pending W-9 receipt.* The accounting department is supposed to issue a Form 1099 to its suppliers following the end of the calendar year. This can be a problem if suppliers have not submitted a Form W-9, which contains the taxpayer identification number that is included on the Form 1099. To avoid this year-end issue, refuse to pay suppliers if they have not yet submitted a Form W-9.

Only apply the preceding suggestions if they work within the restrictions of your business. Some items are only useful for larger businesses, such as payment factories and automated expense reporting. Other suggestions, such as procurement cards, streamlining approvals, and scrubbing accounts payable, are more generally applicable. Ideally, strive for a system that contains sufficient controls to mitigate the risk of overpaying suppliers, while using the smallest possible amount of staff time.

Three-Way Matching

The classic control over accounts payable is called three-way matching. This involves having an accounting clerk match a supplier's invoice not only to the authorizing purchase order issued by the company's purchasing department, but also to evidence of receipt from the receiving department. By doing so, you know that the purchase was both authorized and received. This initially appears acceptable, but is actually difficult to administer, for the following reasons:

- *Paperwork.* The accounting clerk can only authorize a payment if he or she can find the supplier invoice, purchase order, and evidence of receipt. If any of this paperwork is missing, or if it is not apparent that a document is associated with a specific supplier invoice, then the clerk cannot proceed with matching. This means that the invoice is not paid on time.

- *Matching amounts*. What if the supplier shipped an amount different from the amount authorized, or billed the company an amount different from what was stated in the purchase order? The accounting clerk is usually given some leeway in authorizing payment if these differences are small, but larger variances are sent back to the purchasing department for authorization – which takes more time.
- *Purchase orders*. Three-way matching only works if there is an authorizing purchase order. This means that the purchasing staff must issue *a lot* of purchase orders.

Clearly, there are many problems with three-way matching. It is possible to resolve some of these issues with automation. For example, you can scan all incoming supplier invoices, use image conversion software to extract the key information from each invoice, and match it to the purchasing and receiving information already input into the computer system by the purchasing and receiving departments. Such systems automate a large part of the three-way matching chore. However, these systems also kick out any transactions for which they cannot find a three-way match, so a certain amount of manual processing is still required. In addition, these systems are expensive, and usually require the installation of an enterprise resources planning system that links the activities of the purchasing, receiving, and accounting departments.

A less expensive and easier way to deal with three-way matching is to strip away from it any transactions that are repetitive or too small to be worth the effort of matching. For example, a recurring rent invoice can be exempted from the matching process, while smaller items can be purchased with corporate purchasing cards and approved in bulk. Actions such as these can confine three-way matching to a much smaller group of expensive transactions, thereby reducing the efforts of the accounts payable staff.

Use Taxes

Use tax is the sales tax on purchased goods, where the seller is not responsible for collecting the tax; instead, the buyer calculates the amount of the tax and remits it to the applicable government authorities. If a business is buying goods or services for its own use and is not paying a sales tax on those items, then it is likely that the entity should be paying a use tax instead.

Few companies go to the effort of tracking use tax or paying it to the local government, for two reasons. First, it is usually a painfully manual process to calculate the use tax. Second, once a company starts remitting use tax payments, the local government will come to expect these payments in the future. Thus, the most common treatment of use taxes is to wait for the local government to conduct a use tax audit and remit the funds after the audit, along with a penalty for late payment.

From the perspective of practicality, not paying the use tax may be a reasonable approach for a smaller business, since the local government is unlikely to waste the time of its auditors on a smaller company that is unlikely to generate a large use tax payment. However, this is not the case for a larger business, where the cost-benefit tradeoff for the local government's audit staff is quite a bit more favorable. In the latter situation, it is probably easier to develop a defensible system for calculating the use tax and remit the payment at regular intervals, thereby avoiding a possibly higher payment imposed by auditors.

A simplistic method for calculating the use tax is to use the report writer associated with the company's accounting software to print a custom report that lists all supplier invoices within a certain date range for which sales tax has not been paid. You can then refine the report to exclude any items for which the local government does not impose a sales tax, and then calculate the use tax based on the remaining invoices in the report.

Tip: When preparing the use tax payment, be sure to compare it to the payments made in prior periods. If there is a substantial decline in the amount paid from the prior period, be sure that you can justify the decline. Otherwise, the payment reduction may trigger a use tax audit.

Accounting for Accounts Payable

The day-to-day accounting for accounts payable is relatively simple. Whenever the company receives an invoice from a supplier, the accounting staff enters the vendor number of the supplier into the accounting software, which automatically assigns a default general ledger account number from the vendor master file to the invoice.

EXAMPLE

Milagro Corporation receives an invoice from Maid Marian, which provides the company with janitorial services. In the vendor master file, the accounts payable staff has already assigned general ledger account number 4550, Janitorial Expenses, to Maid Marian. Thus, when the accounting staff enters the invoice into the accounts payable module of its accounting software, the system automatically assigns the invoice to account 4550.

If the invoice is for goods or services other than the predetermined general ledger account number, the accounts payable staff can manually enter a different account number, which is only good for that specific invoice – it does not become the new default account for that supplier. In short, the pre-assignment of account numbers to suppliers greatly simplifies the accounting for accounts payable.

Tip: At the end of each accounting period, print a report that shows the amount of expense charged to each account in each of the past 12 months. Compare the expense balance in the most current period to prior periods; if there is a significant difference, it may be caused by the incorrect assignment of a supplier invoice to an account. If so, investigate the account and see if a different default account should be assigned to the supplier whose invoice caused the discrepancy.

The accounting software should automatically create a credit to the accounts payable account whenever the accounting staff records a supplier invoice. Thus, a typical entry might be:

	Debit	Credit
Supplies expense	xxx	
Accounts payable		xxx

Later, when the company pays suppliers, the accounting system eliminates the accounts payable balance with the following entry:

	Debit	Credit
Accounts payable	xxx	
Cash		xxx

It is possible that small debit or credit residual balances may appear in the accounts payable account. These balances may be caused by any number of issues, such as credit memos issued by suppliers which the company does not plan to use, or amounts that the company had valid cause not to pay. It can be useful to occasionally run the aged accounts payable report to spot these items. Do not use journal entries to clear them out, since this will not be recognized by the report writing software that generates the aged accounts payable report. Instead, always create debit or credit memo transactions that are recognized by the report writer; this will flush the residual balances from the aged accounts payable report.

At month-end, you may need to accrue for expenses when goods or services have been received by the company, but for which no supplier invoice has yet been received. To do so, examine the receiving log just after month-end to see which receipts do not have an associated invoice. Also, consider reviewing the expense accruals for the preceding month; a supplier that issues invoices late will do so on a repetitive basis, so the last set of expense accruals typically provides clues to what should be included in the next set of accruals.

When you create a month-end expense accrual, do so with a reversing journal entry, so that the accounting system automatically reverses the expense at the beginning of the following month. Otherwise, you will be at risk of forgetting that an expense was accrued, and may leave it on the books for a number of months. Also, charge the accrued expense to a liability account separate from the accounts payable account, so that you can separately track all accruals. A common liability account for this is Accrued Accounts Payable. Thus, a typical accrued expense entry might be:

	Debit	Credit
Rent expense	xxx	
Accrued accounts payable		xxx

Accounts Payable Controls

There are a number of controls available for accounts payable. The primary goal of most of these controls is to avoid paying more to suppliers than the company is required to pay. These controls are:

- *Check for duplicate invoices.* The accounts payable module of your accounting software should automatically flag any invoice number that you attempt to enter that already exists in the system. In addition, implement the invoice numbering system recommended earlier in the Accounts Payable Management section, to avoid duplicate payments for those invoices that contain no invoice number.
- *Conduct three-way matching.* We described three-way matching in the earlier Three-Way Matching section, along with the reasons why it is so labor-intensive to use. Nonetheless, it may be a necessary control for more expensive purchases.
- *Review unmatched documents.* If you use three-way matching, maintain a close review of all unmatched documents. These invoices, purchase orders, and receiving reports indicate that there are payments to be made that have not yet been approved, and which likely require investigation by the accounts payable staff.
- *Audit expense reports.* Most expense reports contain only minimal errors, or expenditures that are out of compliance with company policies. Thus, it is usually sufficient to only audit a small number of expense reports, rather than conducting in-depth reviews of all such reports. If the auditors find that a particular employee continually submits incorrect expense reports, it can conduct a more detailed and ongoing review for that individual.
- *Use purchase orders.* When the purchasing department issues a purchase order for goods or services, this represents proper authorization for the accounting department to pay for the items (once received). However, purchase orders are expensive to prepare and track, so this control is only economical for more expensive purchases.
- *Lock the vendor master file.* The payment address for each supplier is maintained in the vendor master file. If an employee could gain access to this file, he could change the address to his home address, wait for checks to be printed and mailed, and then change the address back to the supplier's normal address. This action routes payments directly to the employee. You can avoid this issue by using password protection for the vendor master file.
- *Review procurement card purchases.* Procurement cards represent a simplified purchasing technique that can radically reduce the amount of purchasing and accounts payable paperwork; nonetheless, it is also much

easier for an employee to use a procurement card to slip through a fraudulent purchase. These issues are difficult to spot, but you can at least engage in periodic procurement card audits, as well as department manager reviews. Even if these audits and reviews do not find all illicit purchases, they make employees aware of the risks of engaging in unauthorized purchases.

- *Check signer review.* A common control is to attach supplier invoices and other supporting documentation to checks, so that check signers can peruse this material as they sign checks, and possibly spot problems. In reality, this is a poor control, since most check signers do not review the supporting materials; and even if they did, the purchase has already been made, so the company probably has an obligation to pay.

The controls shown in this section do not constitute the full range of controls available, but they are among the more important controls to integrate into the accounts payable system. The check signer review is the least effective, and is the least necessary, as long as there are other expense approvals built into the system prior to payment. The exact mix of controls that you elect to implement will depend upon the type of purchases made, as well as the robustness of the purchasing function.

Accounts Payable Record Keeping

The accounts payable function is one of the largest generators of paperwork in the accounting department. It should be organized to meet the following two goals:

- To make documents easily accessible for payment purposes
- To make documents easily accessible for auditors

The second requirement, to have paperwork available for auditors, does not just refer to the auditors who examine the company's financial statements at year-end. In addition, the local government may send use tax auditors who will also review the records. The following systems of records should be maintained to meet the preceding needs:

- *Supplier files.* There should be one file for each supplier that has been paid within the past year. Within each file, staple all paid invoices and related documents to the remittance advice for each paid check. These checks should be filed by date, with the most recent payment in front.
- *Unpaid invoices file.* There should be a separate file of unpaid invoices, which is usually sorted alphabetically by the name of the supplier. If there is more than one unpaid invoice for a supplier, sort them by date for each supplier.
- *Unmatched documents file.* If the company is using three-way matching, have separate files for unmatched invoices, purchase orders, and receiving documentation.

Tip: It is not necessary to maintain a separate supplier folder for every supplier. If a supplier only issues invoices a few times a year, include them in an "Other" folder that applies to a letter range of suppliers. For example, there may be an "Other A-C" folder, followed by an "Other D-F" folder, and so forth. Review these "Other" folders periodically, extract the invoices of any suppliers that are generating an increasing volume of invoices, and prepare separate folders for these suppliers.

It is useful to maintain supplier files on the premises of the accounting department for at least the current year, if not for the preceding year. The needs of the department are likely going to be met by just maintaining records for the past few months, but auditors may also want these records for a longer period of time. Older records can be stored elsewhere.

Summary

Accounts payable is one of the more difficult responsibilities of the controller, because it relies upon the cooperation of the purchasing and receiving departments for supporting documentation, as well as all company managers for document approvals. If there are failures in any of these other areas, it reflects poorly upon the controller. Consequently, it is useful to construct a system that reduces the use of purchase orders, receiving documentation, and approvals, thereby giving the controller greater control over the success of the function.

The ideal accounts payable function aggregates smaller payments onto procurement cards, leaving only larger purchases for special handling to ensure that payments should be made. This approach vastly reduces the amount of paperwork in the department, and should require less staff time to pay suppliers in a timely manner.

Chapter 8
Equity Management

Introduction

Despite the name of this chapter, the controller does not really manage equity. Instead, he or she records any dividends granted by the board of directors, or stock sold or repurchased by the chief financial officer. Thus, this chapter is really about how to account for the various components of equity.

Controller Responsibilities

The responsibilities of the controller regarding equity topics involve only two items:

- Properly account for any transactions involving company shares.
- Properly account for any transactions involving dividends issued by the company.

Accounting for Stock

Stock is an ownership share in an entity, representing a claim against its assets and profits. The owner of stock is entitled to a proportionate share of any dividends declared by an entity's board of directors, as well as to any residual assets if the entity is liquidated. Depending upon the type of stock issued, the holder of stock may be entitled to vote on certain entity decisions. There are three main types of stock transactions, which are:

- The sale of stock for cash
- Stock issued in exchange for non-cash assets or services
- The repurchase of stock

We will address the accounting for each of these stock transactions below.

The Sale of Stock for Cash

The structure of the journal entry for the cash sale of stock depends upon the existence and size of any par value. Par value is the legal capital per share, and is printed on the face of the stock certificate.

If you are selling common stock, which is the most frequent scenario, then record a credit into the Common Stock account for the amount of the par value of each share sold, and an additional credit for any additional amounts paid by investors in the Additional Paid-In Capital account. Record the amount of cash received as a debit to the Cash account.

EXAMPLE

Milagro Corporation sells 10,000 shares of its common stock for $8 per share. The stock has a par value of $0.01. Milagro records the share issuance with the following entry:

	Debit	Credit
Cash	80,000	
Common stock ($0.01 par value)		100
Additional paid-in capital		79,900

If Milagro were to only sell the stock for an amount equal to the par value, then the entire credit would be to the Common Stock account. There would be no entry to the Additional Paid-In Capital account.

If a company were selling preferred stock instead of common stock, the entry would be the same, except that the accounts in which the entries are made would be identified as preferred stock accounts, not common stock.

Stock Issued in Exchange for Non-Cash Assets or Services

If a company issues stock in exchange for non-cash assets or services received, it uses the following decision process to assign a value to the shares:

1. First, determine the market value of the shares, if there is a trading market for them;
2. If there is no trading market for the shares, instead assign a value to the shares based on the fair market value of the non-cash assets received or services received.

After determining the value of the shares using one of the two methods just noted, the journal entry is the same as was just described, except that a different account is debited, rather than the Cash account.

EXAMPLE

Milagro Corporation goes public, and its stock trades at $9 per share. It issues 5,000 shares to its product design firm for services rendered. The stock has a par value of $0.01. Milagro records the share issuance with the following entry:

	Debit	Credit
Outside services expense	45,000	
Common stock ($0.01 par value)		50
Additional paid-in capital		44,950

The Repurchase of Stock (Treasury Stock)

Treasury stock arises when the board of directors elects to have a company buy back shares from shareholders. This purchase reduces the amount of outstanding stock on the open market.

The most common treasury stock accounting method is the *cost method.* Under this approach, the cost at which shares are bought back is listed in a treasury stock account, which is reported in the stockholders' equity section of the balance sheet as a deduction. When the shares are subsequently sold again, any sale amounts exceeding the repurchase cost are credited to the additional paid-in capital account, while any shortfalls are first charged to any remaining additional paid-in capital remaining from previous treasury stock transactions, and then to retained earnings if there is no additional paid-in capital of this type remaining.

EXAMPLE

The board of directors of Milagro Corporation chooses to buy back 1,000 of its common shares at $10 per share. The entry is:

	Debit	Credit
Treasury stock	10,000	
Cash		10,000

If management later decides to permanently retire treasury stock that was originally recorded under the cost method, it backs out the original par value and additional paid-in capital associated with the initial stock sale, and charges any remaining difference to the retained earnings account.

EXAMPLE

To continue with the previous example, if the 1,000 shares had a par value of $0.01 each, had originally been sold for $8,000 and all were to be retired, the entry would be as follows:

	Debit	Credit
Common stock	10	
Additional paid-in capital	7,990	
Retained earnings	2,000	
Treasury stock		10,000

If instead Milagro subsequently chooses to sell the shares back to investors at a price of $12 per share, the transaction is:

	Debit	Credit
Cash	12,000	
Treasury stock		10,000
Additional paid-in capital		2,000

If treasury stock is later sold at a price higher than it was originally purchased, the excess amount can also be recorded in an additional paid-in capital account that is used specifically for treasury stock transactions; by doing so, subsequent treasury stock sales for less than the original buy-back price requires the accountant to make up the difference from any gains recorded into this account; if the account is zeroed out and a difference still remains, the shortage is made up first from the additional paid-in capital account for the same class of stock, and secondarily from the retained earnings account.

Accounting for Dividends

A dividend is generally considered to be a cash payment to the holders of company stock. However, there are several types of dividends, several of which do not involve the payment of cash to shareholders. These dividend types are:

- *Cash dividend.* The cash dividend is by far the most common of the dividend types used. On the date of declaration, the board of directors resolves to pay a certain dividend amount in cash to those investors holding the company's stock on a specific date. The date of record is the date on which dividends are assigned to the holders of the company's stock. On the date of payment, the company issues dividend payments.
- *Stock dividend.* A stock dividend is the issuance by a company of its common stock to its common shareholders without any consideration. If the company issues less than 25 percent of the total number of previously outstanding shares, treat the transaction as a stock dividend. If the transaction is for a greater proportion of the previously outstanding shares, then treat the transaction as a stock split. To record a stock dividend, transfer from retained earnings to the capital stock and additional paid-in capital accounts an amount equal to the fair value of the additional shares issued. This fair value is based on their fair market value when the dividend is declared.
- *Property dividend.* A company may issue a non-monetary dividend to investors, rather than making a cash or stock payment. Record this distribution at the fair market value of the assets distributed. Since the fair market value is likely to vary somewhat from the book value of the assets, the company will likely record the variance as a gain or loss.

- *Scrip dividend.* A company may not have sufficient funds to issue dividends in the near future, so instead it issues a scrip dividend, which is essentially a promissory note (which may or may not include interest) to pay shareholders at a later date. This dividend creates a note payable.
- *Liquidating dividend.* When the board of directors wishes to return the capital originally contributed by shareholders as a dividend, it is called a liquidating dividend, and may be a precursor to shutting down the business. The accounting for a liquidating dividend is similar to the entries for a cash dividend, except that the funds are considered to come from the additional paid-in capital account.

EXAMPLE – CASH DIVIDEND

On February 1, Milagro Corporation's board of directors declares a cash dividend of $0.50 per share on the company's 2,000,000 outstanding shares, to be paid on June 1 to all shareholders of record on April 1. On February 1, the company records this entry:

	Debit	Credit
Retained earnings	1,000,000	
Dividends payable		1,000,000

On June 1, Milagro pays the dividends and records the transaction with this entry:

	Debit	Credit
Dividends payable	1,000,000	
Cash		1,000,000

EXAMPLE – STOCK DIVIDEND

Milagro Corporation declares a stock dividend to its shareholders of 10,000 shares. The fair value of the stock is $5.00, and its par value is $1. Milagro records the following entry:

	Debit	Credit
Retained earnings	50,000	
Common stock, $1 par value		10,000
Additional paid-in capital		40,000

EXAMPLE – PROPERTY DIVIDEND

Milagro Corporation's board of directors elects to declare a special issuance of 500 identical, signed prints by Pablo Picasso, which the company has stored in a vault for a number of years. The company originally acquired the prints for $500,000, and they have a fair market value as of the date of dividend declaration of $4,000,000. Milagro records the following entry as of the date of declaration to record the change in value of the assets, as well as the liability to pay the dividends:

	Debit	Credit
Long-term investments - artwork	3,500,000	
Gain on appreciation of artwork		3,500,000

	Debit	Credit
Retained earnings	4,000,000	
Dividends payable		4,000,000

On the dividend payment date, Milagro records the following entry to record the payment transaction:

	Debit	Credit
Dividends payable	4,000,000	
Long-term investments - artwork		4,000,000

EXAMPLE – SCRIP DIVIDEND

Milagro Corporation declares a $250,000 scrip dividend to its shareholders that has a 10 percent interest rate. At the dividend declaration date, it records the following entry:

	Debit	Credit
Retained earnings	250,000	
Notes payable		250,000

The date of payment is one year later, so that Milagro has accrued $25,000 in interest expense on the notes payable. On the payment date (assuming no prior accrual of the interest expense), Milagro records the payment transaction with this entry:

	Debit	Credit
Notes payable	250,000	
Interest expense	25,000	
Cash		275,000

EXAMPLE – LIQUIDATING DIVIDEND

Milagro Corporation's board of directors declares a liquidating dividend of $1,600,000. It records the dividend declaration with this entry:

	Debit	Credit
Additional paid-in capital	1,600,000	
Dividends payable		1,600,000

On the dividend payment date, Milagro records the following entry to record the payment transaction:

	Debit	Credit
Dividends payable	1,600,000	
Cash		1,600,000

Summary

The sample accounting transactions described in this chapter for equity transactions will cover most of the equity transactions that a typical controller will see. However, there are more esoteric equity transactions, such as stock options and warrants, for which a GAAP or IFRS guidebook should be consulted that has been updated through the most recent release of accounting standards. See the author's *GAAP Guidebook* or *IFRS Guidebook* for further information.

Chapter 9
Payroll Management

Introduction

In a traditional payroll department that is indifferently managed, the payroll staff spends most of its time on payroll data entry for the next scheduled payroll, and cleaning up errors and mistakes from the last payroll. The nature of this work has two ramifications:

- The payroll staff works on nothing but data entry-level tasks; and
- The department is so inundated with the high volume of transactions that it never has any time to spare for systemic improvements.

This chapter describes a fundamental change in the responsibilities and work flow of the payroll department, which results in the automation of many tasks. It also addresses the proper accounting for payroll transactions, and addresses a selection of payroll controls.

Related Podcast Episodes: Episodes 26, 54, and 126 through 129 of the Accounting Best Practices Podcast discuss payroll metrics, payroll cycles, and streamlining payroll. You can listen to them at: **accountingtools.com/podcasts** or **iTunes**

Controller Responsibilities

The payroll function is a key responsibility of the controller. This is an area where excellent work tends not to be noticed, but where errors are immediately evident to the rest of the company. Also, a traditional payroll system usually requires a significant amount of expensive accounting staff time. These two issues have an impact on the controller's responsibilities, which are:

- Maintain an efficient and cost-effective timekeeping system that accumulates required pay information without errors.
- Correctly calculate net pay and distribute it to employees on designated pay dates.
- Ensure that the correct amounts of payroll taxes are remitted by the required due dates.
- Account for all payroll expenditures and accrued expenses, so that expenses are recorded in the appropriate accounting periods.
- Maintain a system of controls that ensures the proper payment of wages earned, and that garnishments and advances are handled correctly.

Payroll Cycle Duration

One of the more important payroll management decisions is how long to set the payroll cycle. A payroll cycle is the length of time between payrolls. Thus, if you pay employees once a month, the payroll cycle is one month. Each payroll requires a great deal of effort by the payroll staff to collect information about time worked, locate and correct errors, process wage rate and deduction changes, calculate pay, and issue payments. Consequently, it makes a great deal of sense to extend the duration of payroll cycles.

If payrolls are spaced at short intervals, such as weekly, then the payroll staff has to prepare 52 payrolls per year. Conversely, paying employees once a month reduces the payroll staff's payroll preparation activities by approximately three-quarters. Since paying employees just once a month can be a burden on the employees, companies frequently adopt a half-way measure, paying employees either twice a month (the *semimonthly* payroll) or once every two weeks (the *biweekly* payroll). The semimonthly payroll cycle results in processing 24 payrolls per year, while the biweekly payroll cycle requires you to process 26 payrolls per year.

An example of a weekly payroll cycle is shown below, where employees are paid every Tuesday for the hours they worked in the preceding week.

Weekly Payroll Cycle

January						
S	M	T	W	T	F	S
	1	2	3	4	5	6
7	8	9	10	11	12	13
14	15	16	17	18	19	20
21	22	23	24	25	26	27
28	29	30	31			

An example of a biweekly payroll cycle is shown below, where employees are paid every other Tuesday for the hours worked in the preceding two weeks:

Biweekly Payroll Cycle

January						
S	M	T	W	T	F	S
	1	2	3	4	5	6
7	8	9	10	11	12	13
14	15	16	17	18	19	20
21	22	23	24	25	26	27
28	29	30	31			

An example of a semimonthly payroll cycle is shown below, where employees are paid on the 15th and last days of the month.

Semimonthly Payroll Cycle

January						
S	M	T	W	T	F	S
	1	2	3	4	5	6
7	8	9	10	11	12	13
14	15	16	17	18	19	20
21	22	23	24	25	26	27
28	29	30	31			

An example of a monthly payroll cycle is next, where employees are paid on the last day of the month.

Monthly Payroll Cycle

January						
S	M	T	W	T	F	S
	1	2	3	4	5	6
7	8	9	10	11	12	13
14	15	16	17	18	19	20
21	22	23	24	25	26	27
28	29	30	31			

An argument in favor of the biweekly payroll is that employees become accustomed to receiving two paychecks per month, plus two "free" paychecks during the year, which has a somewhat more positive impact on employee morale. Nonetheless, the semimonthly payroll represents a slight improvement over the biweekly payroll from the perspective of payroll department efficiency, and is therefore recommended.

If employees are accustomed to a weekly payroll cycle and you switch them to one of a longer duration, expect to have some employees complain about not having enough cash to see them through the initial increased payroll cycle. You can mitigate this problem by extending pay advances to employees during the initial conversion to the longer payroll cycle. Once employees receive their larger paychecks under the new payroll cycle, they should be able to support themselves and will no longer need an advance.

A further issue is when a company operates a different payroll cycle for different groups of employees. For example, hourly employees may be paid on a weekly cycle and salaried employees on a semimonthly cycle. To complicate matters further, a company may have acquired other businesses and retained the payroll cycles used for their employees. Retaining all of these payroll cycles places the payroll staff in the position of perpetually preparing payrolls, so that it never has time for other activities. To avoid this problem, convert all of the different payroll cycles to a single one that applies to all employees. This may take a large amount of effort, but is mandatory if you wish to unburden the payroll staff from base-level data entry activities.

In short, paying employees at roughly half-month intervals and not allowing any additional payroll cycles can greatly reduce the work load of the payroll department. Once achieved, the staff will have more time available to address the improvement possibilities described in the following sections.

Streamlined Timekeeping

It is entirely common for the payroll department to be mired in the accumulation of timekeeping information; this encompasses the error-laden steps of coaxing timesheets from employees, correcting their submissions, and cajoling supervisors to approve the timesheets – followed by manually entering the information into the payroll software.

You must address several issues in order to break free of the timekeeping data entry trap. These issues are:

1. *Who submits information.* There is no need to collect hours-worked information from salaried employees, so they should not submit timesheets for payroll purposes. Further, if those employees who are paid on an hourly basis nearly always work a standard 40-hour work week, then they should only be reporting on an exception basis, when their hours worked vary from this baseline amount.
2. *How much information to collect.* The main protest against the last point is that employees must submit information irrespective of their salary or wage status, because the company is also tracking hours billed to customers or hours worked on specific jobs. This brings up two sub-issues:

    - *Is the information needed at all?* In many cases, the information collected through the payroll system was originally needed for a specific project or report. The data collection continues, though the project has long since been completed or the report is no longer used. Thus, one should periodically question the need for any information being collected through the payroll system.
    - *Can the information be separated from the payroll system?* In those cases where the information *must* be collected (such as hours worked that will be billed to customers), does the payroll staff need to collect it? For example, if a company has a large number of salaried consultants whose hours are billed to customers, the payroll staff can pay them without any timekeeping data collection at all –

the collection of billed hours is more appropriately a function of the billing staff.

3. *How to automate timekeeping.* The automation of timekeeping involves two sub-issues, which are:
    - *How to automate data collection.* There are a number of solutions available that allow employees to directly enter their hours worked and a selection of additional data into a timekeeping database, thereby eliminating the traditional timesheet or time card and the need for the payroll staff to manually collect and enter this information. Technologies to choose from include computerized time clocks and online timekeeping systems, as described in the next section.
    - *How to create an interface to the payroll system.* The automation of data collection only means that the information is stored in a computer database – you still need to shift it into the correct fields within the payroll system, so that you can process payroll. This calls for a custom interface that automatically shifts the data with no manual intervention.

Note that the automation of timekeeping is presented as the *last* action to take when streamlining timekeeping. That is because the *need* for timekeeping should be explored first, so that the timekeeping requirement can be whittled down to the bare minimum before investing any funds in an automated timekeeping solution.

The impact of streamlined timekeeping on the payroll department can be extraordinary - there may be no data entry work for the payroll staff at all. Instead, the department is more concerned with operating the timekeeping systems and monitoring entered information for discrepancies, missing fields, and errors. Ultimately, this means that the type of knowledge required of the payroll staff will shift away from data entry skills and toward data analysis and computer systems.

Note: The cost of the equipment, software, and training related to an automated timekeeping solution may appear excessive for a company with a small number of employees, since the cost of manually collecting timekeeping information is not large for them. If you are in this position, consider outsourcing payroll to a supplier that also provides an online timekeeping service. This solution is not expensive, and still gives the benefit of shifting timekeeping data entry away from the payroll staff.

Timekeeping Systems

If you choose to acquire a modern timekeeping solution, the two primary systems available are computerized time clocks and Internet-based time tracking. Both are excellent choices, but apply to different circumstances. Both solutions are addressed in the following sub-sections.

Computerized Time Clocks

The computerized time clock is a specialized computer terminal that is linked to the central payroll database, and which has an employee badge scanner attached to it. The scanner can accept either a bar coded or magnetic stripe employee card. An employee swipes his badge through the scanner, and the terminal automatically records his time. The central payroll system periodically polls the terminal and downloads the recorded scans. Thus, the computerized time clock incorporates a very fast and error-free data entry system that requires no rekeying by the payroll staff.

The automated time clock has several additional features. You can set up specific time periods during which employees are authorized to swipe their badges; outside of that period, the system will not accept their entries, which eliminates unauthorized overtime. The system can also spot any cases where an employee did not clock in (or out), and send a report to that person's supervisor, who can resolve the situations. Further, some models have additional data entry modes, so that employees can enter job codes to which their hours are assigned. Thus, the automated time clock also offers a number of built-in controls and an expanded data collection capability.

The computerized time clock has been the time tracking device of choice for a number of years, but do not automatically assume that it is the best time tracking solution. It is one of the higher-cost solutions available, and so is most cost-effective only under certain circumstances, which are as follows:

- *Highly concentrated employees*. Given the high cost of an automated time clock, most companies only budget for a small number of them, which means that they are most cost-effective when there are a large number of employees using each one. Thus, the best environment for such a clock is a facility with a large number of employees who pass through a choke point where the clock is located.
- *Computer interface*. There should be a payroll computer database which polls the various time clocks and downloads information from them. This may require the use of shielded network cables (for a heavy industrial environment), or a wireless connection, or even a cellular phone linkage.
- *Data rekeying reduction*. An automated time clock can eliminate a vast amount, if not all, of the rekeying of payroll data into the payroll system. This is a particular advantage where there are many employees, and when the time period between the end of a pay period and the pay date is very small.
- *Longer pay periods*. There is no theoretical limit to the duration of a pay period for which an automated time clock can accumulate information, so a company is not limited to the one-week pay period that is very nearly a requirement under a time sheet or time card system.

Tip: Though the computerized time clock is certainly a high-speed data entry device, there is an upper limit to how many employees can use it at the start of a work shift. If the queue in front of the clock is too long, some employees will be late for work. Consequently, you may need to install multiple clocks or stagger shift start times in order to reduce the queue in front of each clock.

The preceding list is based on a general view of a full-function automated time clock. Such clocks cost in excess of $1,000 each, and may require shielded network cabling to tie them back into the payroll computer system. However, there are many lower-cost variations on this basic concept. For example, there are wireless automated time clocks available that eliminate the cost of cabling, and which can work well in a light industrial environment. Similarly, there are touchpad systems that can be set up at individual workstations, so that employees can enter their time and related job information without moving from their assigned work areas. Further, automated time clocks with less functionality can be acquired for much less than $1,000. These variations on the basic concept make automated time clocks workable within a relatively broad range of environments.

EXAMPLE

Milagro Corporation has concentrated all of its production in one massive facility, which can be accessed from parking lots on three sides of the building. The 1,000 employees can enter or exit from three sides of the building. There is no need for job costing, so the company is only interested in collecting each employee's start time and ending time.

The ideal solution for this situation is to issue badges to employees and install a computerized time clock at each of the entrances. The employees can then swipe their badges as they enter and exit the building at the beginning and end of their shifts.

Internet-Based Time Tracking

An Internet-based timekeeping system is a website which employees can access in order to enter their hours worked. These systems are routinely offered by the larger payroll outsourcing companies, and can also be custom-designed by any company with a knowledgeable web design staff. A web-based time tracking system can be configured to accept any type of information, such as task codes. These systems are also useful from an employee feedback perspective, because they can notify employees of any data entry errors, and may also allow them to view additional information, such as the time sheets from previous periods and their remaining unused vacation time. It is most useful under the following circumstances:

- *Dispersed staff.* Employees can access the system wherever there is Internet access, anywhere in the world.
- *Large staff.* Many of the available time tracking systems are massively scalable, so they can be used by very large numbers of employees.

- *Full integration*. If you are outsourcing your payroll to a supplier and also using the supplier's web-based time tracking system, then there will be an interface between the two, so there is no need to rekey information into the payroll system.

There are several issues with web-based time tracking that make it a less-than-optimum solution in some situations. They are:

- *Internet access*. If some employees do not have ready access to the Internet, this is not a viable solution for them.
- *Efficiency*. A web-based system requires more manual data entry than a more efficient computerized time clock.

The pros and cons noted here point toward the use of web-based time tracking in companies where employees are dispersed, and especially when they are traveling constantly. Conversely, this is a more problematic solution in the production area, where efficient timekeeping is at a premium. Web-based time tracking could work well in a professional environment, such as consulting or software development, where employees typically have Internet access and need to record some additional task information along with their hours worked.

EXAMPLE

Milagro Corporation employs a group of software programmers for its on-line coffee testing website. Milagro only hires the best programmers, no matter where they may live, so its small staff is spread across 11 countries, and they all work from home.

Given its widely distributed work force, all of whom have access to the Internet, Milagro creates a simplified web-based time tracking system, which it also markets outside the company as a product.

Electronic Payments

After timekeeping, the next largest use of payroll staff time is paying employees. There are a number of controls and processing steps associated with payments using paychecks, and an even greater number if employees are paid with cash. You can greatly reduce this labor by shifting employees to either direct deposit or pay cards. In both cases, funds are shifted electronically to employees, so there is no paycheck distribution.

Some state governments do not allow employers to switch to electronic payments without the consent of their employees. You can work through this problem by requiring new employees to opt out of electronic payments, by issuing reminders to those still receiving paychecks, and by having educational meetings to show the benefits of electronic payments. While the target should be 100% electronic payments, even a smaller percentage results in less work for the payroll staff.

To fully implement electronic payments, send remittance advices to employees by e-mail, or send them an e-mail notification of where they can access this information in a secure online data repository. Similarly, issue the annual Form W-2 to employees by storing the forms in an online data repository that employees can access.

By using online systems to pay employees and send them reports, the payroll department can completely avoid the time-consuming steps of printing checks, having them approved, and handing them out to employees.

Payments by Direct Deposit

Direct deposit involves the electronic transfer of funds from the company to the bank accounts of its employees, using the Automated Clearing House (ACH) system. The payment process is to calculate pay in the same manner as for check payments, but to then send the payment information to a direct deposit processing service, which initiates electronic payments to the bank accounts of those employees being paid in this manner. The processing service deducts the funds from a company bank account in advance of the direct deposits, so cash flow tends to be somewhat more accelerated than is the case if a company were to issue checks and then wait several days for the amounts on the checks to be withdrawn from its bank account.

Direct deposit is more efficient than payments by check, because it does not require a signature on each payment, there are no checks to be delivered, and employees do not have to waste time depositing them at a bank. Further, employees who are off-site can still rely upon having cash paid into their accounts in a timely manner. Finally, all of the controls used to monitor checks are eliminated.

Direct deposit can also be more efficient from the perspective of the remittance advice. A number of payroll suppliers offer an option to notify employees by e-mail when their pay has been sent to them, after which employees can access a secure website to view their remittance advice information. This approach is better than sending a paper version of a remittance advice, because employees can also access many years of historical pay information on-line, as well as their W-2 forms.

Despite its efficiency advantages, direct deposit is not perfect, for it requires employees to have bank accounts. If this is an issue, consider using a blended solution with pay cards for those employees who do not have a bank account. Also, banks charge a fee for direct deposit payments, though the net cost of this fee is less than the cost of check stock, mailing costs, and check processing fees if you were to instead pay employees by check.

Tip: You can reduce the cost of ACH transactions by reducing the number of pay periods per year. Thus, if you switch from a weekly payroll to a semi-monthly payroll, there are 26 fewer payrolls, so that the cost of direct deposit is reduced by half.

The implementation of direct deposit can cause some initial difficulties, because you must correctly set up each person's bank account information in the direct deposit module of the payroll software (or software provided by the payroll supplier). This initial setup is remarkably prone to error, and also usually requires a test transaction (the *pre-notification*) that delays implementation by one pay period. Consequently, even if a new employee signs up for direct deposit immediately, you must still print a paycheck for that person's first payroll, after which direct deposit can be used.

> **Tip:** If employees want to be paid by direct deposit, require them to submit a voided check for the checking account into which they want you to send funds. You can more reliably take the routing and account numbers directly from such a check, rather than risking a transposition error if an employee copies this information onto a form. Also, do not accept a deposit slip instead of a check – the information on the deposit slip may not match the routing and account number information on the check.

> **Tip:** Employees periodically switch bank accounts, close their old accounts, and do not inform you of the change, resulting in payments bouncing from the closed accounts. If you have a company newsletter, include an occasional notice, reminding employees to notify the payroll department if they want their direct deposit payments to go into a different account.

A final issue with direct deposit is being able to do so from an in-house payroll processing function. If the payroll software does not provide for direct deposit, you will have to contract with a third party to make the payments on behalf of the company. Direct deposit is much easier to implement if you are outsourcing payroll, since direct deposit is part of the standard feature set for all payroll suppliers.

Payments by Pay Card

If you have employees who do not have a bank account and who do not want one, they are either asking for payment in cash or are taking their paychecks to a check cashing service that charges a high fee. You can improve the situation for these workers by offering them a *pay card*, which is also known as a *payroll card* or *debit card*. The company transfers funds directly into the pay card, so there is no need for a check cashing service. Employees can make purchases directly with the card, or use it to obtain cash through an ATM. The company still issues a remittance advice to all pay card holders, so they can see the detail behind the amounts being paid to them.

Here are several additional advantages of using pay cards:

- *Check fees*. Pay cards eliminate the possibility of having to pay the occasional stop payment fee for a lost paycheck.
- *First payment*. Direct deposit is not usually possible for an employee's first payment, but can be achieved with a pay card.
- *Low fees*. ATM cash withdrawal fees are much lower than the fees charged by check cashing services.

- *Security*. The pay card is protected by a personal identification number.
- *Special payments*. There is no need to cut a check for special payments, such as for an award or pay adjustment. Instead, simply the send the cash to the pay card.
- *Statement*. Employees receive a monthly statement, detailing payments into and withdrawals from their account.
- *Unclaimed property*. Once funds are transferred to a pay card, they are the property of the recipient, so the company no longer has to concern itself with remitting unclaimed pay to the state government under escheatment laws.

When compared to direct deposit, pay cards are the more attractive option for many employees. However, since direct deposit has been available far longer, pay cards have not gained as much traction in the marketplace.

Employee Self-Service

Employees sometimes need to change the information used to compile their net pay, such as benefits that require pay deductions, or their marriage status, or withholding allowances. Traditionally, employees fill out a form in which they authorize these changes to their payroll records, and the payroll staff enters the information into the payroll system. This is not a large chore in a smaller company, but can involve full-time staff in a larger company where the sheer volume of employees results in a great many changes.

You can eliminate this data entry task by having employees enter the information directly into the payroll system themselves, using an online portal. The types of information they can enter include the items just noted, as well as changes to their addresses and bank account information. The self-service portal is a common feature if you outsource payroll processing to a major payroll supplier, though there is usually an extra fee charged to use it.

The payroll staff should still monitor the information being entered by employees for errors. This can be done by reviewing a change log or by creating custom reports that only report changes that exceed predetermined "normal" entries (such as entering a withholding allowance that is inordinately high).

Manager Self-Service

Department managers are the source of a different set of payroll information. They submit changes to employee pay rates, department codes, and shift differentials, as well as start and termination dates. As was the case with employee self-service, it is possible to construct an online portal through which managers can make these changes themselves. And as was the case for employee self-service, the payroll staff should monitor these changes.

It is critical for the payroll staff to monitor changes made by managers, since these alterations will impact the company's compensation and payroll tax expenses.

Monitoring may include comparing pay changes to the authorized pay change percentages assigned to each manager, and verifying pay rates with senior management if the rates exceed authorized levels.

Manager self-service is not as easy a feature to find in many payroll systems, since it is considered to have a smaller cost-benefit than employee self-service. Nonetheless, if you have completed the improvement steps noted in the preceding sections, this is the next logical step to pursue.

Transaction Error Analysis

It requires far more time to track down a payroll error and correct it than it does to initially enter the transaction correctly. Further, you typically assign the more experienced (and expensive) staff to investigate and correct errors. Thus, the cost of transaction errors is high, and is worthy of considerable analysis to find the causes of errors and prevent them from occurring again.

Transaction error analysis begins with the summarization of all payroll errors into a single document, so that you can classify and prioritize the errors. This may call for an informal system where the payroll staff forwards to you any complaints received regarding pay problems, and you translate this information into a standard format. Then select a single error type to pursue, and investigate it with the goal of isolating the specific issue that caused the error to occur. Then fix the issue, and monitor it to see if the error has now been eliminated. Examples of errors and their causes and possible corrections are shown in the following table.

Sample Payroll Errors and Corrections

Error	Source of Error	Error Correction
Timesheet not recorded	Employee did not submit timesheet	Send automated e-mail notification
Incorrect timesheet total	Clerk incorrectly added hours	Switch to computerized time clock
Overtime not approved	Supervisor did not sign card	Switch to computerized time clock
No benefits deduction	Clerk did not add deduction	Use standard deductions checklist
Allowance not updated	Clerk did not enter allowance change	Install employee self-service
Paycheck not signed	Checks stuck together	Use signature stamp
Paycheck issued for terminated employee	Clerk did not update pay status to terminated	Install manager self-service

> **Tip:** Do not turn transaction error analysis into a witch hunt, where you assign blame for an error to a specific person. If this approach is taken, the payroll staff will not inform you of any errors. Instead, make it clear that you are pursuing changes to the underlying systems that will keep errors from arising again.

Staff Training Program

An employee in the payroll department needs a considerable skill set in order to work at an optimal level of efficiency. These skills become more broad-ranging over time, as the department moves away from data entry tasks and into data analysis and system installations. Also, the legal requirements associated with payroll are significant, and are increasing in complexity every year. Further, as the department rolls out a variety of payroll tools for employees to use throughout the company, the payroll staff must enter into a training role, where they show employees how to use these tools. Clearly, there is a need for a comprehensive and ongoing training program for the entire payroll staff.

In a modern, thoroughly computerized payroll department, the staff should receive training in the following areas:

- *Payroll software.* Every payroll software package has a different set of commands, modules, file structures, and so forth, and employees must be fully aware of how to handle transactions through the software. This usually involves a separate training class for each module of the software. Even if you outsource payroll, you must still access the supplier's online software, so training in its software is still required.
- *Payroll processes.* There is a particular flow to payroll processes that is driven by the level of automation, the type of software, and payroll regulations. Employees must be thoroughly familiar with these processes.
- *Regulatory changes.* There are regulatory changes every year that impact the payroll department. While the controller could simply send everyone to a conference to learn about the most recent changes, a more cost-effective approach is to have a consultant monitor the changes and create a custom in-house training class to convey these changes to the staff. This latter approach requires a significant consulting fee, but keeps the staff in-house for the training, thereby avoiding travel and conference fees. It also results in a seminar that is expressly designed for the needs of the company and the locations where it has employees.
- *Data analysis.* As the department shifts away from data entry, there is a greater need for the payroll staff to review data entered by others, to verify that it is correct. This calls for training in report writing software, so that they can create a set of standard analysis reports that highlight possible data entry issues.
- *Training skills.* When the payroll department pushes software and hardware out from the department for use by other employees to enter information, it

must also take on the task of training employees in their use. Consequently, several members of the department should be taught how to train others.

It is difficult to standardize payroll training for everyone in the payroll department, since some people are specialized on specific tasks, and their skill sets do not need to extend beyond those areas. Also, some people have more experience than others. Consequently, ascertain the skill set required by each person, and the specific areas in which extra training is needed to bring them up to the standard that you require. Then create a training plan for everyone in the department, and go over it with them on a regular basis to review their progress in meeting their training goals.

The Payroll Calendar

The payroll department's activities are driven by a large number of deadlines – for paying employees, depositing taxes, issuing reports, and so forth. Without a proper amount of documentation, it would be impossible to go through a year without missing some deadlines, and likely incurring both the wrath of employees and government-imposed penalties.

The solution to these problems is the departmental payroll calendar. This is a full-year schedule, on which is recorded all due dates and who is responsible for them. The controller retains this full schedule, and may issue a subset of the calendar to his employees, so that each one has a calendar containing only those activities for which he or she is responsible. An example of a master department payroll calendar for a single month is shown next.

Note that the calendar also includes a scheduled week of vacation for one employee. This information provides the staff with notice of a capacity reduction during that week, which it will need to plan around.

The payroll calendar is particularly important if there are new employees in the department who do not yet have experience with those deadlines pertaining to the operations of the department – it is a useful reminder for these individuals.

Ideally, the controller should consult the payroll calendar for the following day, and verify that the staff is aware of the deadlines for that day, and how any issues will be addressed. If a specific date is likely to require a larger amount of work than usual (such as the final day of the month in the preceding example), the controller can use the calendar to plan well in advance for how to handle the work load.

Sample Payroll Calendar

Monday	Tuesday	Wednesday	Thursday	Friday
1 Issue metrics Process payroll Fund bank acct Journal entry	2 State deposit	3 Forward garnishments	4	5 Timesheets EFTPS deposit
8 Process payroll Fund bank acct Journal entry	9 Issue checks State deposit	10 Forward garnishments Form 4070	11	12 Timesheets EFTPS deposit
15 Process payroll Fund bank acct Journal entry Jones vacation	16 Issue checks State deposit Jones vacation	17 Forward garnishments Jones vacation	18 Jones vacation	19 Timesheets EFTPS deposit Jones vacation
22 Process payroll Fund bank acct Journal entry	23 Issue checks State deposit	24 Forward garnishments	25	26 Timesheets EFTPS deposit
29 Process payroll Fund bank acct Journal entry	30 Issue checks State deposit	31 Forms W-2 Forms 1099 Form 940 Form 941 Form 945 FUTA deposit		

Information Confidentiality

A major issue for any payroll department is to ensure that a large part of the information it processes remains confidential. Most employees would consider it disastrous if information about their wages, pension plans, garnishments, social security numbers, and so forth were to be made public. This information is located in the payroll register and employee files, and may be scattered among other payroll reports, as well. The following are recommended methods for improving the confidentiality of payroll information:

- *Locked storage.* Clearly, the best single action you can take to enhance confidentiality is to keep payroll documents in a locked storage area. This can be a locked storage cabinet, or locked room with a door that automatically closes and locks.
- *Password protection.* Anyone using the payroll software must input a password to access the system. Further, set the software to require a new password at frequent intervals.

- *Limit authorization.* Even within the payroll department, it is not necessary for every employee to have full access to payroll information. For example, if there is a clerk who only handles employee timesheets, do not give that person access to other types of payroll information.
- *Shred documents.* Once the company is no longer required to continue archiving old payroll files, do not throw them in the trash; instead, shred them. There are shredding services in most major cities that can handle this task for you.
- *Dissemination policy.* Have a department policy that no one ever gives out confidential information without specific authorization. In all cases, this should involve the approval of the controller.

Accounting for Payroll

There are a number of journal entries that you may use to record payroll transactions. In this section, we cover the primary payroll entry, as well as the entries for accrued wages, accrued bonuses, accrued commissions, manual paychecks, employee advances, and accrued vacation pay.

Primary Payroll Journal Entry

The primary journal entry for payroll is the summary-level entry that is compiled from the payroll register, and which is recorded in either the payroll journal or the general ledger. This entry usually includes debits for the direct labor expense, wages, and the company's portion of payroll taxes. There will also be credits to a number of other accounts, each detailing the liability for payroll taxes that have not been paid, as well as for the amount of cash already paid to employees for their net pay. The basic entry (assuming no further breakdown of debits by individual department) is:

	Debit	Credit
Direct labor expense	xxx	
Wages expense	xxx	
Payroll taxes expense	xxx	
Cash		xxx
Federal withholding taxes payable		xxx
Social security taxes payable		xxx
Medicare taxes payable		xxx
Federal unemployment taxes payable		xxx
State unemployment taxes payable		xxx
Garnishments payable		xxx

Note: The reason for the payroll taxes expense line item in this journal entry is that the company incurs the cost of matching the social security and Medicare amounts paid by employees, and directly incurs the cost of unemployment insurance. The employee-paid portions of the social security and Medicare taxes are not recorded as expenses; instead, they are liabilities for which the company has an obligation to remit cash to the taxing government entity.

A key point with this journal entry is that the direct labor expense and salaries expense contain employee gross pay, while the amount actually paid to employees through the cash account is their net pay. The difference between the two figures (which can be substantial) is the amount of deductions from their pay, such as payroll taxes and withholdings to pay for benefits.

There may be a number of additional employee deductions to include in this journal entry. For example, there may be deductions for 401(k) pension plans, health insurance, life insurance, vision insurance, and for the repayment of advances.

When you later pay the withheld taxes and company portion of payroll taxes, use the following entry to reduce the balance in the cash account, and eliminate the balances in the liability accounts.

	Debit	Credit
Federal withholding taxes payable	xxx	
Social security taxes payable	xxx	
Medicare taxes payable	xxx	
Federal unemployment taxes payable	xxx	
State withholding taxes payable	xxx	
State unemployment taxes payable	xxx	
Garnishments payable	xxx	
Cash		xxx

Thus, when a company initially deducts taxes and other items from an employee's pay, the company incurs a liability to pay the taxes to a third party. This liability only disappears from the company's accounting records when it pays the related funds to the entity to which they are owed.

Note: If your payroll system is tightly integrated into the accounting system, it is not necessary to create the entries just described. Instead, the software will automatically transfer detailed payroll information into the payroll journal, which will eventually be transferred to the general ledger.

Accrued Wages

It is quite common to have some amount of unpaid wages at the end of an accounting period, so accrue this expense (if it is material). The accrual entry, as shown next, is simpler than the comprehensive payroll entry already shown, because you typically clump all payroll taxes into a single expense account and offsetting liability account. After recording this entry, reverse it at the beginning of the following accounting period, and then record the actual payroll expense whenever it occurs.

	Debit	Credit
Direct labor expense	xxx	
Wages expense	xxx	
Accrued salaries and wages		xxx
Accrued payroll taxes		xxx

Companies with predominantly salaried staffs may avoid making the accrued wages entry, on the grounds that the wages due to a small number of hourly personnel at the end of the reporting period have a minimal impact on reported financial results.

The information for the wage accrual entry is most easily derived from a spreadsheet that itemizes all employees to whom the calculation applies, the number of unpaid days or hours, and the standard pay rate for each individual. It is generally not necessary to also calculate the cost of overtime hours earned during an accrual period, if the amount of such hours is relatively small. A sample spreadsheet for calculating accrued wages is:

Hourly Employees	Unpaid Days	Hourly Rate	Pay Accrual
Anthem, Jill	4	$20.00	$640
Bingley, Adam	4	18.25	584
Chesterton, Elvis	4	17.50	560
Davis, Ethel	4	23.00	736
Ellings, Humphrey	4	21.50	688
Fogarty, Miriam	4	16.00	512
		Total	$3,720

Accrued Bonuses

A bonus expense should be accrued whenever there is an expectation that the financial or operational performance of a company at least equals the performance levels required in any active bonus plans.

The decision to accrue a bonus calls for a certain amount of judgment, for the entire period of performance may encompass many future months, during which time a person may *not* continue to achieve his bonus plan objectives, in which case any prior bonus accrual should be reversed. Here are some alternative ways to treat a bonus accrual during the earlier stages of a bonus period:

- Accrue no expense at all until there is a reasonable probability that the bonus will be achieved.
- Accrue a smaller bonus expense during the early months of a performance period to reflect the higher risk of performance failure, and accrue a larger expense later, if the probability of success improves.

One thing you should *not* do is accrue a significant bonus expense in a situation where the probability that the bonus will be awarded is low; such an accrual is essentially earnings management, since it creates a false expense that is later reversed when the performance period is complete.

EXAMPLE

The management team of Milagro Corporation will earn a year-end group bonus of $240,000 if profits exceed 12 percent of revenues. There is a reasonable probability that the team will earn this bonus, so the controller records the following accrual in each month of the performance year:

	Debit	Credit
Bonus expense	20,000	
Accrued bonus liability		20,000

The management team does not quite meet the profit criteria required under the bonus plan, so the group instead receives a $150,000 bonus. This results in the following entry to eliminate the liability and pay out the bonus:

	Debit	Credit
Accrued bonus liability	240,000	
Bonus expense		90,000
Cash		150,000

The actual payout of $150,000 would be reduced by any social security and Medicare taxes applicable to each person in the management group being paid.

Tip: Employee performance plans are usually maintained by the human resources department. The controller should summarize these plans into a format that the payroll staff can consult when calculating its estimates of bonus accruals.

Accrued Commissions

Accrue an expense for a commission in the same period as you record the sale generated by the salesperson, *and* when you can calculate the amount of the commission. This is a debit to the commission expense account and a credit to a commission liability account. You can classify the commission expense as part of the cost of goods sold, since it directly relates to the sale of goods or services. It is also acceptable to classify it as part of the expenses of the sales department.

EXAMPLE

Wes Smith sells a $1,000 item for Milagro Corporation. Under the terms of his commission agreement, he receives a 5% commission on the revenue generated by the transaction, and will be paid on the 15th day of the following month. At the end of the accounting period in which Mr. Smith generates the sale, Milagro creates the following entry to record its liability for the commission:

	Debit	Credit
Commission expense	50	
Accrued commissions (liability)		50

Milagro then reverses the entry at the beginning of the following accounting period, because it is going to record the actual payment on the 15th of the month. Thus, the reversing entry is:

	Debit	Credit
Accrued commissions (liability)	50	
Commission expense		50

On the 15th of the month, Milagro pays Mr. Smith his commission and records this entry:

	Debit	Credit
Commission expense	50	
Cash		50

Manual Paycheck Entry

It is all too common to create a manual paycheck, either because an employee was short-paid in a prior payroll, or because the company is laying off or firing an employee, and so is obligated to pay that person before the next regularly scheduled payroll. This check may be paid through the corporate accounts payable bank account, rather than its payroll account, so you may need to make this entry through the accounts payable system. If you are recording it directly into the general ledger or the payroll journal, use the same line items already noted for the primary payroll journal entry.

EXAMPLE

Milagro Corporation lays off Mr. Jones. Milagro owes Mr. Jones $5,000 of wages at the time of the layoff. The payroll staff calculates that it must withhold $382.50 from Mr. Jones' pay to cover the employee-paid portions of social security and Medicare taxes. Mr. Jones has claimed a large enough number of withholding allowances that there is no income tax withholding. Thus, the company pays Mr. Jones $4,617.50. The journal entry it uses is:

	Debit	Credit
Wage expense	5,000	
Social security taxes payable		310.00
Medicare taxes payable		72.50
Cash		4,617.50

At the next regularly-scheduled payroll, the payroll staff records this payment as a notation in the payroll system, so that it will properly compile the correct amount of wages for Mr. Jones for his year-end Form W-2. In addition, the payroll system calculates that Milagro must pay a matching amount of social security and Medicare taxes (though no unemployment taxes, since Mr. Jones already exceeded his wage cap for these taxes). Accordingly, an additional liability of $382.50 is recorded in the payroll journal entry for that payroll. Milagro pays these matching amounts as part of its normal tax remittances associated with the payroll.

Employee Advances

When an employee asks for an advance, this is recorded as a current asset in the company's balance sheet. There may not be a separate account in which to store advances, especially if employee advances are infrequent; possible asset accounts you can use are:

- Employee advances (for high-volume situations)
- Other assets (probably sufficient for smaller companies that record few assets other than trade receivables, inventory, and fixed assets)
- Other receivables (useful if you are tracking a number of different types of assets, and want to segregate receivables in one account)

EXAMPLE

Milagro Corporation issues a $1,000 advance to employee Wes Smith. Milagro issues advances regularly, and so uses a separate account in which to record advances. It records the transaction as:

	Debit	Credit
Other assets	1,000	
Cash		1,000

One week later, Mr. Smith pays back half the amount of the advance, which is recorded with this entry:

	Debit	Credit
Cash	500	
Other assets		500

No matter what method is later used to repay the company – a check from the employee, or payroll deductions – the entry will be a credit to whichever asset account was used, until such time as the balance in the account has been paid off.

Employee advances require ongoing vigilance by the accounting staff, because employees who have limited financial resources will tend to use the company as their personal banks, and so will be reluctant to pay back advances unless pressed repeatedly. Thus, it is essential to continually monitor the remaining amount of advances outstanding for every employee.

Accrued Vacation Pay

Accrued vacation pay is the amount of vacation time that an employee has earned as per a company's employee benefit manual, but which he has not yet used. The calculation of accrued vacation pay for each employee is:

1. Calculate the amount of vacation time earned through the beginning of the accounting period. This should be a roll-forward balance from the preceding period.
2. Add the number of hours earned in the current accounting period.
3. Subtract the number of vacation hours used in the current period.
4. Multiply the ending number of accrued vacation hours by the employee's hourly wage to arrive at the correct accrual that should be on the company's books.
5. If the amount already accrued for the employee from the preceding period is lower than the correct accrual, record the difference as an addition to the accrued liability. If the amount already accrued from the preceding period is higher than the correct accrual, record the difference as a reduction of the accrued liability.

A sample spreadsheet follows that uses the preceding steps, and which can be used to compile accrued vacation pay:

Name	Vacation Roll-Forward Balance	+ New Hours Earned	- Hours Used	= Net Balance	× Hourly Pay	= Accrued Vacation $
Hilton, David	24.0	10	34.0	0.0	$25.00	$0.00
Idle, John	13.5	10	0.0	23.5	17.50	411.25
Jakes, Jill	120.0	10	80.0	50.0	23.50	1,175.00
Kilo, Steve	114.5	10	14.0	110.5	40.00	4,420.00
Linder, Alice	12.0	10	0.0	22.0	15.75	346.50
Mills, Jeffery	83.5	10	65.00	28.5	19.75	562.88
					Total	$6,915.63

It is not necessary to reverse the vacation pay accrual in each period if you choose to instead record just incremental changes in the accrual from month to month.

EXAMPLE

There is already an existing accrued balance of 40 hours of unused vacation time for Wes Smith on the books of Milagro Corporation. In the most recent month that has just ended, Mr. Smith accrued an additional five hours of vacation time (since he is entitled to 60 hours of accrued vacation time per year, and 60 ÷ 12 = five hours per month). He also used three hours of vacation time during the month. This means that, as of the end of the month, Milagro should have accrued a total of 42 hours of vacation time for him (calculated as 40 hours existing balance + 5 hours additional accrual – 3 hours used).

Mr. Smith is paid $30 per hour, so his total vacation accrual should be $1,260 (42 hours × $30/hour), so Milagro accrues an additional $60 of vacation liability.

What if a company has a "use it or lose it" policy? This means that employees must use their vacation time by a certain date (such as the end of the year), and can only carry forward a small number of hours (if any) into the next year. One issue is that this policy may be illegal, since vacation is an earned benefit that cannot be taken away (which depends on state law). If this policy is considered to be legal, it is acceptable to reduce the accrual as of the date when employees are supposed to have used their accrued vacation, thereby reflecting the reduced liability to the company as represented by the number of vacation hours that employees have lost.

What if an employee receives a pay raise? Then increase the amount of his entire vacation accrual by the incremental amount of the pay raise. This is because, if the employee were to leave the company and be paid all of his unused vacation pay, he would be paid at his most recent rate of pay.

Payroll Controls

The payroll function is a prime source of fraud, since it is designed to disburse large amounts of money, and there are many ways to "game" the system to pay out funds that exceed the amounts actually earned by employees. Given the large transaction volume associated with a payroll system, there is also a strong likelihood that errors will arise at various points in the process that yield incorrect payment amounts. This section describes a number of controls to consider installing to mitigate losses due to fraud and errors.

General Controls

Consider using a selection of the following controls for nearly all payroll systems, irrespective of how timekeeping information is accumulated or how employees are paid:

- *Change authorizations.* Only allow a change to an employee's marital status, withholding allowances, or deductions if the employee has submitted a written and signed request for the company to do so. Otherwise, there is no proof that the employee wanted a change to be made. The same control applies for any pay rate changes requested by a manager.
- *Error-checking reports.* Some types of payroll errors can be spotted by running reports that only show items that fall outside of the normal distribution of payroll results. These may not all indicate certain errors, but the probability of underlying errors is higher for the reported items. The controller or a third party not involved in payroll activities should review these reports. Examples of error-checking reports are:
    - *Activity for terminated employees.* Shows payments being made to an employee who has left the company or is on leave; may indicate a case of fraud, or that the status of the employee should be changed to active.
    - *Negative deductions.* Shows employees being paid through a negative deduction; usually indicates either a data entry error or fraud.
    - *Negative vacation.* Shows employees being paid for vacation time they have not accrued; should require supervisory approval in these cases.
    - *Net pay exceeds boundary.* Flags any net pay that exceeds a predetermined trigger point; may indicate a data entry error or fraud.
    - *No payments.* Shows active employees who received no pay; may indicate missing timesheets.
    - *Pay rate exceeds boundary.* Flags any pay rate that exceeds a predetermined trigger point; may indicate a data entry error or fraud.
- *Expense trend lines.* Look for fluctuations in payroll-related expenses in the financial statements, and investigate the reasons for the fluctuations. This analysis involves creating financial statements that list the results of multi-

ple periods side-by-side (known as *horizontal analysis*), and doing so at the department level, so that you can spot fluctuations at the most granular level of detail. An alternative approach is to conduct this same analysis, but at the individual general ledger account level. The difference between account-level and financial statement line-item analysis is that several accounts may be clustered into a single financial statement line item, resulting in a more aggregate level of analysis.

- *Issue payment report to supervisors.* Send a list of payments made to employees to each department supervisor, with a request to review it for correct payment amounts and unfamiliar names. They may identify payments being made to employees who no longer work for the company.
- *Separation of duties.* Have one person prepare the payroll, another authorize it, and another create payments, thereby reducing the risk of fraud unless multiple people collude in doing so. In smaller companies where there are not enough personnel for a proper separation of duties, at least insist on having someone review and authorize the payroll before payments are sent to employees.

Payroll Calculation Controls

Without even considering the challenges posed by fraudulent payroll transactions, it is sufficiently hard enough to calculate payroll to insist on installing a number of controls – just to spot errors. The following list of possible controls address such issues as missing timesheets, incorrect time worked, and incorrect pay calculations. They are:

- *Automated timekeeping systems.* Depending on the circumstances, consider installing a computerized time clock. These clocks have a number of built-in controls, such as only allowing employees to clock in or out for their designated shifts and not allowing overtime without a supervisory override. Also, send any exception reports generated by these clocks to supervisors for review.
- *Hours worked verification.* Always have a supervisor approve hours worked by employees, to prevent employees from charging more time than they actually worked.
- *Match payroll register to supporting documents.* The payroll register shows gross wages, deductions, and net pay, and so is a good summary document from which to trace back to the supporting documents for verification purposes. This is hardly a good control for *every* payroll, since it is time-consuming, but use it occasionally as a deterrent to anyone intending to commit payroll fraud.
- *Match timecards to employee list.* There is a risk that an employee will not turn in a timesheet in a timely manner, and so will not be paid. To avoid this problem, print a list of active employees at the beginning of payroll processing, and check off the names on the list when you receive their timesheets.

- *Overtime worked verification.* Even if you do not require supervisors to approve the hours worked by employees, at least have supervisors approve overtime hours worked. There is a pay premium associated with these hours, so the cost to the company is higher, as is the temptation for employees to claim them.

Check Payment Controls

When you pay employees with checks, this calls for quite a large number of controls, as noted in the following bullet points. The controls are necessary, because there are risks of fraud and errors in multiple places during the storage, printing, and distribution of checks. You will not need *all* of the following controls, but consider a robust subset of them to provide a significant amount of protection:

- *Fill space.* When creating a check, be sure to fill all of the empty spaces on the payment amount line, so that no one can add to the amount of the payment. For example, this can be a line of hyphens. Also, write the numerical amount of the payment as close to the dollar sign as possible, so that no one can insert another number in front of those already recorded.
- *Hand checks to employees.* Where possible, hand checks directly to employees. Doing so prevents a type of fraud where a payroll clerk creates a check for a fake employee, and pockets the check. If this is too inefficient a control, consider distributing checks manually on an occasional basis.
- *Limit access to signature stamp.* If you use a signature stamp to authorize payroll checks, lock up the stamp, and not in the same location as unused checks. Having two separate, locked locations makes it more difficult to fraudulently create payroll checks.
- *Limit access to unused checks.* Lock up all unused checks to mitigate the risk that someone could remove blank checks and use them to steal funds.
- *Lock up undistributed paychecks.* If you are issuing paychecks directly to employees and someone is not present, then lock up their check in a secure location. Such a check might otherwise be stolen and cashed.
- *Match addresses.* If the company mails checks to its employees, match the addresses on the checks to employee addresses. If more than one check is going to the same address, it may be because a payroll clerk is routing illicit payments for fake employees to his or her address.
- *Reconcile the checking account.* Conduct a monthly reconciliation of the bank account to detect any unauthorized transactions and undocumented bank charges. The person who creates the reconciliation should not be the same person who prepares or signs the checks.
- *Segregation of duties.* The person who signs paychecks should not be the person who prepares the paychecks. Doing so gives the check signer an opportunity to review paychecks for problems.

Direct Deposit Controls

The number of controls required for direct deposit are fewer (and less intrusive) than those needed for check payments, largely because the authorization to pay cash (e.g., the check) has been removed from the payment process. Still, there are a few controls to consider, mostly involving the accuracy and security of bank account information. The controls are:

- *Authorization signature.* Have employees sign a form, stating their authorization for the company to pay them by direct deposit, to which is stapled a copy of a cancelled check for the designated account. This makes it more difficult for someone to fraudulently alter the bank account information.
- *Lock up direct deposit information.* Since direct deposit authorization forms include an employee's bank account information, lock them in a secure location, probably with the employee personnel folders.
- *Require a cancelled check.* Employees must submit a cancelled check, from which you extract the bank routing number and account number. This is a key point, for many employees find it easier to submit a deposit slip instead – but the information on a deposit slip does not always match the information on a check.

Self-Service Controls

If a company allows employees or their managers to alter certain information in their pay records through on-line access, there is a possibility that they will enter incorrect information that will hinder the proper processing of wages. To avoid these problems, consider using the following controls:

- *Confirm changes.* The system should send a confirming e-mail to the person who made changes to an employee record, describing the changes made.
- *Limit checks.* The system should either not allow excessively large pay rate changes, or route them to a more senior supervisor for review and approval.
- *Notify of pre-note failures.* If an employee enters new bank account information for a direct deposit payment and the pre-notification fails, the system should sent a notification of the failure by e-mail to the employee.

Garnishment Controls

A cause for concern is garnishments, since a company is liable for garnishments if the payroll staff does not deduct garnished amounts from employee pay as required by court orders. To mitigate this risk, consider the following controls:

- *Garnishment tracking log.* Maintain a tracking log that itemizes which garnishments have been received, the amount to be deducted, and the start and termination dates of the garnishment. The accounting staff should periodically compare this log to the payroll register to ensure that required garnishments are being acted upon.

- *Deduction to payables matching.* In addition to the control just noted, the accounting staff should periodically compare the garnishment deductions from the payroll system to the checks issued through the accounts payable system to the garnishing entity, to ensure that deductions are being forwarded in the correct amounts and by the required dates.

Employee Advances Controls

Those employees who are short on funds may ask for an advance on their pay. This transaction can be lost in a poorly-organized payroll department, so that an employee receiving an advance effectively receives additional pay, and does not even pay taxes on it. Here are several controls to combat the problem:

- *Approval requirement.* Never pay an advance without the approval of the manager of the person requesting the advance. This is needed, since an advance is essentially a transfer of company assets to a third party, and if it is not paid back, the manager's department is charged the amount of the unrecovered funds.
- *Periodic advances review.* Require that all advances be recorded in a designated asset account, and have someone review the contents of the account regularly and follow up on outstanding amounts.
- *Repayment policy.* Have a corporate policy that all advances are to be repaid as part of the next scheduled payroll. Doing so cuts down on the risk of any advances remaining on the books for a long time, and also reduces the attractiveness of advances to employees.

Summary

This chapter has addressed a number of general management concepts that are designed to improve the efficiency and effectiveness of the payroll department. Ultimately, this can result in a department that has shifted almost entirely away from data entry activities, and instead spends most of its time monitoring payroll transactions, installing new systems, and issuing reports related to payroll expenses. This sweeping change will also result in a department whose employees have a much higher knowledge of payroll regulations, controls, and systems.

The sections presented near the beginning of this chapter were sorted in order by the importance of their impact on the payroll department. Thus, consider implementing changes in the following order:

1. *Reduce and consolidate the number of payrolls.* This can substantially reduce the work load of the department, giving it more time to implement additional changes.
2. *Streamline timekeeping.* The time savings from eliminating data entry tasks is potentially enormous.
3. *Shift to electronic payments.* The payroll staff can avoid printing and distributing paychecks if it can persuade employees to switch to direct deposit or pay cards.

4. *Install self-service.* Employees can enter information directly into the payroll system related to their withholding allowances, benefits, bank accounts, mailing information, and so forth.
5. *Install manager self-service.* Managers can enter information directly into the payroll system related to employee pay rates, department codes, shift differentials, and so forth.

You will need to implement a comprehensive staff training program as you gradually work through the preceding steps, because the nature of the employees' work will diverge more and more from their original data entry-oriented tasks and into areas that require more knowledge. They will also need training skills, since they must show employees throughout the company how to use the new timekeeping and self-service systems to enter information into the payroll system. Thus, the training program may begin as a relatively small effort, and gradually change into a major undertaking that involves all of the payroll staff on an ongoing basis.

This chapter also described almost 30 controls that could be imposed on the payroll function. They are not all needed! As the controller, you need to determine which ones mitigate identifiable risks, and whether there is a sufficiently strong benefit to offset the cost of each one. In short, evaluate the situation based on both theoretical risks and actual experience, to determine which controls to install.

Chapter 10
Department Management

Introduction

If there is one department that responds well to a high level of organizational structure, it is the accounting department. This area involves a large number of scheduled activities, procedures, and controls, so the new controller can take a number of steps to ensure that everything is completed both on-time and without error. In this chapter, we cover several management techniques that a new controller can use to improve department operations.

Related Podcast Episodes: Episodes 165 and 180 of the Accounting Best Practices Podcast discuss how to set up an accounting department, and training, respectively. The episodes are available at: **accountingtools.com/podcasts** or **iTunes**

Controller Responsibilities

The issues described in this chapter are mostly of a tactical, day-to-day variety, and so represent responsibilities that are likely to appear regularly in the controller's work schedule. Those responsibilities are:

- Monitor and plan for all due dates associated with the accounting department.
- Examine and streamline the flow of accounting information.
- Examine and streamline the physical flow of work in the accounting department.
- Consolidate accounting operations to the extent needed to minimize overall costs.

Schedule of Activities

The controller should collect information about when accounting activities must be completed, reports issued, payments made, and so forth, and organize them into a department-wide schedule of activities. It is quite likely that each member of the accounting department is well aware of when their work is supposed to be done, so this may not initially appear to improve the situation in the department. However, there are three good reasons for creating it:

- *Vacations*. Employees leave for vacations and forget to tell their replacements about due dates.

- *Departures*. An experienced employee leaves the company, and the rest of the department has to scramble to figure out when that person's work should be done.
- *MBWA*. This is management by wandering around. The controller can use the schedule of activities to chat with the staff about upcoming due dates. This may sometimes detect issues that would otherwise have been forgotten, and is also an excellent excuse to talk to the staff, which may bring up other issues worth investigating.

Error Tracking System

The accounting department handles an enormous number of business transactions, and some of those transactions will be processed incorrectly. Fixing them requires a considerable amount of time by an experienced accounting person. Further, if an erroneous transaction is visible outside of the accounting department (such as an error on an employee paycheck), it gives the department a reputation for substandard work. Thus, one of the first steps for a new controller should be to set up an error tracking system.

An error tracking system is a manual one, and involves digging through the accounting records each month for adjusting transactions, such as special journal entries to correct an improper expense accrual, or a credit memo to a customer to correct the price stated on an invoice. Examples of accounting errors are:

- Compiling an incorrect number of hours worked by an employee
- Deducting the incorrect amount from an employee's wages
- Not remitting payroll taxes to the government
- Not recording a supplier invoice
- Paying a supplier invoice when the amount was not authorized
- Not taking an early payment discount on a supplier invoice
- Recording a supplier invoice in the wrong expense account
- Sending a supplier payment to the wrong address
- Billing the incorrect amount to a customer
- Not charging sales taxes to a customer
- Applying a cash payment to the wrong customer account
- Incorrectly completing the monthly bank reconciliation
- Incorrectly calculating depreciation expense on a new fixed asset
- Not reversing an expense accrual in the following period
- Incorrectly applying overhead to inventory and the cost of goods sold

The preceding list of errors is by no means complete, and yet is so long that one can see how possible it may be for the accounting department to be buried under an avalanche of errors. Consequently, it is critical to obtain an understanding of transactional errors.

Once uncovered, compile all errors in a spreadsheet or more formal database. This database should include the following information:

- Type of error
- Description of error
- Date when error occurred
- Person responsible for error

A sample error database is:

Error Area	Description	Date of Occurrence	Person Responsible for
Timekeeping	Overtime recorded as regular time (Rogers paycheck)	Mar. 15	P. Doyle
Timekeeping	Hours not totaled correctly (Smith paycheck)	Mar. 15	P. Doyle
Billings	Incorrect pricing on invoice (Verity invoice)	Mar. 18	C. Breeze
Billings	Incorrect pricing on invoice (Standard invoice)	Mar. 18	C. Breeze
Payables	Early payment discount not taken (Arnold Distributors)	Mar. 19	K. Dithers
Payables	Invoice charged to wrong account (Lightspeed invoice)	Mar. 20	Q. Mathers
Payables	Invoice charged to wrong account (Casey invoice)	Mar. 20	S. Jingle
Timekeeping	Overtime recorded as regular time (Elinora paycheck)	Mar. 22	P. Doyle
Billings	Customer invoice not sent (Bosley customer)	Mar. 27	C. Breeze
Closing	Depreciation entry not made	Mar. 30	R. Sommers
Closing	Accrued wages not set to reverse	Mar. 31	R. Sommers
Payroll	Insurance not deducted from pay (Marlowe paycheck)	Mar. 31	P. Doyle

Tip: A "severity of error" column might also be included in the database, which reveals those items causing either a great deal of investigative work to fix or which cost the company money. In the preceding sample error database, not sending a customer invoice would likely have received a high score for error severity.

By using this format to collect error information, the information can be sorted several ways to see if there are clusters of errors. If a particular accounting area is revealing a cluster of errors, there may be a procedural issue that can be readily fixed. Alternatively, if errors appear to be clustering around a specific individual, the solution is likely to be the application of training, though fraud is also a possibility. For example, sorting the preceding report by name shows that P. Doyle appears to be causing a variety of problems in the timekeeping and payroll areas, which will likely call for more training, and perhaps the application of new controls. Similarly, C. Breeze is causing a number of errors on customer invoices, which may require a similar solution.

Tip: Do not use the error tracking system to fire employees, unless their performance cannot be improved by any reasonable means. Otherwise, the system will be looked upon by employees as the basic tool used for an ongoing witch hunt in the accounting department.

The most effective way to use the error tracking tool is to look for clusters of errors that have a common solution, and then implement that solution in order to eliminate an entire swathe of errors. This is a cost-effective approach, since all of the error correction activities associated with multiple errors can be avoided by implementing just one correcting activity. This approach rapidly reduces the grand total number of errors, which allows the accounting staff to concentrate their attention on a reduced pool of errors.

Process Reviews

There are a number of processes that run through the accounting department. For example, it is involved with customer billings, cash disbursements, and payroll. These processes change periodically to accommodate changes elsewhere in the business. Each incremental change may alter the efficiency with which transactions can be completed, usually making them slower. Over time, a series of these incremental changes can seriously impact the efficiency of the accounting department.

To counteract the ongoing decline in process efficiency, schedule periodic process reviews that are designed to root out inefficiencies and streamline processes. A typical review involves documenting each step in a process, including an examination of all forms, reports, and controls, as well as the movement of paperwork between personnel. The process review team then documents errors created by the system, the time required to complete an average transaction, and the queue time during which a transaction sits between processing activities. Based on this information, the team configures a new process flow that may contain any of the following improvements:

- *Eliminate approvals.* A process may require multiple approvals, where only one is needed.
- *Eliminate data.* A transaction may call for the entry of more data into the accounting system than is actually needed.
- *Process moves.* A process may require the movement of paperwork between employees, so concentrate activities with fewer people. By doing so, queue times are eliminated from the process.
- *Automation.* In a few cases, it may be possible to shift manual processing to an automated solution. However, only use this approach when there is a solidly favorable cost-benefit tradeoff. In many cases, an expensive automation solution will not yield much of an overall benefit to the company as a whole.

- *Report reductions*. Are reports really needed? In many cases, a process may result in a variety of reports being issued that are not used by the recipients. Interview recipients to determine which reports can be eliminated, or which information on specific reports can be eliminated.
- *Eliminate controls*. Some controls are redundant, and so only interfere with a process without reducing risk. However, only eliminate controls after having consulted with the auditors, who may have a different opinion.

A process review is a time-consuming activity that involves a number of people both within and outside of the accounting department. For this reason, it is impossible to engage in a continual review of processes. Instead, consider scheduling reviews on a rotating basis, so that a single process is reviewed in detail perhaps every six months to a year. The exact review interval will depend upon the amount of change within a company. If little has changed in the past few years, there may be little reason to invest in a process review. However, if there have been substantial changes, such as acquisitions, it may be necessary to engage in an ongoing series of reviews.

Queue Management

Certain employees may operate with a perpetual backlog of work, or do so at certain times of the month or year. This may not be a problem, as long as these queues do not interfere with cash flow. For example, an accounts payable clerk may have a five-day backlog of supplier invoices to enter into the accounting system, but this is not a problem if payment terms state that the company does not have to pay its suppliers for 30 days. However, if a billings clerk has a two-day backlog of customer invoices that have not yet been issued, this is a much greater concern, since customers will now pay the company a few days later, which impacts cash flow. This latter case may call for an alteration in the work load of the billings clerk, or the use of additional staff. Consider using the following techniques to improve the management of work queues:

- Narrowly define the job description of the person who has a persistently large queue, thereby permanently offloading some work. This is a common solution when transaction volumes gradually increase to the point where an employee is persistently using overtime to complete his or her work.
- Shift work temporarily when the work in a queue is time sensitive. This can involve shifting work to other full-time employees or bringing in part-time help. For example, this works well when processing month-end customer invoices.
- Examine the process flow to see if the activities related to a work queue can be streamlined. This may involve an investment in technology. This approach is more cost-effective when there is a persistent work queue.
- Structure jobs so that some employees are scheduled to have little required work at the same time that there are spikes in the work load elsewhere in the

department. This allows employees with low utilization levels to assist those in the reverse situation.

- Compare scheduled vacation times to expected changes in work queue levels. Restrict the use of vacation time during those periods when work queues are expected to be high.
- Delay the performance of routine tasks that have no impact on cash flow, so that staff can concentrate on reducing queues during peak work periods. This is a common solution during the month-end close, when the department stops all other work in order to create financial statements.

Queue management is a nearly daily activity that requires constant attention to workloads throughout the department, as well as anticipation of queue levels in the near future. Proper scheduling and shifting of personnel among tasks can reduce the most crucial queues and makes the department run more efficiently.

Department Layout

If the accounting department appears to be operating at near-maximum capacity, with employees working furiously throughout the day, then it may be possible to squeeze some extra capacity out of the department by altering its layout. The goals are a combination of improving the workflow within the department and reducing the amount of employee travel time within the building. Here are several layout improvements to consider:

- *Printers*. Provide employees with decent-quality printers that are positioned adjacent to their computers. Doing so eliminates the startling amount of travel time between employee work areas and a central printer; employees may travel back and forth many times during the day. Retain the central printer for higher-speed printing jobs.
- *Furniture*. If there is unused furniture or office equipment cluttering the department, then dispose of it. By doing so, not only can the traffic flow within the department be improved, but (better yet) the department can be compressed into a smaller work area, so that total travel times within the department are reduced.
- *Clustering*. Monitor the travel patterns of employees within the department. It is likely that some people must interact with others on the far side of the department, or must access filing cabinets located well away from where they sit. Based on this information, configure the department to cluster together those employees who interact most frequently. This may also result in the central document storage area being broken up and distributed closer to users.
- *Cubicles*. It is difficult to reconfigure the accounting department into clusters when everyone uses cubicles, since they require skilled furniture movers to disassemble and rebuild. Instead, eliminate the cubicles in favor

of clusters of desks, which can more easily be moved around in the department.

- *Carts*. An enhancement on the concept of clustering is to issue mobile office carts to employees. They can then shift any documents they need from fixed storage locations into the carts, and roll the carts to where they are working. If employees switch to different workstations during the day, they can just move the carts along with them.
- *Supplies*. Stock an office supplies cabinet, and place it in the middle of the accounting area. Then forbid anyone to keep an excess "stash" of office supplies at their desks. By doing so, some clutter in employee work areas can be eliminated.

The reconfiguring recommendations just noted do not preclude the use of offices. There is still a need for private meetings from time to time, as well as meeting rooms. However, the proportion of offices to the general work area assigned to the accounting department should be low.

Once a realignment of the department has been completed, undertake a formal review of the situation about once a year, which may even involve the use of a consultant who specializes in office workflow. In addition, make minor reconfiguration tweaks to the office layout whenever an opportunity presents itself, possibly at the suggestion of an employee, or as the workload shifts among employees.

Tip: If you have a highly configurable office where most employees use desk clusters, consider shifting them for each month-end close, so that the closing team is positioned in a group. Then move employees back to their usual positions as soon as the financial statements have been issued. This improves the level of coordination during the closing process.

The improvements outlined in this section will be much less useful in situations where there is clearly excess capacity in the accounting department, since the incremental improvement in efficiency afforded by changing the department's layout will only create a moderate increase in the level of available capacity.

Skills Review and Training

It is common practice to decide which accounting employees are deficient in certain skill areas, and then give them training in those areas. However, doing so can involve additional (and expensive) training, much of which may never be used. If a company pays for some portion of an employee's college education, then this cost-benefit effect becomes even more glaring. In short, many training programs result in employees learning skills for which they have no use within the company.

A more prudent view of training is to use the error tracking system described in a preceding section to determine where employees require additional training *in their current jobs*, and apply the exact amount of specific training to reduce the number of errors that they are causing. Or, consider linking training to specific upgrades that will be made to the department's systems. Here are several examples of targeted training:

- The department's error tracking system reveals that the accounts payable staff is not using the automated three-way matching feature in the accounting software, which has resulted in several payments to suppliers that should not have been made. The controller has a trainer come to the company's offices to train the accounts payable staff in this feature, as well as to monitor their usage of it over the next few days.
- A company is planning to install direct deposit as a new feature in its in-house payroll system, so it provides training to only those employees involved with employee paychecks, to give them sufficient knowledge to set up direct deposit payments, investigate errors, and answer employee questions pertaining to direct deposit.
- A company has just upgraded its accounting system to a new version of the same software. The controller pays the software supplier to send a consultant to the company to give users a training session on the specific changes that were made to system features, and how best to take advantage of them.

In short, avoid broad-based training, such as paying for accounting degrees at the local university, or sending employees to conferences. Instead, expend funds on training that very specifically improves the operations of the department. Also, as you may have noticed in the examples of targeted training, it is more effective if conducted on-site, where employees can use the training immediately. It may be more expensive to bring in consultants to conduct such training, but the results easily offset the costs.

Because of the need to engage in extremely specific training, it is nearly impossible to create a long-term training plan for employees. Instead, training needs are usually uncovered and addressed in the short term. The only case where employees can be involved in a longer-term training plan is when there is an intention to promote someone to a different position, and a course of study has been created for them to learn all aspects of their new position.

Consolidate Accounting

A business may have a divisional organizational structure, where all business functions are duplicated within an operating division. While this approach works well for localized decision-making, it has the following failings from the perspective of the corporate controller:

- *Cost.* Functional duplication requires headcount duplication, so each division has its own controller, assistant controller, payroll staff, cost accountant, and so forth.
- *Closing speed.* Local accounting departments need to close their books first before sending their results to corporate headquarters. Thus, it only takes a

delayed submission from one division to delay the release of financial statements for the entire company.

- *Procedures.* When there are many divisions, there are many different procedures for handling essentially identical business processes, which can lead to both inefficiencies and control problems.
- *Knowledge.* When there are only a few accounting staff at the division level, they are unlikely to be up-to-date on the most recent work efficiencies.

These issues can be eliminated by centralizing the accounting function in a single area that services the entire company. Doing so eliminates redundant positions, improves the speed at which the company closes its books, improves the uniformity of procedures, and results in the most efficient operational practices.

A move to consolidate accounting may very well be met with resistance from the division managers, who like to have control over their accounting functions. If so, point out the reduced overall accounting cost that will be assigned to their divisions, since the cost of the entire accounting function will decline. Also, it may be necessary to maintain a small local accounting presence to appease the local managers.

If accounting is to be consolidated, the best way to do so is by centralizing one functional area at a time. For example, aggregate all accounts payable functions into one location, then centralize payroll, and then move on to billing and collections – the exact items consolidated and the timing for doing so will depend on the circumstances of the company.

Tip: Consolidation does not necessarily work well for all accounting functions when a company is a conglomeration of many different types of businesses. Accounting systems vary by industry, so they cannot always be easily consolidated. In these cases, it is best to restrict centralization to only those activities that are similar across divisions, such as payroll processing.

A variation on the consolidation concept is to outsource certain types of accounting work away from the divisions, rather than to a central location. A prime example is employee expense report processing, where employees submit their expense reports to a website that automatically matches submissions against company travel policies, and then sends all approved expenses back to the company's accounts payable system through a custom interface. This approach works well if the corporate accounting department does not have the expertise, and the price offered by the supplier is reasonable.

Tip: When acquiring businesses, insist upon moving their entire accounting functions into the corporate accounting group. This is easier to do in an acquisition situation, since the acquiring entity has most of the power; local managers are less likely to resist the change.

Summary

The new controller faces a number of opportunities for improving the accounting department. Scheduling and work queue analysis can be used to improve the allocation of labor among the various work products that the department must complete, while workflow improvements, process reviews, and functional consolidations can be used to achieve a substantially higher degree of efficiency. All of the management issues noted in this chapter are not to be treated as one-time events, however. It will be necessary to continually monitor and adjust the condition of the department to achieve a state where the accounting staff is completing its assigned tasks in the most efficient and effective manner possible.

Chapter 11
Closing the Books

Introduction

A great many steps are required to close the books and issue financial statements. In this chapter, we give an overview of the most prevalent closing activities that you are likely to need.

The closing process does not begin after a reporting period has been completed. Instead, be prepared for it well in advance. By doing so, you can complete a number of activities in a leisurely manner before the end of the month, leaving fewer items for the busier period immediately following the end of the period. Accordingly, we have grouped closing steps into the following categories:

1. *Prior steps*. These are steps needed to complete the processing of the financial statements, and which can usually be completed before the end of the reporting period.
2. *Core steps*. These are the steps that are required for the creation of financial statements, and which cannot be completed prior to the end of the reporting period.
3. *Delayed steps*. These are the activities that can be safely delayed until after the issuance of the financial statements, but which are still part of the closing process.

The sections in this chapter do not necessarily represent the exact sequence of activities to follow when closing the books; you may want to alter the sequence based on the processes of the company and the availability of employees to work on them.

Related Podcast Episodes: Episodes 17 through 25, 77, 160, and 199 of the Accounting Best Practices Podcast discuss the fast close, the soft close, and the year-end book, respectively. These podcasts are available at: **accountingtools.com/podcasts** or **iTunes**

Controller Responsibilities

Closing the books quickly and accurately is the hallmark of an excellent controller. Management expects the department to issue financial statements, along with a pertinent analysis of the key issues, within a few days of month-end. Thus, the key controller responsibilities are:

- Issue financial statements shortly after the end of each accounting period.
- Provide an analysis of the financial results of the business.

Prior Steps: Update Reserves

Under the accrual basis of accounting, create a reserve in the expectation that expenses will be incurred in the future that are related to revenues generated now. This concept is called the matching principle. Under the matching principle, the cause and effect of a business transaction are recorded at the same time. Thus, when recording revenue, also record within the same accounting period any expenses directly related to that revenue.

The most common of all reserves is the allowance for doubtful accounts. It is used to charge to expense the amount of bad debts expected from a certain amount of sales, before you know precisely which invoices will not be paid. Update this allowance as part of the closing process.

There are several possible ways to estimate the allowance, which are:

- *Risk classification.* Assign a risk score to each customer, and assume a higher risk of default for those having a higher risk score.
- *Historical percentage.* If a certain percentage of accounts receivable became bad debts in the past, then use the same percentage in the future. This method works best for large numbers of small account balances.
- *Pareto analysis.* Review the largest accounts receivable that make up 80% of the total receivable balance, and estimate which specific customers are most likely to default. Then use the preceding historical percentage method for the remaining smaller accounts. This method works best if there are a small number of large account balances.

Review the balance in the allowance for doubtful accounts as part of the month-end closing process, to ensure that the balance is reasonable in comparison to the latest bad debt forecast. For companies having minimal bad debt activity, a quarterly update may be sufficient. The accounting for this allowance was described in the Credit and Collection Management chapter.

There are a number of other reserves to consider, such as:

- *Inventory obsolescence reserve.* If there is an expectation that there are some higher-cost items in inventory that will be rendered obsolete and disposed of, even if there is no certainty about which items they are, then create an obsolescence reserve and charge any losses against the reserve as you locate and dispose of these items.
- *Reserve for product returns.* If there is a history of significant product returns from customers, estimate the percentage of these returns based on prior history, and create a reserve using that percentage whenever related sales are recorded.
- *Reserve for warranty claims.* If the company has experienced a material amount of warranty claims in the past, and it can reasonably estimate the amount of these claims in the future, create a reserve in that amount whenever related sales are recorded.

The reserves just noted are among the more common ones. You may find a need for more unique types of reserves that are specific to your company's industry or business model. If so, it is quite acceptable to maintain other reserves.

There is no need to create a reserve if the balance in the account is going to be immaterial. Instead, many businesses can generate perfectly adequate financial statements that only have a few reserves, while charging all other expenditures to expense as incurred.

Core Steps: Issue Customer Invoices

Part of the closing process nearly always includes the issuance of month-end invoices to customers, especially in situations (such as consulting) where billable hours are compiled throughout the month and then billed at one time, or where a company has a practice of shipping most of its products near the end of the month. In other cases, invoices may have been issued throughout the month, leaving only a residual number to be issued as part of the closing process.

Irrespective of the number of invoices to be issued, invoices are always an important part of the closing process, because they are the primary method for recognizing revenue. Consequently, you normally spend a significant part of the closing process verifying that all possible invoices have, in fact, been created. This verification process may include a comparison of the shipping log to the invoice register, or a comparison of the shipping log to the timekeeping system where billable hours are stored or to a listing of open contracts.

If some revenues are considered to not yet be billable, but to have been fully earned by the company, then accrue the revenue with a journal entry. If this approach is used, be sure to address the following issues:

- *Auditor documentation.* Auditors do not like accrued revenue, since there are a number of restrictions placed on its use under Generally Accepted Accounting Principles (GAAP). Consequently, document the reasons for accruing revenue, with complete backup of the revenue calculations. The auditors will review this information. However, if revenue is only being accrued partway through a year, it may not be necessary to document the transactions in detail, since they should no longer be present on the balance sheet by the end of the fiscal year.
- *Reversing entry.* When revenue is accrued, the assumption is that you are likely to issue an invoice soon thereafter, probably in the next month. Consequently, set up every revenue accrual journal entry to automatically reverse in the next month. This clears the revenue accrual from the books, leaving room to record the revenue on the invoice. The following example illustrates the technique.

EXAMPLE

Milagro Corporation has fulfilled all of the terms of a contract with a customer to deliver a coffee bean roasting facility, but is unable to issue an invoice until July, which is the following month. Accordingly, the controller creates a revenue accrual with the following entry in June:

	Debit	Credit
Accrued revenue receivable (asset)	6,500,000	
Accrued revenue (revenue)		6,500,000

The controller sets the journal entry to automatically reverse in the next month, so the accounting software creates the following entry at the beginning of July:

	Debit	Credit
Accrued revenue (revenue)	6,500,000	
Accrued revenue receivable (asset)		6,500,000

In July, Milagro is now able to issue the invoice to the customer. When the invoice is created, the billing module of the accounting software creates the following entry:

	Debit	Credit
Accounts receivable	6,500,000	
Revenue		6,500,000

Thus, the net impact of these transactions is:

June:	Accrued revenue =	$6,500,000
July:	Accrued revenue reversal =	-$6,500,000
	Invoice generated =	+6,500,000
	Net effect in July =	$0

Core Steps: Value Inventory

Potentially the most time-consuming activity in the closing process is valuing ending inventory. This involves the following steps:

1. *Physical count.* Either conduct an ending inventory count or have an adequate perpetual inventory system in place that yields a verifiable ending inventory.
2. *Determine the cost of the ending inventory.* There are several methods available for assigning a cost to the ending inventory, such as the first in first out method, the last in first out method, and standard costing.
3. *Allocate overhead.* Allocate the costs of manufacturing overhead to any inventory items that are classified as work-in-process or finished goods. Overhead is not allocated to raw materials inventory, since the operations

giving rise to overhead costs only impact work-in-process and finished goods inventory. The following items are usually included in manufacturing overhead:

Depreciation of factory equipment	Quality control and inspection
Factory administration expenses	Rent, facility and equipment
Indirect labor and production supervisory wages	Repair expenses
Indirect materials and supplies	Rework labor, scrap and spoilage
Maintenance, factory and production equipment	Taxes related to production assets
Officer salaries related to production	Uncapitalized tools and equipment
Production employees' benefits	Utilities

The typical procedure for allocating overhead is to accumulate all manufacturing overhead costs into one or more cost pools, and to then use an activity measure to apportion the overhead costs in the cost pools to inventory. Thus, the overhead allocation formula is:

Cost pool ÷ Total activity measure = Overhead allocation per unit

4. *Adjust the valuation.* It may be necessary to reduce the amount of ending inventory due to the lower of cost or market rule, or for the presence of obsolete inventory. The lower of cost or market rule is required by GAAP, and requires that the cost of inventory be recorded at whichever cost is lower – the original cost or its current market price. This situation typically arises when inventory has deteriorated, or has become obsolete, or market prices have declined. The "current market price" is defined as the current replacement cost of the inventory, as long as the market price does not exceed net realizable value; also, the market price shall not be less than the net realizable value, less the normal profit margin. Net realizable value is defined as the estimated selling price, minus estimated costs of completion and disposal.

EXAMPLE

Milagro Corporation has a small production line for toy coffee roasters. During April, it incurs costs for the following items:

Cost Type	Amount
Building rent	$65,000
Building utilities	12,000
Factory equipment depreciation	8,000
Production equipment maintenance	7,000
Total	$92,000

All of these items are classified as manufacturing overhead, so Milagro creates the following journal entry to shift these costs into an overhead cost pool, for later allocation:

	Debit	Credit
Overhead cost pool	92,000	
Depreciation expense		8,000
Maintenance expense		7,000
Rent expense		65,000
Utilities expense		12,000

EXAMPLE

Milagro Corporation resells five major brands of coffee, which are noted in the following table. At the end of its reporting year, Milagro calculates the lower of its cost or net realizable value in the following table:

Product Line	Quantity on Hand	Unit Cost	Inventory at Cost	Market per Unit	Lower of Cost or Market
Arbuthnot	1,000	$190	$190,000	$230	$190,000
Bagley	750	140	105,000	170	105,000
Chowdry	200	135	27,000	120	24,000
Dingle	1,200	280	336,000	160	192,000
Ephraim	800	200	160,000	215	160,000

Based on the table, the market value is lower than cost on the Chowdry and Dingle coffee lines. Consequently, Milagro recognizes a loss on the Chowdry line of $3,000 ($27,000 - $24,000), as well as a loss of $144,000 ($336,000 - $192,000) on the Dingle line.

There are many steps because of the complexity of inventory valuation, but also because the investment in inventory may be so large that you simply cannot afford to arrive at an incorrect valuation – an error here could require a large adjustment to the financial statements in a later period.

If there is a relatively small investment in inventory, then it may not be so necessary to invest a large amount of time in closing inventory, since the size of potential errors is substantially reduced.

Core Steps: Calculate Depreciation

Once all fixed assets have been recorded in the accounting records for the month, calculate the amount of depreciation (for tangible assets) and amortization (for intangible assets). This is a significant issue for companies with a large investment in fixed assets, but may be so insignificant in other situations that it is sufficient to only record depreciation at the end of the year.

The basic depreciation entry is to debit the depreciation expense account (which appears in the income statement) and credit the accumulated depreciation account (which appears in the balance sheet as a contra account that reduces the amount of fixed assets). Over time, the accumulated depreciation balance will continue to increase as more depreciation is added to it, until such time as it equals the original cost of the asset. At that time, stop recording any depreciation expense, since the cost of the asset has now been reduced to zero.

The journal entry for depreciation can be a simple two-line entry designed to accommodate all types of fixed assets, or it may be subdivided into separate entries for each type of fixed asset.

EXAMPLE

Milagro Corporation calculates that it should have $25,000 of depreciation expense in the current month. The entry is:

	Debit	Credit
Depreciation expense	25,000	
Accumulated depreciation		25,000

In the following month, Milagro's controller decides to show a higher level of precision at the expense account level, and instead elects to apportion the $25,000 of depreciation among different expense accounts, so that each class of asset has a separate depreciation charge. The entry is:

	Debit	Credit
Depreciation expense – Automobiles	4,000	
Depreciation expense – Computer equipment	8,000	
Depreciation expense – Furniture and fixtures	6,000	
Depreciation expense – Office equipment	5,000	
Depreciation expense – Software	2,000	
Accumulated depreciation		25,000

An intangible asset is a non-physical asset having a useful life greater than one year. Examples of intangible assets are trademarks, patents, and non-competition agreements. The journal entry to record the amortization of intangible assets is fundamentally the same as the entry for depreciation, except that the accounts used substitute the word "amortization" for depreciation.

EXAMPLE

Milagro Corporation calculates that it should have $4,000 of amortization expense in the current month that is related to intangible assets. The entry is:

	Debit	Credit
Amortization expense	4,000	
Accumulated amortization		4,000

If fixed assets are being constructed (as would be the case for a factory or company headquarters) and the company has incurred debts to do so, it may be necessary to capitalize some interest expense into the cost of the fixed assets. Interest capitalization is the inclusion of any interest expense directly related to the construction of a fixed asset in the cost of that fixed asset.

Follow these steps to calculate the amount of interest to be capitalized for a specific project:

1. Construct a table itemizing the amounts of expenditures made and the dates on which the expenditures were made.
2. Determine the date on which interest capitalization ends.
3. Calculate the capitalization period for each expenditure, which is the number of days between the specific expenditure and the end of the interest capitalization period.
4. Divide each capitalization period by the total number of days elapsed between the date of the first expenditure and the end of the interest capitalization period to arrive at the capitalization multiplier for each line item.
5. Multiply each expenditure amount by its capitalization multiplier to arrive at the average expenditure for each line item over the capitalization measurement period.
6. Add up the average expenditures at the line item level to arrive at a grand total average expenditure.
7. If there is project-specific debt, multiply the grand total of the average expenditures by the interest rate on that debt to arrive at the capitalized interest related to that debt.
8. If the grand total of the average expenditures exceeds the amount of the project-specific debt, multiply the excess expenditure amount by the weighted average of the company's other outstanding debt to arrive at the remaining amount of interest to be capitalized.
9. Add together both capitalized interest calculations. If the combined total is more than the total interest cost incurred by the company during the calculation period, then reduce the amount of interest to be capitalized to the total interest cost incurred by the company during the calculation period.
10. Record the interest capitalization with a debit to the project's fixed asset account and a credit to the interest expense account.

EXAMPLE

Milagro Corporation is building a company headquarters building. Milagro makes payments related to the project of $10,000,000 and $14,000,000 to a contractor on January 1 and July 1, respectively. The building is completed on December 31.

For the 12-month period of construction, Milagro can capitalize all of the interest on the $10,000,000 payment, since it was outstanding during the full period of construction. Milagro can capitalize the interest on the $14,000,000 payment for half of the construction period, since it was outstanding during only the second half of the construction period. The average expenditure for which the interest cost can be capitalized is calculated in the following table:

Date of Payment	Expenditure Amount	Capitalization Period*	Capitalization Multiplier	Average Expenditure
January 1	$10,000,000	12 months	12 ÷ 12 months = 100%	$10,000,000
July 1	14,000,000	6 months	6 ÷ 12 months = 50%	7,000,000
				$17,000,000

* In the table, the capitalization period is defined as the number of months that elapse between the expenditure payment date and the end of the interest capitalization period.

The only debt that Milagro has outstanding during this period is a line of credit, on which the interest rate is 8%. The maximum amount of interest that Milagro can capitalize into the cost of the building project is $1,360,000, which is calculated as:

8% Interest rate × $17,000,000 Average expenditure = $1,360,000

Milagro records the following journal entry:

	Debit	Credit
Buildings (asset)	1,360,000	
Interest expense		1,360,000

Tip: There may be an inordinate number of expenditures related to a larger project, which could result in a large and unwieldy calculation of average expenditures. To reduce the workload, consider aggregating these expenses by month, and then assume that each expenditure was made in the middle of the month, thereby reducing all of the expenditures for each month to a single line item.

It is not possible to capitalize more interest cost in an accounting period than the total amount of interest cost incurred by the business in that period. If there is a corporate parent, this rule means that the amount capitalized cannot exceed the total amount of interest cost incurred by the business on a consolidated basis.

Core Steps: Create Accruals

An accrual allows you to record expenses and revenues for which there is an expectation to expend cash or receive cash, respectively, in a future reporting period. The offset to an accrued expense is an accrued liability account, which appears in the balance sheet. The offset to accrued revenue is an accrued asset account (such as unbilled consulting fees), which also appears in the balance sheet. Examples of accruals are:

- *Revenue accrual.* A consulting company works billable hours on a project that it will eventually invoice to a client for $5,000. It can record an accrual in the current period so that its current income statement shows $5,000 of revenue, even though it has not yet billed the client.
- *Expense accrual – general.* A supplier provides $10,000 of services before month-end, but does not issue an invoice to the company by the time it closes its books. Accordingly, the company accrues a $10,000 expense to reflect the receipt of services.
- *Expense accrual – interest.* A company has a loan with the local bank for $1 million, and pays interest on the loan at a variable rate of interest. The invoice from the bank for $3,000 in interest expense does not arrive until the following month, so the company accrues the expense in order to show the amount on its income statement in the proper month.
- *Expense accrual – wages.* A company pays its employees at the end of each month for their hours worked through the 25th day of the month. To fully record the wage expense for the entire month, it also accrues $32,000 in additional wages, which represents the cost of wages for the remaining days of the month.

Most accruals are initially created as reversing entries, so that the accounting software automatically creates a reverse version of them in the following month. This happens when you are expecting revenue to actually be billed, or supplier invoices to actually arrive, in the next month.

Core Steps: Consolidate Division Results

If there are company divisions that forward their financial results to the parent company, the largest issue from the perspective of the close is simply obtaining the information in a timely manner. This information may be provided in the format of a trial balance report. Then input the summary totals for all accounts provided into the general ledger of the parent company. This process is repeated for all of the divisions.

If the company uses the same accounting software throughout the business, then it may be quite simple to consolidate the division results, but only if the software is networked together. Otherwise, it will be necessary to create a separate journal entry to record the results of each division.

> **Tip:** If division results are recorded with a journal entry, the transaction likely involves a large number of line items. To reduce the risk of recording this information incorrectly, create a journal entry template in the accounting software that includes only the relevant accounts. If the entries for the various divisions are substantially different, then consider creating a separate template for each one.

Core Steps: Eliminate Intercompany Transactions

If there are several divisions within a company for which accounting transactions are recorded separately, it is possible that they do business with each other. For example, if a company is vertically integrated, some subsidiaries may sell their output to other subsidiaries, which in turn sell their output to other subsidiaries. If this is the case, they are generating intercompany transactions to record the sales. Intercompany transactions must be eliminated from the consolidated financial statements of the business, since not doing so would artificially inflate the revenue of the company as a whole. This elimination requires you to reverse the sale and offsetting account receivable for each such transaction.

Intercompany transactions can be difficult to spot, especially in businesses where such transactions are rare, and therefore not closely monitored. In a larger business, it is relatively easy to flag these transactions as being intercompany when they are created, so that the system automatically reverses them when the financial statements are consolidated. However, this feature is usually only available in the more expensive accounting software packages.

Core Steps: Review Journal Entries

It is entirely possible that some journal entries were made incorrectly, in duplicate, or not at all. Print the list of standard journal entries and compare it to the actual entries made in the general ledger, just to ensure that they were entered in the general ledger correctly. Another test is to have someone review the detailed calculations supporting each journal entry, and trace them through to the actual entries in the general ledger. This second approach takes more time, but is quite useful for ensuring that all necessary journal entries have been made correctly.

If there is an interest in closing the books quickly, the latter approach could interfere with the speed of the close; if so, you could authorize this detailed review at a later date, when someone can conduct the review under less time pressure. However, any errors found can only be corrected in the *following* accounting period, since the financial statements will already have been issued.

Core Steps: Reconcile Accounts

It is very important to examine the contents of the balance sheet accounts to verify that the recorded assets and liabilities are supposed to be there. It is quite possible that some items are still listed in an account that should have been flushed out of the balance sheet a long time ago, which can be quite embarrassing if they are still on record when the auditors review the company's books at the end of the year. Here are several situations that a proper account reconciliation would have caught:

- *Prepaid assets.* A company issues a $10,000 bid bond to a local government. The company loses the bid, but is not repaid. The asset lingers on the books until year-end, when the auditors inquire about it, and the company then recovers the funds from the local government.
- *Accrued revenue.* A company accrues revenue of $50,000 for a services contract, but forgets to reverse the entry in the following month, when it invoices the full $50,000 to the customer. This results in the double recordation of revenue, which is not spotted until year-end. The controller then reverses the accrual, thereby unexpectedly reducing revenues for the full year by $50,000.
- *Depreciation.* A company calculates the depreciation on several hundred assets with an electronic spreadsheet, which unfortunately does not track when to stop depreciating assets. A year-end review finds that the company charged $40,000 of excess depreciation to expense.
- *Accumulated depreciation.* A company has been disposing of its assets for years, but has never bothered to eliminate the associated accumulated depreciation from its balance sheet. Doing so reduces both the fixed asset and accumulated depreciation accounts by 50%.
- *Accounts payable.* A company does not compare its accounts payable detail report to the general ledger account balance, which is $8,000 lower than the detail. The auditors spot the error and require a correcting entry at year-end, so that the account balance matches the detail report.

These issues and many more are common problems encountered at year-end. To prevent the error correction work caused by these problems, conduct account reconciliations every month for the larger accounts, and occasionally review the detail for the smaller accounts, too. The following are some of the account reconciliations to conduct, as well as the specific issues to look for:

Sample Account Reconciliation List

Account	Reconciliation Discussion
Cash	There can be a number of unrecorded checks, deposits, and bank fees that will only be spotted with a bank reconciliation. It is permissible to do a partial bank reconciliation a day or two before the close, but completely ignoring it is not a good idea.
Accounts receivable, trade	The accounts receivable detail report should match the account balance. If not, you probably created a journal entry that should be eliminated from this account.

Account	Reconciliation Discussion
Accounts receivable, other	This account usually includes a large proportion of accounts receivable from employees, which are probably being deducted from their paychecks over time. This is a prime source of errors, since payroll deductions may not have been properly reflected in this account.
Accrued revenue	It is good practice to reverse all accrued revenue out of this account at the beginning of every period, so that you are forced to create new accruals every month. Thus, if there is a residual balance in the account, it probably should not be there.
Prepaid assets	This account may contain a variety of assets that will be charged to expense in the short term, so it may require frequent reviews to ensure that items have been flushed out in a timely manner.
Inventory	If a periodic inventory system is being used, you must match the inventory account to the ending inventory balance, which calls for a monthly reconciliation. However, if a perpetual inventory system is being used, inadequate cycle counting can lead to incorrect inventory balances. Thus, the level of reconciliation work depends upon the quality of the supporting inventory tracking system.
Fixed assets	It is quite likely that fixed assets will initially be recorded in the wrong fixed asset account, or that they are disposed of incorrectly. Reconcile the account to the fixed asset detail report at least once a quarter to spot and correct these issues.
Accumulated depreciation	The balance in this account may not match the fixed asset detail if accumulated depreciation has not been removed from the account upon the sale or disposal of an asset. This is not a critical issue, but still warrants occasional review.
Accounts payable, trade	The accounts payable detail report should match the account balance. If not, you probably included the account in a journal entry, and should reverse that entry.
Accrued expenses	This account can include a large number of accruals for such expenses as wages, vacations, and benefits. It is good practice to reverse all of these expenses in the month following recordation. Thus, if there is a residual balance, there may be an excess accrual still on the books.
Sales taxes payable	If state and local governments mandate the forwarding of collected sales taxes every month, this means that beginning account balances should have been paid out during the subsequent month. Consequently, there should not be any residual balances from the preceding month, unless payment intervals are longer than one month.

Account	Reconciliation Discussion
Income taxes payable	The amount of income taxes paid on a quarterly basis does not have to match the accrued liability, so there can be a residual balance in the account. However, the account should still be examined, if only to verify that scheduled payments have been made.
Notes payable	The balance in this account should exactly match the account balance of the lender, barring any exceptions for in-transit payments to the lender.
Equity	In an active equity environment where there are frequent stock issuances or treasury stock purchases, these accounts may require detailed and ongoing reviews to ensure that the account balances can be verified. However, if there is only sporadic account activity, it may be acceptable to reconcile at much longer intervals.

The number of accounts that can be reconciled makes it clear that this is one of the larger steps involved in closing the books. Some reconciliations can be skipped from time to time, but doing so presents the risk of an error creeping into the financial statements and not being spotted for quite a few months. Consequently, there is a significant risk of issuing inaccurate financial statements if some reconciliations are continually avoided.

Core Steps: Close Subsidiary Ledgers

Depending on the type of accounting software being using, it may be necessary to resolve any open issues in subsidiary ledgers, create a transaction to shift the totals in these balances to the general ledger (called *posting*), and then close the accounting periods within the subsidiary ledgers and open the next accounting period. This may involve ledgers for inventory, accounts receivable, and accounts payable.

Other accounting software systems (typically those developed more recently) do not have subsidiary ledgers, or at least use ones that do not require posting, and so are essentially invisible from the perspective of closing the books. Posting is the process of copying either summary-level or detailed entries in an accounting journal into the general ledger. Posting is needed in order to have a complete record of all accounting transactions in the general ledger.

Core Steps: Create Financial Statements

When all of the preceding steps have been completed, print the financial statements, which include the following items:

- Income statement
- Balance sheet
- Statement of cash flows

- Statement of retained earnings
- Disclosures

If the financial statements are only to be distributed internally, it may be acceptable to only issue the income statement and balance sheet, and dispense with the other items just noted. Reporting to people outside of the company generally calls for issuance of the complete set of financial statements.

Core Steps: Review Financial Statements

Once all of the preceding steps have been completed, review the financial statements for errors. There are several ways to do so, including:

- *Horizontal analysis*. Print reports that show the income statement, balance sheet, and statement of cash flows for the past twelve months on a rolling basis. Track across each line item to see if there are any unusual declines or spikes in comparison to the results of prior periods, and investigate those items. This is the best review technique.
- *Budget versus actual*. Print an income statement that shows budgeted versus actual results, and investigate any larger variances. This is a less effective review technique, because it assumes that the budget is realistic, and also because a budget is not usually available for the balance sheet or statement of cash flows.

There will almost always be problems with the first iteration of the financial statements. Expect to investigate and correct several items before issuing a satisfactory set of financials. To reduce the amount of time needed to review financial statement errors during the core closing period, consider doing so a few days prior to month-end; this may uncover a few errors, leaving a smaller number to investigate later on.

Core Steps: Accrue Tax Liabilities

Once you have created the financial statements and have finalized the information in it, there may be a need to accrue an income tax liability based on the amount of net profit or loss. There are several issues to consider when creating this accrual:

- *Income tax rate*. In most countries that impose an income tax, the tax rate begins at a low level and then gradually moves up to a higher tax rate that corresponds to higher levels of income. When accruing income taxes, use the average income tax rate that you expect to experience for the full year. Otherwise, the first quarter of the year will have a lower tax rate than later months, which is caused by the tax rate schedule, rather than any changes in company operational results.
- *Losses*. If the company has earned a profit in a prior period of the year, and has now generated a loss, accrue for a tax rebate, which will offset the tax

expense that was recorded earlier. Doing so creates the correct amount of tax liability when looking at year-to-date results. If there was no prior profit and no reasonable prospect of one, then do not accrue for a tax rebate, since it is more likely than not that the company will not receive the rebate.

- *Net operating loss carryforwards*. A net operating loss (NOL) carryforward is a loss experienced in an earlier period that could not be completely offset against prior-period profits. If the company has a net operating loss carryforward on its books, you may be able to use it to offset income taxes in the current period. If so, there is no need to accrue for an income tax expense.

Once the income tax liability has been accrued, print the complete set of financial statements.

Core Steps: Close the Month

Once all accounting transactions have been entered in the accounting system, close the month in the accounting software. This means prohibiting any further transactions in the general ledger in the old accounting period, as well as allowing the next accounting period to accept transactions. These steps are important, so that you do not inadvertently enter transactions into the wrong accounting periods.

Tip: There is a risk that an accounting person might access the accounting software to re-open an accounting period to fraudulently adjust the results from a prior period. To avoid this, password-protect the relevant data entry screens in the software.

Core Steps: Add Disclosures

If financial statements are being issued to readers other than the management team, consider adding disclosures to the basic set of financial statements. There are many disclosures required under GAAP and International Financial Reporting Standards. It is especially important to include a complete set of disclosures if the financial statements are being audited. If so, the auditors will offer advice regarding which disclosures to include. Allocate a large amount of time to the proper construction and error-checking of disclosures, for they contain a number of references to the financial statements and subsets of financial information extracted from the statements, and this information could be wrong. Thus, every time a new iteration of the financial statements is created, update the disclosures.

If financial statements are being issued solely for the management team, do not include any disclosures. By avoiding them, a significant amount of time can be cut from the closing process. Further, the management team is already well aware of how the business is run, and so presumably does not need the disclosures. If there are disclosure items that are unusual (such as violating the covenants on a loan), then attach just those items to the financial statements, or note them in the cover letter that accompanies the financials (see the next section).

Core Steps: Write Cover Letter

When you issue financial statements, readers are receiving several pieces of information that they may not have the time, interest, or knowledge to properly interpret. Accordingly, create a cover letter that itemizes the key aspects of the financial results and position of the business during the reporting period. This should not be an exhaustive analysis. Instead, point out the *key* changes in the business that might be of interest to the readers. Conversely, if changes were expected but did not occur, point that out. Further, discuss events that will occur in the near future, and their financial impact. Finally, use a standard format for the cover letter that lists all major topic areas, just so that you can refer to each topic while writing the contents of the letter. Doing so ensures that no areas will be missed. A sample cover letter follows.

Sample Cover Letter

To: Milagro Management Team
Fr: Controller
Re: April Financial Statements

Income statement: The profit for the past month was $100,000 below budget, because we did not ship the ABC widget order on time. This was caused by a quality problem that was not spotted until the final quality review at the shipping dock. The order could have shipped on time if the quality review had been positioned after the widget trimming machine.

We also paid $20,000 more than expected for rent, because we leased 12 storage trailers to accommodate a work-in-process overflow that did not fit into the warehouse. This was caused by the failure of the widget stamping machine. A replacement machine will arrive next week, and we expect it to require two months to eliminate the backlog of stored items. Thus, we will incur most of these leasing costs again through the next two months.

Balance Sheet: Accounts receivable were lower than expected by $180,000, primarily because of the ABC widget order just noted. This means that incoming cash flows will be reduced by that amount in one month. In anticipation of this cash shortfall, we have finalized an increase in the company's line of credit of $200,000.

Future Events: We expect to hear from the Marine Corps regarding the Combat Coffee order in late May. That order could increase the backlog by $1,000,000. Also, the office rent agreement expires on June 1. Market rates have increased, so we expect the replacement lease to cost at least $8,000 more per month.

Note that the sample cover letter addressed three key areas: the income statement, the balance sheet, and future events. These general categories are used as reminders to review each area for discussion topics. If there are areas of particular ongoing concern, such as cash or debt, it is acceptable to list these items as separate categories.

Tip: When writing the cover letter, always round up the numbers in the report to the nearest thousand (if not higher). Managers will not change their decision if a variance is reported as $82,000 or as $81,729.32, and the report will be much easier to read.

Whenever possible, state the causes of issues in the cover letter, so that recipients do not have to spend time conducting their own investigations. In essence, the ideal cover letter should highlight key points, discuss why they happened, and perhaps even point out how to correct them in the future.

Core Steps: Issue Financial Statements

The final core step in closing the books is to issue the financial statements. There are several ways to do this. If you are interested in reducing the total time required for someone to receive the financial statements, convert the entire package to PDF documents and e-mail them to the recipients. Doing so eliminates the mail float that would otherwise be required. If a number of reports are being incorporated into the financial statement package, this may require the purchase of a document scanner.

When issuing financial statements, always print a copy for yourself and store it in a binder. This gives you ready access to the report during the next few days, when managers from around the company are most likely to call with questions about it.

Delayed Steps: Issue Customer Invoices

From the perspective of closing the books, it is more important to formulate all customer invoices than it is to issue those invoices to customers.

Taking this delaying step can delay a company's cash flow. The problem is that a customer is supposed to pay an invoice based on pre-arranged terms that may also be stated on the invoice, so a delayed receipt of the invoice delays the corresponding payment. However, this is not necessarily the case. The terms set with customers should state that they must pay the company following a certain number of days from the invoice date, not the date when they receive the invoices. Thus, if invoices are printed that are dated as of the last day of the month being closed, and are then mailed a few days later, you should still be paid on the usual date.

From a practical perspective, this can still be a problem, because the accounting staff of the customer typically uses the current date as the default date when it enters supplier invoices into its accounting system. If they do so, you will likely be paid late. You can follow up with any customers that appear to being paying late for this reason, but this could be a continuing problem.

Delayed Steps: Closing Metrics

If there is an interest in closing the books more quickly, consider tracking a small set of metrics related to the close. The objective of having these metrics is not necessarily to attain a world-class closing speed, but rather to spot the bottleneck areas of the close that are preventing a more rapid issuance of the financial statements. Thus, there should be a set of metrics that delve sufficiently far into the workings of the closing process to spot the bottlenecks. An example of such metrics follows. Note that the total time required to close the books and issue financial statements is six days, but that the closing time for most of the steps needed to close the books is substantially shorter. Only the valuation of inventory and the bank reconciliation metrics reveal long closing intervals. Thus, this type of metric measurement and presentation allows you to quickly spot where there are opportunities to compress the closing process.

Sample Metrics Report for Closing the Books

	Day 1	Day 2	Day 3	Day 4	Day 5	Day 6
Issue financials	xxx	xxx	xxx	xxx	xxx	**Done**
Supplier invoices	xxx	**Done**				
Customer invoices	xxx	xxx	**Done**			
Accrued expenses	xxx	xxx	**Done**			
Inventory valuation	xxx	xxx	xxx	xxx	**Done**	
Bank reconciliation	xxx	xxx	xxx	**Done**		
Fixed assets	xxx	**Done**				
Payroll	**Done**					

Delayed Steps: Document Future Closing Changes

After reviewing the closing metrics in the preceding step, you will likely want to make some improvements to the closing process. Incorporate these changes into a schedule of activities for the next close, and review any resulting changes in responsibility with the accounting staff. Do this as soon after the close as possible, since this is the time when any problems with the close will be fresh in your mind, and you will be most interested in fixing them during the next close.

Even if you are satisfied with the timing of closing activities, it is possible that one or more employees in the accounting department will be on vacation during the next close, so you will need to incorporate their absence into the plan. Further, if there are inexperienced people in the department, consider including them in peripheral closing activities, and then gradually shifting them into positions of greater responsibility within the process. Thus, from the perspective of improvements, employee absences, and training, it is important to document any changes to the next closing process.

Delayed Steps: Update Closing Procedures

When you first implement a rigorous set of closing procedures, you will find that they do not yield the expected results. Some steps may be concluded too late to feed into another step, or some activities may be assigned to the wrong employee. As you gradually sort through these issues, update the closing procedures and schedule of events. This process will require a number of iterations, after which the closing procedures will yield more satisfactory results. Further, every time the company changes its operations, the procedures will require further updating. Examples of situations that may require a change in the closing procedures are noted in the following table.

Situation	Impact on Closing Procedure
New accounting software	Every accounting package has a different built-in methodology for closing the books, which must be incorporated into the closing procedures.
New business transaction procedures	If other parts of the business alter their approaches to processing purchasing, inventory counts, shipping, and so forth, you will need to adjust the closing procedures for them.
Acquisition or sale of a subsidiary	Add procedures to encompass new lines of business, while shutting down closing activities for those segments that have been disposed of.
Change in bank accounts	Different banks have different systems for providing on-line access to bank account information, which may alter the bank reconciliation procedure.
Change in credit policy	This may require a different method for compiling the allowance for doubtful accounts.
Change in inventory management system	If a business changes to just-in-time inventory management, it may flush out many older LIFO inventory layers, or uncover more obsolete inventory. These changes may also require different inventory costing methods, new overhead allocation methodologies, or altered obsolescence reserves.

The preceding list is by no means all-encompassing. It merely illustrates the fact that you should consider the impact of almost *any* change in the business on the closing procedures. It is quite likely that at least minor tweaking will be needed every few months for even the most finely-tuned closing procedures. In particular, be wary of closing steps that are no longer needed, or whose impact on the financial statements have become so minor that their impact is immaterial; such steps clutter up the closing process and can significantly delay the issuance of financial statements.

The Soft Close

A soft close refers to closing the books at the end of a reporting period without many of the more rigorous steps used in a normal closing process. By doing so, the accounting department can issue financial statements with minimal effort and then return to its normal day-to-day activities. The soft close approach has the added advantage of allowing the accounting staff to issue financial statements very quickly – usually the day after the end of a reporting period.

This enhanced closing speed comes at a cost, for the accuracy of the financial statements is reduced by the various revenue and expense accruals that are no longer being applied to the financial statements. This means that the results reported through a soft close may be materially inaccurate. Or, they may have more variable results from month to month because accruals are not being used to smooth out results over multiple periods.

The reduced accuracy level makes the soft close impractical for reviewed or audited financial statements that are read by outsiders. Auditors would likely refuse to render a favorable opinion on such financial statements. Also, outsiders would be receiving information for which there would be a heightened risk of material errors, which places the company at risk of knowingly issuing inaccurate financial statements.

However, it may be perfectly acceptable to use the soft close for internal management reporting, where total accuracy is not entirely necessary. Internal recipients would be more familiar with the areas in which the soft close provides less accurate information, and could build this knowledge into how they interpret the reports. For example, if the accounting department is only bothering to record depreciation at the end of the year, recipients of the report can be made aware of this fact, and adjust their estimates of the company's results accordingly for all interim periods.

A reasonable compromise is to use a more thorough closing process whenever a complete set of financial statements is needed for the use of outsiders, and the soft close for all other months. This means that, for example, a publicly-held company could adopt a detailed closing process for its quarterly financial statements (which are issued to the public), and a soft close for all other months. A privately-held company could get away with eleven months of soft closes, and a more detailed close at the end of its fiscal year. This means that, depending on the circumstances, the majority of the monthly closes could potentially be reported under a soft close procedure.

The majority of closing steps are typically avoided during a soft close. For example, the following actions might be skipped:

- Account reconciliations
- Expense accruals
- Intercompany eliminations
- Overhead allocations
- Physical inventory counts

- Reserve account updates
- Revenue accruals

Many of these steps involve reversing entries that are created specifically for the financial statements, and then reversed at the beginning of the next reporting period. Other steps, such as physical inventory counts and account reconciliations, are designed to detect errors. If a company elects to conduct a long series of soft closes, this means the error detection steps are being turned off for a long time, which increases the risk of significant errors finding their way into the financial statements.

Tip: If there are to be a number of consecutive soft closes, consider conducting some of the error-checking routines at intervals, to see if any errors have occurred that should be corrected.

If the results of a business are particularly susceptible to an item that has been removed from the soft close checklist, add the item back onto the list of closing tasks. For example, if the wage accrual is a large one, consider calculating and accruing it in every reporting period, irrespective of the type of close that the company uses.

The nature of a business may mandate that certain closing steps cannot be avoided, or else there will be material errors in the financial statements. For example:

- *Asset-intensive business*. If there is a large investment in fixed assets, and these assets are routinely being acquired or disposed of, it may be necessary to update the depreciation journal entries on a regular basis.
- *Inventory inaccuracies*. If there is a large investment in inventory and the inventory tracking system is primitive, a relatively frequent physical count may be necessary.
- *Irregular profits*. If profit levels are difficult to predict, it may be necessary to engage in extra closing steps in order to gain some assurance that the quarterly income tax liability is accurate.

If these issues can be surmounted, then the closing process for a soft close essentially involves completing all periodic billings to customers, recording billings from suppliers, and paying employees through the payroll system. The most problematic remaining activity is the accrual of supplier invoices that have not yet been received. If a company has a system in place for comparing received goods to authorizing purchase orders, it can readily calculate the amount of this accrual as soon as a reporting period is over, yielding accurate payable and expense figures for amounts due to its suppliers.

In short, a company can use the soft close concept to produce somewhat less accurate financial statements for selected reporting periods, thereby reducing the time required to close the books. This can be a useful concept if employed with caution, and when the recipients of the resulting reports have been warned about the potential shortcomings of the information they are receiving.

Summary

This chapter has outlined a large number of steps that are needed to close the books. You may feel that the level of organization required to close the books in this manner is overkill. However, consider that the primary work product of the accounting department as a whole, and the controller in particular, is the financial statements. If you can establish a reputation for consistently issuing high-quality financial statements within a reasonable period of time, this will likely be the basis for the company's view of the entire department.

You may find that additional closing steps are needed beyond the extensive list noted in this chapter. This is particularly common when a business has an unusual operating model, or operates in an industry with unique accounting rules. If so, incorporate the additional closing steps into the list described in this chapter.

If you would like to peruse a more in-depth analysis of closing the books, see the author's *Closing the Books*, which is available at accountingtools.com. This book provides more detail about all aspects of the closing process.

Chapter 12
The Financial Statements

Introduction

The controller *may* be judged on his or her administration of the accounting function, but will *absolutely* be judged on the quality and presentation of the financial statements issued by the accounting staff. For this reason, be thoroughly familiar with the contents of each component of the financial statements, the different formats available, and how to construct them. We address these issues in the following sections for the income statement, balance sheet, statement of cash flows, and statement of retained earnings. The process of closing the books is addressed in the Closing the Books chapter.

Controller Responsibilities

The responsibilities of the controller for issuing the financial statements are noted in the Closing the Books chapter. In addition, we include the following responsibility related to the format of the financial statements:

- Prepare financial statement layouts that are understandable and clearly present the financial results, financial position, and cash flows of the business.

The Income Statement

In most organizations, the income statement is considered the most important of the financial statements, and may even be the only one of the financial statements that is produced (though we do not recommend doing so). Given its importance, we spend extra time in this section addressing different income statement formats, and then walk through the steps needed to create an income statement.

Income Statement Overview

The income statement is an integral part of an entity's financial statements, and contains the results of its operations during an accounting period, showing revenues and expenses and the resulting profit or loss.

There are two ways to present the income statement. One method is to present all items of revenue and expense for the reporting period in a statement of comprehensive income. Alternatively, you can split this information into an income statement and a statement of other comprehensive income. Other comprehensive income contains all changes that are not permitted in the main part of the income statement. These items include unrealized gains and losses on available-for-sale securities, cash flow hedge gains and losses, foreign currency translation adjustments, and pension plan gains or losses. Smaller companies tend to ignore the distinction and simply aggregate the information into a document that they call the income statement; this is sufficient for internal reporting, but auditors will require the expanded version before they will certify the financial statements.

There are no specific requirements for the line items to include in the income statement, but the following line items are typically used, based on general practice:

- Revenue
- Tax expense
- Post-tax profit or loss for discontinued operations and their disposal
- Profit or loss
- Other comprehensive income, subdivided into each component thereof
- Total comprehensive income

A key additional item is to present an analysis of the expenses in profit or loss, using a classification based on their nature or functional area; the goal is to maximize the relevance and reliability of the presented information. If you elect to present expenses by their nature, the format looks similar to the following:

Sample Presentation by Nature of Items

Revenue		$xxx
Expenses		
Direct materials	$xxx	
Direct labor	xxx	
Salaries expense	xxx	
Payroll taxes	xxx	
Employee benefits	xxx	
Depreciation expense	xxx	
Telephone expense	xxx	
Other expenses	xxx	
Total expenses		$xxx
Profit before tax		$xxx

Alternatively, if you present expenses by their functional area, the format looks similar to the following, where most expenses are aggregated at the department level:

Sample Presentation by Function of Items

Revenue	$xxx
Cost of goods sold	xxx
Gross profit	xxx
Administrative expenses	$xxx
Distribution expenses	xxx
Research and development expenses	xxx
Sales and marketing expenses	xxx
Other expenses	xxx
Total expenses	$xxx
Profit before tax	$xxx

Of the two methods, presenting expenses by their nature is easier, since it requires no allocation of expenses between functional areas. Conversely, the functional area presentation may be more relevant to users of the information, who can more easily see where resources are being consumed.

Add additional headings, subtotals, and line items to the items noted above if doing so will increase the user's understanding of the entity's financial performance.

An example follows of an income statement that presents expenses by their nature, rather than by their function.

EXAMPLE

Milagro Corporation presents its results in two separate statements by their nature, resulting in the following format, beginning with the income statement:

Milagro Corporation
Income Statement
For the years ended December 31

(000s)	20x2	20x1
Revenue	$900,000	$850,000
Expenses		
Direct materials	$270,000	$255,000
Direct labor	90,000	85,000
Salaries	300,000	275,000
Payroll taxes	27,000	25,000
Depreciation expense	45,000	41,000

(000s)	20x2	20x1
Telephone expense	30,000	20,000
Other expenses	23,000	22,000
Finance costs	29,000	23,000
Other income	-25,000	-20,000
Profit before tax	$111,000	$124,000
Income tax expense	38,000	43,000
Profit from continuing operations	$73,000	$81,000
Loss from discontinued operations	42,000	0
Profit	$31,000	$81,000

Milagro Corporation then continues with the following statement of comprehensive income:

Milagro Corporation
Statement of Comprehensive Income
For the years ended December 31

(000s)	20x2	20x1
Profit	$31,000	$81,000
Other comprehensive income		
Exchange differences on translating foreign operations	$5,000	$9,000
Available-for-sale financial assets	10,000	-2,000
Actuarial losses on defined benefit pension plan	-2,000	-12,000
Other comprehensive income, net of tax	$13,000	-$5,000
Total comprehensive income	$18,000	$76,000

The Single-Step Income Statement

The simplest format in which you can construct an income statement is the single-step income statement. In this format, you present a single subtotal for all revenue line items, and a single subtotal for all expense line items, with a net gain or loss appearing at the bottom of the report. A sample single-step income statement follows:

Sample Single-Step Income Statement

Revenues	$1,000,000
Expenses:	
Cost of goods sold	350,000
Advertising	30,000
Depreciation	20,000
Rent	40,000
Payroll taxes	28,000
Salaries and wages	400,000
Supplies	32,000
Travel and entertainment	50,000
Total expenses	950,000
Net income	$50,000

The single-step format is not heavily used, because it forces the reader to separately summarize information for subsets of information within the income statement. For a more readable format, try the following multi-step approach.

The Multi-Step Income Statement

The multi-step income statement involves the use of multiple sub-totals within the income statement, which makes it easier for readers to aggregate selected types of information within the report. The usual subtotals are for the gross margin, operating expenses, and other income, which allow readers to determine how much the company earns just from its manufacturing activities (the gross margin), what it spends on supporting operations (the operating expense total) and which components of its results do not relate to its core activities (the other income total). A sample format for a multi-step income statement follows:

Sample Multi-Step Income Statement

Revenues	$1,000,000
Cost of goods sold	350,000
Gross margin	$650,000
Operating expenses	
Advertising	30,000
Depreciation	20,000
Rent	40,000
Payroll taxes	28,000

Salaries and wages	380,000
Supplies	32,000
Travel and entertainment	50,000
Total operating expenses	$580,000
Other income	
Interest income	-5,000
Interest expense	25,000
Total other income	$20,000
Net income	$50,000

The Condensed Income Statement

A condensed income statement is simply an income statement with many of the usual line items condensed down into a few lines. Typically, this means that all revenue line items are aggregated into a single line item, while the cost of goods sold appears as one line item, and all operating expenses appear in another line item. A typical format for the statement is:

Sample Condensed Income Statement

Revenues	$1,000,000
Cost of goods sold	350,000
Sales, general, and administrative expenses	580,000
Financing income and expenses	20,000
Net income	$50,000

A condensed income statement is typically issued to those external parties who are less interested in the precise sources of a company's revenues or what expenses it incurs, and more concerned with its overall performance. Thus, bankers and investors may be interested in receiving a condensed income statement.

The Contribution Margin Income Statement

A contribution margin income statement is an income statement in which all variable expenses are deducted from sales to arrive at a contribution margin, from which all fixed expenses are then subtracted to arrive at the net profit or loss for the period. This income statement format is a superior form of presentation, because the contribution margin clearly shows the amount available to cover fixed costs and generate a profit (or loss).

In essence, if there are no sales, a contribution margin income statement will have a zero contribution margin, with fixed costs clustered beneath the contribution margin line item. As sales increase, the contribution margin will increase in conjunction with sales, while fixed costs remain approximately the same.

A contribution margin income statement varies from a normal income statement in the following three ways:

- Fixed production costs are aggregated lower in the income statement, after the contribution margin;
- Variable selling and administrative expenses are grouped with variable production costs, so that they are a part of the calculation of the contribution margin; and
- The gross margin is replaced in the statement by the contribution margin.

Thus, the format of a contribution margin income statement is:

Sample Contribution Margin Income Statement

+	Revenues
-	Variable production expenses (such as materials, supplies, and variable overhead)
-	Variable selling and administrative expenses
=	Contribution margin
-	Fixed production expenses (including most overhead)
-	Fixed selling and administrative expenses
=	Net profit or loss

In many cases, direct labor is categorized as a fixed expense in the contribution margin income statement format, rather than a variable expense, because this cost does not always change in direct proportion to the amount of revenue generated. Instead, management needs to keep a certain minimum staffing in the production area, which does not vary even if there are lower production volumes.

The key difference between gross margin and contribution margin is that fixed production costs are included in the cost of goods sold to calculate the gross margin, whereas they are not included in the same calculation for the contribution margin. This means that the contribution margin income statement is sorted based on the variability of the underlying cost information, rather than by the functional areas or expense categories found in a normal income statement.

It is useful to create an income statement in the contribution margin format when you want to determine that proportion of expenses that truly varies directly with revenues. In many businesses, the contribution margin will be substantially higher than the gross margin, because such a large proportion of production costs are fixed and few of its selling and administrative expenses are variable.

The Multi-Period Income Statement

A variation on any of the preceding income statement formats is to present them over multiple periods, preferably over a trailing 12-month period. By doing so, readers of the income statement can see trends in the information, as well as spot changes in the trends that may require investigation. This is an excellent way to present the income statement, and is highly recommended. The following sample shows the layout of a multi-period income statement over a four-quarter period.

Sample Multi-Period Income Statement

	Quarter 1	Quarter 2	Quarter 3	Quarter 4
Revenues	$1,000,000	$1,100,000	$1,050,000	$1,200,000
Cost of goods sold	350,000	385,000	368,000	**480,000**
Gross margin	$650,000	$715,000	$682,000	$720,000
Operating expenses				
Advertising	30,000	**0**	**60,000**	30,000
Depreciation	20,000	21,000	22,000	24,000
Rent	40,000	40,000	**50,000**	50,000
Payroll taxes	28,000	28,000	28,000	26,000
Salaries and wages	380,000	385,000	385,000	370,000
Supplies	32,000	30,000	31,000	33,000
Travel and entertainment	50,000	45,000	40,000	60,000
Total operating expenses	$580,000	$549,000	$616,000	$593,000
Other income				
Interest income	-5,000	-5,000	-3,000	-1,000
Interest expense	25,000	25,000	30,000	**39,000**
Total other income	$20,000	$20,000	$27,000	$38,000
Net income	$50,000	$146,000	$39,000	$89,000

The report shown in the sample reveals several issues that might not have been visible if the report had only spanned a single period. These issues are:

- *Cost of goods sold.* This cost is consistently 35% of sales until Quarter 4, when it jumps to 40%.
- *Advertising.* There was no advertising cost in Quarter 2 and double the amount of the normal $30,000 quarterly expense in Quarter 3. The cause could be a missing supplier invoice in Quarter 2 that was received and recorded in Quarter 3.

- *Rent.* The rent increased by $10,000 in Quarter 3, which may indicate a scheduled increase in the rent agreement.
- *Interest expense.* The interest expense jumps in Quarter 3 and does so again in Quarter 4, while interest income declined over the same periods. This indicates a large increase in debt.

In short, the multi-period income statement is an excellent tool for spotting anomalies in the presented information from period to period.

How to Construct the Income Statement

If you use an accounting software package, it is quite easy to construct an income statement. Just access the report writing module, select the time period for which you want to print the income statement, and print it.

Tip: If you have used a report writer to create an income statement in your accounting software, there is a good chance that the first draft of the report will be wrong, due to some accounts being missed or duplicated. To ensure that the income statement is correct, compare it to the default income statement report that is usually provided with the accounting software, or compare the net profit or loss on your report to the current year earnings figure listed in the equity section of the balance sheet. If there is a discrepancy, the customized income statement report is incorrect.

The situation is more complex if you choose to create the income statement by hand. This involves the following steps:

1. Create the trial balance report (available through the accounting software as a standard report).
2. List each account pertaining to the income statement in a separate column of the trial balance.
3. Aggregate these lines into those you want to report in the income statement on a separate line.
4. Shift the result into the format of the income statement that you prefer.

The following example illustrates the construction of an income statement.

EXAMPLE

The accounting software for Milagro Corporation breaks down at the end of July, and the controller has to create the financial statements by hand. He has a copy of Milagro's trial balance, which is shown below. He transfers this information to an electronic spreadsheet, creates separate columns for accounts to include in the income statement, and copies those balances into these columns. This leaves a number of accounts related to the balance sheet, which he can ignore for the purposes of creating the income statement.

Milagro Corporation Extended Trial Balance

	Adjusted Trial Balance		Income Statement		Aggregation	
	Debit	Credit	Debit	Credit	Debit	Credit
Cash	$60,000					
Accounts receivable	230,000					
Inventory	300,000					
Fixed assets (net)	210,000					
Accounts payable		$90,000				
Accrued liabilities		75,000				
Notes payable		420,000				
Equity		350,000				
Revenue		450,000		$450,000		$450,000
Cost of goods sold	290,000		$290,000		$290,000	
Salaries expense	225,000		225,000		245,000	
Payroll tax expense	20,000		20,000			
Rent expense	35,000		35,000			
Other expenses	15,000		15,000		50,000	
Totals	$1,385,000	$1,385,000	$585,000	$450,000	$585,000	$450,000

In the "Aggregation" columns of the extended trial balance, the controller has aggregated the expenses for salaries and payroll taxes into the salaries expense line, and aggregated the rent expense and other expenses into the other expenses line. He then transfers this information into the following condensed income statement:

Milagro Corporation
Income Statement
For the month ended July 31, 20X1

Revenue	$450,000
Cost of goods sold	290,000
Salaries expenses	245,000
Other expenses	50,000
Net loss	-$135,000

The Balance Sheet

In most organizations, the balance sheet is considered the second most important of the financial statements, after the income statement. A common financial reporting package is to issue the income statement and balance sheet, along with supporting materials. This does not comprise a complete set of financial statements, but it is considered sufficient for internal reporting purposes in many organizations.

In this section, we explore several possible formats for the balance sheet, and also describe how to create it.

Overview of the Balance Sheet

A balance sheet (also known as a statement of financial position) presents information about an entity's assets, liabilities, and shareholders' equity, where the compiled result must match this formula:

Total assets = Total liabilities + Equity

The balance sheet reports the aggregate effect of transactions as of a specific date. The balance sheet is used to assess an entity's liquidity and ability to pay its debts.

There is no specific requirement for the line items to be included in the balance sheet. The following line items, at a minimum, are normally included in it:

Current Assets:

- Cash and cash equivalents
- Trade and other receivables
- Investments
- Inventories
- Assets held for sale

Non-Current Assets:

- Property, plant, and equipment
- Intangible assets
- Goodwill

Current Liabilities:

- Trade and other payables
- Accrued expenses
- Current tax liabilities
- Current portion of loans payable
- Other financial liabilities
- Liabilities held for sale

Non-Current Liabilities:

- Loans payable
- Deferred tax liabilities
- Other non-current liabilities

Equity:

- Capital stock
- Additional paid-in capital
- Retained earnings

Here is an example of a balance sheet which presents information as of the end of two fiscal years:

Milagro Corporation
Balance Sheet
As of December 31, 20X2 and 20X1

(000s)	12/31/20X2	12/31/20x1
ASSETS		
Current assets		
Cash and cash equivalents	$270,000	$215,000
Trade receivables	147,000	139,000
Inventories	139,000	128,000
Other current assets	15,000	27,000
Total current assets	$571,000	$509,000
Non-current assets		
Property, plant, and equipment	551,000	529,000
Goodwill	82,000	82,000
Other intangible assets	143,000	143,000
Total non-current assets	$776,000	$754,000
Total assets	$1,347,000	$1,263,000
LIABILITIES AND EQUITY		
Current liabilities		
Trade and other payables	$217,000	$198,000
Short-term borrowings	133,000	202,000
Current portion of long-term borrowings	5,000	5,000
Current tax payable	26,000	23,000
Accrued expenses	9,000	13,000
Total current liabilities	$390,000	$441,000

(000s)	12/31/20X2	12/31/20x1
Non-current liabilities		
Long-term debt	85,000	65,000
Deferred taxes	19,000	17,000
Total non-current liabilities	$104,000	$82,000
Total liabilities	$494,000	$523,000
Shareholders' equity		
Capital	100,000	100,000
Additional paid-in capital	15,000	15,000
Retained earnings	738,000	625,000
Total equity	$853,000	$740,000
Total liabilities and equity	$1,347,000	$1,263,000

Classify an asset on the balance sheet as current when an entity expects to sell or consume it during its normal operating cycle or within 12 months after the reporting period. If the operating cycle is longer than 12 months, use the longer period to judge whether an asset can be classified as current. Classify all other assets as non-current.

Classify all of the following as current assets:

- *Cash*. This is cash available for current operations, as well as any short-term, highly liquid investments that are readily convertible to known amounts of cash and which are so near their maturities that they present an insignificant risk of value changes. Do not include cash whose withdrawal is restricted, to be used for other than current operations, or segregated for the liquidation of long-term debts; such items should be classified as longer-term.
- *Accounts receivable*. This includes trade accounts, notes, and acceptances that are receivable. Also, include receivables from officers, employees, affiliates, and others if they are collectible within a year. Do not include any receivable that you do not expect to collect within 12 months; such items should be classified as longer-term.
- *Marketable securities*. This includes those securities representing the investment of cash available for current operations, including trading securities.
- *Inventory*. This includes merchandise, raw materials, work-in-process, finished goods, operating supplies, and maintenance parts.
- *Prepaid expenses*. This includes prepayments for insurance, interest, rent, taxes, unused royalties, advertising services, and operating supplies.

Classify a liability as current when the entity expects to settle it during its normal operating cycle or within 12 months after the reporting period, or if it is scheduled for settlement within 12 months. Classify all other liabilities as non-current.

Classify all of the following as current liabilities:

- *Payables*. This is all accounts payable incurred in the acquisition of materials and supplies that are used to produce goods or services.
- *Prepayments*. This is amounts collected in advance of the delivery of goods or services by the entity to the customer. Do not include a long-term prepayment in this category.
- *Accruals*. This is accrued expenses for items directly related to the operating cycle, such as accruals for compensation, rentals, royalties, and various taxes.
- *Short-term debts*. This is debts maturing within the next 12 months.

Current liabilities include accruals for amounts that can only be determined approximately, such as bonuses, and where the payee to whom payment will be made cannot initially be designated, such as a warranty accrual.

The Common Size Balance Sheet

A common size balance sheet presents not only the standard information contained in a balance sheet, but also a column that notes the same information as a percentage of the total assets (for asset line items) or as a percentage of total liabilities and shareholders' equity (for liability or shareholders' equity line items).

It is extremely useful to construct a common size balance sheet that itemizes the results as of the end of multiple time periods, so that you can construct trend lines to ascertain changes over longer time periods. The common size balance sheet is also useful for comparing the proportions of assets, liabilities, and equity between different companies, particularly as part of an industry or acquisition analysis.

For example, if you were comparing the common size balance sheet of your company to that of a potential acquiree, and the acquiree had 40% of its assets invested in accounts receivable versus 20% by your company, this may indicate that aggressive collection activities might reduce the acquiree's receivables if your company were to acquire it.

The common size balance sheet is not required under the GAAP or IFRS accounting frameworks. However, being a useful document for analysis purposes, it is commonly distributed within a company for review by management.

There is no mandatory format for a common size balance sheet, though percentages are nearly always placed to the right of the normal numerical results. If you are reporting balance sheet results as of the end of many periods, you may even dispense with numerical results entirely, in favor of just presenting the common size percentages.

EXAMPLE

Milagro Corporation creates a common size balance sheet that contains the balance sheet as of the end of its fiscal year for each of the past two years, with common size percentages to the right:

Milagro Corporation
Common Size Balance Sheet
As of 12/31/20x02 and 12/31/20x1

	($) 12/31/20x2	($) 12/31/20x1	(%) 12/31/20x2	(%) 12/31/20x1
Current assets				
Cash	$1,200	$900	7.6%	7.1%
Accounts receivable	4,800	3,600	30.4%	28.3%
Inventory	3,600	2,700	22.8%	21.3%
Total current assets	$9,600	$7,200	60.8%	56.7%
Total fixed assets	6,200	5,500	39.2%	43.3%
Total assets	$15,800	$12,700	100.0%	100.0%
Current liabilities				
Accounts payable	$2,400	$41,800	15.2%	14.2%
Accrued expenses	480	360	3.0%	2.8%
Short-term debt	800	600	5.1%	4.7%
Total current liabilities	$3,680	$2,760	23.3%	21.7%
Long-term debt	9,020	7,740	57.1%	60.9%
Total liabilities	$12,700	$10,500	80.4%	82.7%
Shareholders' equity	3,100	2,200	19.6%	17.3%
Total liabilities and equity	$15,800	$12,700	100.0%	100.0%

The Comparative Balance Sheet

A comparative balance sheet presents side-by-side information about an entity's assets, liabilities, and shareholders' equity as of multiple points in time. For example, a comparative balance sheet could present the balance sheet as of the end of each year for the past three years. Another variation is to present the balance sheet as of the end of each month for the past 12 months on a rolling basis. In both cases, the intent is to provide the reader with a series of snapshots of a company's financial condition over a period of time, which is useful for developing trend line analyses.

The comparative balance sheet is not required under the GAAP accounting framework for a privately-held company, but the Securities and Exchange Commission (SEC) does require it in numerous circumstances for the reports issued by publicly-held companies, particularly the annual Form 10-K and the quarterly Form 10-Q. The usual SEC requirement is to report a comparative balance sheet for the past two years, with additional requirements for quarterly reporting.

There is no standard format for a comparative balance sheet. It is somewhat more common to report the balance sheet as of the least recent period furthest to the right, though the reverse is the case when you are reporting balance sheets in a trailing twelve months format.

The following is a sample of a comparative balance sheet that contains the balance sheet as of the end of a company's fiscal year for each of the past three years:

Sample Comparative Balance Sheet

	as of 12/31/20X3	as of 12/31/20X2	as of 12/31/20X1
Current assets			
Cash	$1,200,000	$900,000	$750,000
Accounts receivable	4,800,000	3,600,000	3,000,000
Inventory	3,600,000	2,700,000	2,300,000
Total current assets	$9,600,000	$7,200,000	$6,050,000
Total fixed assets	6,200,000	5,500,000	5,000,000
Total assets	$15,800,000	$12,700,000	$11,050,000
Current liabilities			
Accounts payable	$2,400,000	$1,800,000	$1,500,000
Accrued expenses	480,000	360,000	300,000
Short-term debt	800,000	600,000	400,000
Total current liabilities	$3,680,000	$2,760,000	$2,200,000
Long-term debt	9,020,000	7,740,000	7,350,000
Total liabilities	$12,700,000	$10,500,000	$9,550,000
Shareholders' equity	3,100,000	2,200,000	1,500,000
Total liabilities and equity	$15,800,000	$12,700,000	$11,050,000

The sample comparative balance sheet reveals that the company has increased the size of its current assets over the past few years, but has also recently invested in a large amount of additional fixed assets that have likely been the cause of a significant boost in its long-term debt.

How to Construct the Balance Sheet

If you use an accounting software package, it is quite easy to construct the balance sheet. Just access the report writing module, select the time period for which you want to print the balance sheet, and print it.

Tip: It is generally not necessary to create your own version of the balance sheet in the accounting software package, since the default version is usually sufficient. If you choose to do so, test it by verifying that the total of all asset line items equals the total of all liability and equity line items. An error is usually caused by some accounts not being included in the report, or added to it multiple times.

If you choose to construct the balance sheet manually, follow these steps:

1. Create the trial balance report (usually available through the accounting software as a standard report).
2. List each account pertaining to the balance sheet in a separate column of the trial balance.
3. Add the difference between the revenue and expense line items on the trial balance to a separate line item in the equity section of the balance sheet.
4. Aggregate these line items into those you want to report in the balance sheet as a separate line item.
5. Shift the result into the format of the balance sheet that you prefer.

The following example illustrates the construction of a balance sheet.

EXAMPLE

The accounting software for Milagro Corporation breaks down at the end of July, and the controller has to create the financial statements by hand. He has a copy of Milagro's trial balance, which is shown below. He transfers this information to an electronic spreadsheet, creates separate columns for accounts to include in the balance sheet, and copies those balances into these columns. This leaves a number of accounts related to the income statement, which he can ignore for the purposes of creating the balance sheet. However, he *does* include the net loss for the period in the "Current year profit" row, which is included in the equity section of the balance sheet.

Milagro Corporation Extended Trial Balance

	Adjusted Trial Balance		Balance Sheet		Aggregation	
	Debit	Credit	Debit	Credit	Debit	Credit
Cash	$60,000		$60,000		$60,000	
Accounts receivable	230,000		230,000		230,000	
Inventory	300,000		300,000		300,000	
Fixed assets (net)	210,000		210,000		210,000	
Accounts payable		$90,000		$90,000		$165,000
Accrued liabilities		75,000		75,000		
Notes payable		420,000		420,000		420,000
Equity		350,000		350,000		215,000
Current year profit			135,000			
Revenue		450,000				
Cost of goods sold	290,000					
Salaries expense	225,000					
Payroll tax expense	20,000					
Rent expense	35,000					
Other expenses	15,000					
Totals	$1,385,000	$1,385,000	$935,000	$935,000	$800,000	$800,000

In the "Aggregation" columns of the extended trial balance, the controller has aggregated the liabilities for accounts payable and accrued liabilities in the accounts payable line, and aggregated equity and current year profit into the equity line. He then transfers this information into the following condensed balance sheet:

Milagro Corporation
Balance Sheet
For the month ended July 31, 20X1

Assets	
Cash	$60,000
Accounts receivable	230,000
Inventory	300,000
Fixed assets	210,000
Total assets	$800,000
Liabilities	
Accounts payable	$165,000
Notes payable	420,000
Total liabilities	$585,000
Equity	$215,000
Total liabilities and equity	$800,000

The Statement of Cash Flows

The statement of cash flows is the least used of the primary financial statements, and may not be issued at all for internal financial reporting purposes. The recipients of financial statements seem to be mostly concerned with the profit information on the income statement, and to a lesser degree with the financial position information on the balance sheet. Nonetheless, the cash flows on the statement of cash flows can provide valuable information, especially when combined with the other elements of the financial statements. At a minimum, be prepared to construct a statement of cash flows for the annual financial statements, which will presumably be issued outside of the company.

This section addresses the two formats used for the statement of cash flows, as well as how to assemble the information needed for the statement.

Overview of the Statement of Cash Flows

The statement of cash flows contains information about the flows of cash into and out of a company; in particular, it shows the extent of those company activities that generate and use cash. The primary activities are:

- *Operating activities*. These are an entity's primary revenue-producing activities. Examples of operating activities are cash receipts from the sale of goods, as well as from royalties and commissions, amounts received or paid to settle lawsuits, fines, payments to employees and suppliers, cash payments to lenders for interest, contributions to charity, and the settlement of asset retirement obligations.

- *Investing activities*. These involve the acquisition and disposal of long-term assets. Examples of investing activities are cash receipts from the sale of property, the sale of the debt or equity instruments of other entities, the repayment of loans made to other entities, and proceeds from insurance settlements related to damaged fixed assets. Examples of cash payments that are investment activities include the acquisition of fixed assets, as well as the purchase of the debt or equity of other entities.
- *Financing activities*. These are the activities resulting in alterations to the amount of contributed equity and the entity's borrowings. Examples of financing activities include cash receipts from the sale of the entity's own equity instruments or from issuing debt, proceeds from derivative instruments, and cash payments to buy back shares, pay dividends, and pay off outstanding debt.

The statement of cash flows also incorporates the concept of cash and cash equivalents. A cash equivalent is a short-term, very liquid investment that is easily convertible into a known amount of cash, and which is so near its maturity that it presents an insignificant risk of a change in value because of changes in interest rates.

You can use the *direct method* or the *indirect method* to present the statement of cash flows. These methods are described below.

The Direct Method

The direct method of presenting the statement of cash flows presents the specific cash flows associated with items that affect cash flow. Items that typically do so include:

- Cash collected from customers
- Interest and dividends received
- Cash paid to employees
- Cash paid to suppliers
- Interest paid
- Income taxes paid

The format of the direct method appears in the following example.

EXAMPLE

Milagro Corporation constructs the following statement of cash flows using the direct method:

Milagro Corporation
Statement of Cash Flows
For the year ended 12/31/20X1

Cash flows from operating activities		
Cash receipts from customers	$45,800,000	
Cash paid to suppliers	-29,800,000	
Cash paid to employees	-11,200,000	
Cash generated from operations	4,800,000	
Interest paid	-310,000	
Income taxes paid	-1,700,000	
Net cash from operating activities		$2,790,000
Cash flows from investing activities		
Purchase of fixed assets	-580,000	
Proceeds from sale of equipment	110,000	
Net cash used in investing activities		-470,000
Cash flows from financing activities		
Proceeds from issuance of common stock	1,000,000	
Proceeds from issuance of long-term debt	500,000	
Principal payments under lease obligation	-10,000	
Dividends paid	-450,000	
Net cash used in financing activities		1,040,000
Net increase in cash and cash equivalents		3,360,000
Cash and cash equivalents at beginning of period		1,640,000
Cash and cash equivalents at end of period		$5,000,000

Reconciliation of net income to net cash provided by operating activities:

Net income		$2,665,000
Adjustments to reconcile net income to net cash provided by operating activities:		
Depreciation and amortization	$125,000	
Provision for losses on accounts receivable	15,000	
Gain on sale of equipment	-155,000	
Increase in interest and income taxes payable	32,000	
Increase in deferred taxes	90,000	
Increase in other liabilities	18,000	
Total adjustments		125,000
Net cash provided by operating activities		$2,790,000

The standard-setting bodies encourage the use of the direct method, but it is rarely used, for the excellent reason that the information in it is difficult to assemble; companies simply do not collect and store information in the manner required for this format. Instead, they use the indirect method, which is described next.

The Indirect Method

Under the indirect method of presenting the statement of cash flows, the presentation begins with net income or loss, with subsequent additions to or deductions from that amount for non-cash revenue and expense items, resulting in net income provided by operating activities. The format of the indirect method appears in the following example.

EXAMPLE

Milagro Corporation constructs the following statement of cash flows using the indirect method:

Milagro Corporation
Statement of Cash Flows
For the year ended 12/31/20X1

Cash flows from operating activities		
Net income		$3,000,000
Adjustments for:		
Depreciation and amortization	$125,000	
Provision for losses on accounts receivable	20,000	
Gain on sale of facility	-65,000	
		80,000
Increase in trade receivables	-250,000	
Decrease in inventories	325,000	
Decrease in trade payables	-50,000	
		25,000
Cash generated from operations		3,105,000
Cash flows from investing activities		
Purchase of fixed assets	-500,000	
Proceeds from sale of equipment	35,000	
Net cash used in investing activities		-465,000
Cash flows from financing activities		
Proceeds from issuance of common stock	150,000	
Proceeds from issuance of long-term debt	175,000	
Dividends paid	-45,000	
Net cash used in financing activities		280,000
Net increase in cash and cash equivalents		2,920,000
Cash and cash equivalents at beginning of period		2,080,000
Cash and cash equivalents at end of period		$5,000,000

The indirect method is very popular, because the information required for it is relatively easily assembled from the accounts that a business normally maintains.

How to Prepare the Statement of Cash Flows

The most commonly used format for the statement of cash flows is the indirect method (as just described). The general layout of this statement of cash flows is shown below, along with an explanation of the source of the information in the statement.

Company Name
Statement of Cash Flows
For the year ended 12/31/20X1

Line Item	Derivation
Cash flows from operating activities	
Net income	From the net income line on the income statement
Adjustment for:	
Depreciation and amortization	From the corresponding line items in the income statement
Provision for losses on accounts receivable	From the change in the allowance for doubtful accounts in the period
Gain/loss on sale of facility	From the gain/loss accounts in the income statement
Increase/decrease in trade receivables	Change in trade receivables during the period, from the balance sheet
Increase/decrease in inventories	Change in inventories during the period, from the balance sheet
Increase/decrease in trade payables	Change in trade payables during the period, from the balance sheet
Cash generated from operations	Summary of the preceding items in this section
Cash flows from investing activities	
Purchase of fixed assets	Itemized in the fixed asset accounts during the period
Proceeds from sale of fixed assets	Itemized in the fixed asset accounts during the period
Net cash used in investing activities	Summary of the preceding items in this section
Cash flows from financing activities	
Proceeds from issuance of common stock	Net increase in the common stock and additional paid-in capital accounts during the period
Proceeds from issuance of long-term debt	Itemized in the long-term debt account during the period

Line Item	Derivation
Dividends paid	Itemized in the retained earnings account during the period
Net cash used in financing activities	Summary of the preceding items in this section
Net change in cash and cash equivalents	Summary of all preceding subtotals

A less commonly-used format for the statement of cash flows is the *direct method.* The general layout of this version is shown next, along with an explanation of the source of the information in the statement.

Company Name
Statement of Cash Flows
For the year ended 12/31/20X1

Line Item	Derivation
Cash flows from operating activities	
Cash receipts from customers	Summary of the cash receipts journal for the period
Cash paid to suppliers	Summary of the cash disbursements journal for the period (less the financing and income tax payments noted below)
Cash paid to employees	Summary of the payroll journal for the period
Cash generated from operations	Summary of the preceding items in this section
Interest paid	Itemized in the cash disbursements journal
Income taxes paid	Itemized in the cash disbursements journal
Net cash from operating activities	Summary of the preceding items in this section
Cash flows from investing activities	
Purchase of fixed assets	Itemized in the fixed asset accounts during the period
Proceeds from sale of fixed assets	Itemized in the fixed asset accounts during the period
Net cash used in investing activities	Summary of the preceding items in this section

Line Item	Derivation
Cash flows from financing activities	
Proceeds from issuance of common stock	Net increase in the common stock and additional paid-in capital accounts during the period
Proceeds from issuance of long-term debt	Itemized in the long-term debt account during the period
Dividends paid	Itemized in the retained earnings account during the period
Net cash used in financing activities	Summary of the preceding items in this section
Net change in cash and cash equivalents	Summary of all preceding subtotals

As you can see from the explanations for either the indirect or direct methods, the statement of cash flows is much more difficult to create than the income statement and balance sheet. In fact, a complete statement may require a substantial supporting spreadsheet that shows the details for each line item in the statement.

If the accounting software contains a template for the statement of cash flows, use it! The information may not be aggregated quite correctly, and it may not contain all of the line items required for the statement, but it *will* produce most of the information you need, and is much easier to modify than the alternative of creating the statement entirely by hand.

The Statement of Retained Earnings

The statement of retained earnings, also known as the statement of shareholders' equity, is essentially a reconciliation of the beginning and ending balances in a company's equity during an accounting period. It is not considered an essential part of the monthly financial statements, and so is the least likely of all the financial statements to be issued. However, it is a common part of the annual financial statements. This section discusses the format of the statement and how to create it.

Overview of the Statement of Retained Earnings

The statement of retained earnings reconciles changes in the retained earnings account during an accounting period. The statement starts with the beginning balance in the retained earnings account, and then adds or subtracts such items as profits and dividend payments to arrive at the ending retained earnings balance. The general calculation structure of the statement is:

Beginning retained earnings + Net income – Dividends +/- Other changes

= Ending retained earnings

The statement of retained earnings is most commonly presented as a separate statement, but can also be added to another financial statement. The following example shows a simplified format for the statement.

EXAMPLE

The controller of Milagro Corporation assembles the following statement of retained earnings to accompany his issuance of the financial statements of the company:

Milagro Corporation
Statement of Retained Earnings
For the year ended 12/31/20X1

Retained earnings at December 31, 20X0	$150,000
Net income for the year ended December 31, 20X1	40,000
Dividends paid to shareholders	-25,000
Retained earnings at December 31, 20X1	$165,000

It is also possible to provide a greatly expanded version of the statement of retained earnings that discloses the various elements of retained earnings. For example, it could separately identify the par value of common stock, additional paid-in capital, retained earnings, and treasury stock, with all of these elements then rolling up into the total just noted in the last example. The following example show what the format could look like.

EXAMPLE

The controller of Milagro Corporation creates an expanded version of the statement of retained earnings in order to provide more visibility into activities involving equity. The statement follows:

Milagro Corporation
Statement of Retained Earnings
For the year ended 12/31/20X1

	Common Stock, $1 par	Additional Paid-in Capital	Retained Earnings	Total Shareholders' Equity
Retained earnings at December 31, 20X0	$10,000	$40,000	$100,000	$150,000
Net income for the year ended December 31, 20X1			40,000	40,000
Dividends paid to shareholders			-25,000	-25,000
Retained earnings at December 31, 20X1	$10,000	$40,000	$115,000	$165,000

How to Prepare the Statement of Retained Earnings

A simplified version of the statement of retained earnings was shown in the first of the examples in this section. This format works well if there are few equity transactions during the year. However, a more active environment calls for a considerable amount of detail in the statement. In the latter case, consider following these steps:

1. Create separate accounts in the general ledger for each type of equity. Thus, there should be different accounts for the par value of stock, additional paid-in capital, and retained earnings. Each of these accounts is represented by a separate column in the statement.
2. Transfer every transaction within each equity account to a spreadsheet, and identify it in the spreadsheet.
3. Aggregate the transactions within the spreadsheet into similar types, and transfer them to separate line items in the statement of retained earnings.
4. Complete the statement, and verify that the beginning and ending balances in it match the general ledger, and that the aggregated line items within it add up to the ending balances for all columns.

If you do not use the spreadsheet recommended in the preceding steps, you may find it difficult to compile the aggregated line items in the statement, resulting in incorrect subtotals and totals within the statement.

Summary

This chapter has discussed each of the financial statements, and revealed a number of possible layouts for them. When in doubt, issue the minimal number of financial statements, and use the standard template versions of these statements that are provided with the company's accounting software. There are several reasons for doing so:

- *No value*. The statement of retained earnings is rarely read by internal recipients, with the statement of cash flows taking a close second. If no one reads these statements, why issue them? They only take additional time to prepare and review, so a simplified set of financial statements might be an economical alternative.
- *Errors*. It is entirely possible that if you create customized versions of the financial statements, they will contain errors. Consequently, if the template versions look acceptable, use them instead.

The financial statements are generally considered to be the primary work product of the controller, so you want to issue a quality set of financial statements. Consult the author's *Closing the Books* book for more information on this important topic. It is available at the accountingtools.com website.

Chapter 13
Public Company Financial Reporting

Introduction

If a company is publicly-held, there are several more reporting requirements than the standard set of financial statements. In addition, there are issues related to quarterly interim reports, segment reporting that is added to the financial statement disclosures, and earnings per share to calculate and report. This information is then included in the quarterly Form 10-Q and annual Form 10-K. Additional information may be included in the occasional Form 8-K. All of these financial reporting topics are addressed in the following sections.

Controller Responsibilities

In a publicly-held company, the Forms 10-Q and 10-K are given a *very* high priority, so the following responsibilities are considered among the most important of all job responsibilities for the controller:

- Prepare the additional reports required for public company filings.
- Comply with the additional approval steps required for public-company filings.
- File the Forms 10-Q and 10-K by the designated due dates.

Interim Reporting

If a company is publicly-held, the Securities and Exchange Commission requires that it file a variety of quarterly information on the Form 10-Q. This information is a reduced set of the requirements for the more comprehensive annual Form 10-K. The requirement to issue these additional financial statements may appear to be simple enough, but you must consider whether to report information assuming that quarterly results are stand-alone documents, or part of the full-year results of the business. This section discusses the disparities that these different viewpoints can cause in the financial statements, as well as interim reporting issues related to inventory.

The Integral View

Under the integral view of producing interim reports, you assume that the results reported in interim financial statements are an integral part of the full-year financial results (hence the name of this concept). This viewpoint produces the following accounting issues:

- *Accrue expenses not arising in the period.* If you know that an expense will be paid later in the year that is incurred at least partially in the reporting period, accrue some portion of the expense in the reporting period. Here are several examples:
    - *Advertising.* If you pay in advance for advertising that is scheduled to occur over multiple time periods, recognize the expense over the entire range of time periods.
    - *Bonuses.* If there are bonus plans that may result in bonus payments later in the year, accrue the expense in all accounting periods. Only accrue this expense if you can reasonably estimate the amount of the bonus, which may not always be possible during the earlier months covered by a performance contract.
    - *Contingencies.* If there are contingent liabilities that will be resolved later in the year, and which are both probable and reasonably estimated, accrue the related expense.
    - *Profit sharing.* If employees are paid a percentage of company profits at year-end, and the amount can be reasonably estimated, accrue the expense throughout the year as a proportion of the profits recognized in each period.
    - *Property taxes.* A local government entity issues an invoice to the company at some point during the year for property taxes. These taxes are intended to cover the entire year, so accrue a portion of the expense in each reporting period.
- *Tax rate.* A company is usually subject to a graduated income tax rate that incrementally escalates through the year as the business generates more profit. Under the integral view, use the expected tax rate for the entire year in every reporting period, rather than the incremental tax rate that applies only to the profits earned for the year to date.

EXAMPLE

The board of directors of Milagro Corporation approves a senior management bonus plan for the upcoming year that could potentially pay the senior management team a maximum of $240,000. It initially seems probable that the full amount will be paid, but by the third quarter it appears more likely that the maximum amount to be paid will be $180,000. In addition, the company pays $60,000 in advance for a full year of advertising in *Coffee Times* magazine. Milagro recognizes these expenses as follows:

	Quarter 1	Quarter 2	Quarter 3	Quarter 4	Full Year
Bonus expense	$60,000	$60,000	$30,000	$30,000	$180,000
Advertising	15,000	15,000	15,000	15,000	60,000

The accounting staff spreads the recognition of the full amount of the projected bonus over the year, but then reduces its recognition of the remaining expense starting in the third quarter, to adjust for the lowered bonus payout expectation.

The accounting staff initially records the $60,000 advertising expense as a prepaid expense, and recognizes it ratably over all four quarters of the year, which matches the time period over which the related advertisements are run by *Coffee Times*.

One problem with the integral view is that it tends to result in a significant number of expense accruals. Since these accruals are usually based on estimates, it is entirely possible that adjustments should be made to the accruals later in the year, as the company obtains more precise information about the expenses that are being accrued. Some of these adjustments could be substantial, and may materially affect the reported results in later periods.

The Discrete View

Under the discrete view of producing interim reports, you assume that the results reported for a specific interim period are *not* associated with the revenues and expenses arising during other reporting periods. Under this view, you would record the entire impact of a transaction within the reporting period, rather than ratably over the entire year. The following are examples of the situations that can arise under the discrete method:

- *Reduced accruals.* A substantially smaller number of accruals are likely under the discrete method, since the assumption is that you should not anticipate the recordation of transactions that have not yet arisen.
- *Gains and losses.* Do not spread the recognition of a gain or loss across multiple periods. If you were to do so, it would allow a company to spread a loss over multiple periods, thereby making the loss look smaller on a per-period basis than it really is.

Comparison of the Integral and Discrete Views

The integral view is clearly the better method from a theoretical perspective, since the causes of some transactions can span an entire year. For example, a manager may be awarded a bonus at the end of December, but he probably had to achieve specific results throughout the year to earn it. Otherwise, if you were to adopt the discrete view, interim reporting would yield exceedingly varied results, with some periods revealing inordinately high or low profitability.

However, it is useful to adopt the integral view from the perspective of accounting *efficiency*; that is, it is very time-consuming to maintain a mass of revenue and expense accruals, their ongoing adjustments, and documentation of the reasons for them throughout a year. Instead, use the integral view only for the more material transactions that are anticipated, and use the discrete view for smaller transactions. Thus, you could accrue the expense for property taxes throughout the year if the amount were significant, or simply record it in the month when the invoice is received, if the amount is small.

Interim Reporting Issues

When you are reporting interim results, there are several issues involving the recordation of inventory that vary from the normal handling of inventory for the year-end financial statements.

One issue is the method you are allowed to use for calculating the cost of goods sold. Normally, you would be required to use a periodic or perpetual inventory tracking system to derive the on-hand quantities of inventory. However, this can be too burdensome for interim reporting, so you are allowed to estimate it instead. A good method for doing so is the gross profit method, under which you estimate the cost of goods sold based on the expected gross profit.

Another issue concerns the use of the last in, first out (LIFO) method for calculating the cost of inventory (as described in the Inventory Management chapter). A key issue when using LIFO is that you cannot recover an inventory layer that was liquidated as of year-end. However, you *can* recover such a layer if it is liquidated during an interim period and you expect to replace the layer by year-end. If that is the case, add the expected inventory replacement cost to the cost of sales for the interim period.

Yet another issue is the recognition of any losses that may have been caused by the lower of cost or market (LCM) rule (see the Closing the Books chapter). If you recognized LCM losses during an interim period, you are allowed to offset the full amount of these losses with any gains in subsequent periods within the same year on the same inventory items. Further, you can simply avoid recognizing these losses in an interim period if there are seasonal price fluctuations that you expect to result in an offsetting increase in market prices by the end of the year.

Segment Reporting

A publicly-held company must report segment information, which is part of the disclosures attached to the financial statements. This information is supposedly needed to give the readers of the financial statements more insights into the operations and prospects of a business. In this section, we describe how to determine which business segments to report separately, and how to report that information.

Primary Segment Reporting Issues

A segment is a distinct component of a business that produces revenue, and for which the business produces separate financial information that is regularly reviewed internally by a chief operating decision maker. A chief operating decision maker is a person who is responsible for making decisions about resource allocations to the segments of a business, and for evaluating those segments. The primary issue with segment reporting is determining which business segments to report. The rules for this selection process are quite specific.

Only report segment information if a business segment passes any one of the following three tests:

1. *Revenue.* The revenue of the segment is at least 10% of the consolidated revenue of the entire business; or
2. *Profit or loss.* The absolute amount of the profit or loss of the segment is at least 10% of the greater of the combined profits of all the operating segments reporting a profit, or of the combined losses of all operating segments reporting a loss (see the following example for a demonstration of this concept); or
3. *Assets.* The assets of the segment are at least 10% of the combined assets of all the operating segments of the business.

Some parts of a business are not considered to be reportable business segments under the following circumstances:

- *Corporate overhead.* The corporate group does not usually earn outside revenues, and so is not considered a segment.
- *Post-retirement benefit plans.* A benefit plan can earn income from investments, but it has no operating activities, and so is not considered a segment.
- *One-time events.* If an otherwise-insignificant segment has a one-time event that boosts it into the ranks of reportable segments, do not report it, since there is no long-term expectation for it to remain a reportable segment.

If you run the preceding tests and arrive at a group of reportable segments whose combined revenues are not at least 75% of the consolidated revenue of the entire business, add more segments until the 75% threshold is surpassed.

If you have a business segment that used to qualify as a reportable segment and does not currently qualify, but which you expect to qualify in the future, continue to treat it as a reportable segment.

If you have several smaller segments that would normally be considered too small to be reported separately, combine them for reporting purposes if they have similar regulatory environments, types of customers, production processes, products, distribution methods, *and* economic characteristics. The number of restrictions on this type of reporting makes it unlikely that you would be able to aggregate smaller segments.

Tip: The variety of methods available for segment testing makes it possible that you will have quite a large number of reportable segments. If so, it can be burdensome to create a report for so many segments, and it may be confusing for the readers of the company's financial statements. Consequently, consider limiting the number of reportable segments to ten; you can aggregate the information for additional segments for reporting purposes.

EXAMPLE

Milagro Corporation has six business segments whose results it reports internally. Milagro's controller needs to test the various segments to see which ones qualify as being reportable. He collects the following information:

Segment	(000s) Revenue	(000s) Profit	(000s) Loss	(000s) Assets
Commercial roasters	$120,000	$10,000	$--	$320,000
Home roasters	85,000	8,000	--	180,000
Coffee brokerage	29,000	--	-21,000	90,000
Coffee sales	200,000	32,000		500,000
Coffee storage	15,000	--	-4,000	4,000
International	62,000	--	-11,000	55,000
	$511,000	$50,000	-$36,000	$1,149,000

In the table, the total profit exceeds the total loss, so the controller uses the total profit for the 10% profit test. The controller then lists the same table again, but now with the losses column removed and with test thresholds at the top of the table that are used to determine which segments are reported. An "X" mark below a test threshold indicates that a segment is reportable. In addition, the controller adds a new column on the right side of the table, which is used to calculate the total revenue for the reportable segments.

Segment	(000s) Revenue	(000s) Profit	(000s) Assets	75% Revenue Test
Reportable threshold (10%)	**$51,100**	**$5,000**	**$114,900**	
Commercial roasters	X	X	X	$120,000
Home roasters	X	X	X	85,000
Coffee brokerage				
Coffee sales	X	X	X	200,000
Coffee storage				
International	X			62,000
			Total	$467,000

This analysis shows that the commercial roasters, home roasters, coffee sales, and international segments are reportable, and that the combined revenue of these reportable segments easily exceeds the 75% reporting threshold. Consequently, the company does not need to separately report information for any additional segments.

The Segment Report

The key requirement of segment reporting is that the revenue, profit or loss, and assets of each segment be separately reported. In addition, reconcile this segment information back to the company's consolidated results, which requires the inclusion of any adjusting items. Also disclose the methods by which you determined which segments to report. The essential information to include in a segment report includes:

- The types of products and services sold by each segment
- The basis of organization (such as by geographic region or product line)
- Revenues
- Interest expense
- Depreciation and amortization
- Material expense items
- Equity method interests in other entities
- Income tax expense or income
- Other material non-cash items
- Profit or loss

EXAMPLE

The controller of Milagro Corporation produces the following segment report for the segments identified in the preceding example:

(000s)	Commercial Roasters	Home Roasters	Coffee Sales	International	Other	Consolidated
Revenues	$120,000	$85,000	$200,000	$62,000	$44,000	$511,000
Interest income	11,000	8,000	28,000	8,000	2,000	57,000
Interest expense	--	--	--	11,000	39,000	50,000
Depreciation	32,000	18,000	50,000	6,000	10,000	116,000
Income taxes	4,000	3,000	10,000	-3,000	-7,000	7,000
Profit	10,000	8,000	32,000	-11,000	-25,000	14,000
Assets	320,000	180,000	500,000	55,000	94,000	1,149,000

Earnings per Share

Earnings per share is a company's net income divided by the weighted-average number of shares outstanding. If your company is publicly-held, you are required to report two types of earnings per share information within the financial statements. These can be complex calculations, and so may slow down your closing of the books. In this section, we describe how to calculate both basic and diluted earnings per share, as well as how to present this information within the financial statements.

Basic Earnings per Share

Basic earnings per share is the amount of a company's profit or loss for a reporting period that is available to the shares of its common stock that are outstanding during a reporting period. If a business only has common stock in its capital structure, it presents only its basic earnings per share for income from continuing operations and net income. This information is reported on its income statement.

The formula for basic earnings per share is:

$$\frac{\text{Profit or loss attributable to common equity holders of the parent business}}{\text{Weighted average number of common shares outstanding during the period}}$$

In addition, subdivide this calculation into:

- The profit or loss from continuing operations attributable to the parent company
- The total profit or loss attributable to the parent company

When calculating basic earnings per share, incorporate in the numerator an adjustment for dividends. Deduct from the profit or loss the after-tax amount of any dividends declared on non-cumulative preferred stock, as well as the after-tax amount of any preferred stock dividends, even if the dividends are not declared; this does not include any dividends paid or declared during the current period that relate to previous periods.

Also, incorporate the following adjustments into the denominator of the basic earnings per share calculation:

- *Contingent stock.* If there is contingently issuable stock, treat it as though it were outstanding as of the date when there are no circumstances under which the shares would *not* be issued.
- *Issuance date.* Include shares under any of the following circumstances:
    - A liability is settled in exchange for shares
    - An acquisition paid for with shares is recognized
    - Any shares related to a mandatorily convertible instrument as of the contract date
    - Cash is receivable for sold shares
    - Dividends are reinvested
    - Interest stops accruing on convertible debt instruments on which shares can be issued
    - Services are paid for with shares
- *Weighted-average shares.* Use the weighted-average number of shares during the period in the denominator. You do this by adjusting the number of shares outstanding at the beginning of the reporting period for common shares repurchased or issued in the period. This adjustment is based on the proportion of the days in the reporting period that the shares are outstanding.

EXAMPLE

Milagro Corporation earns a profit of $1,000,000 net of taxes in Year 1. In addition, Milagro owes $200,000 in dividends to the holders of its cumulative preferred stock. Milagro calculates the numerator of its basic earnings per share as follows:

$1,000,000 Profit - $200,000 Dividends = $800,000

Milagro had 4,000,000 common shares outstanding at the beginning of Year 1. In addition, it sold 200,000 shares on April 1 and 400,000 shares on October 1. It also issued 500,000 shares on July 1 to the owners of a newly-acquired subsidiary. Finally, it bought back 60,000 shares on December 1. Milagro calculates the weighted-average number of common shares outstanding as follows:

Date	Shares	Weighting (Months)	Weighted Average
January 1	4,000,000	12/12	4,000,000
April 1	200,000	9/12	150,000
July 1	500,000	6/12	250,000
October 1	400,000	3/12	100,000
December 1	-60,000	1/12	-5,000
			4,495,000

Milagro's basic earnings per share is:

$800,000 adjusted profits ÷ 4,495,000 weighted-average shares = $0.18 per share

---

Diluted Earnings per Share

Diluted earnings per share is the profit for a reporting period per share of common stock outstanding during that period; it includes the number of shares that would have been outstanding during the period if the company had issued common shares for all potential dilutive common stock outstanding during the period.

If a company has more types of stock than common stock in its capital structure, it must present both basic earnings per share and diluted earnings per share information; this presentation must be for both income from continuing operations and net income. This information is reported on the company's income statement.

To calculate diluted earnings per share, include the effects of all dilutive potential common shares. This means that you increase the number of shares outstanding by the weighted average number of additional common shares that would have been outstanding if the company had converted all dilutive potential common stock to common stock. This dilution may affect the profit or loss in the numerator of the dilutive earnings per share calculation. The formula is:

$$\frac{\text{(Profit or loss attributable to common equity holders of parent company + After-tax interest on convertible debt + Convertible preferred dividends)}}{\text{(Weighted average number of common shares outstanding during the period + All dilutive potential common stock)}}$$

You may need to make two adjustments to the numerator of this calculation. They are:

- *Interest expense.* Eliminate any interest expense associated with dilutive potential common stock, since you assume that these shares are converted to common stock. The conversion would eliminate the company's liability for the interest expense.
- *Dividends.* Adjust for the after-tax impact of dividends or other types of dilutive potential common shares.

You may need to make several adjustments to the denominator of this calculation. They are:

- *Contingent shares dependency.* If there is a contingent share issuance that is dependent upon the future market price of the company's common stock, include the shares in the diluted earnings per share calculation, based on the market price at the end of the reporting period; however, only include the issuance if the effect is dilutive. If the shares have a contingency feature, do not include them in the calculation until the contingency has been met.
- *Contingent shares in general.* Treat common stock that is contingently issuable as though it was outstanding as of the beginning of the reporting period, but only if the conditions have been met that would require the company to issue the shares.
- *Anti-dilutive shares.* If there are any contingent stock issuances that would have an anti-dilutive impact on earnings per share, do not include them in the calculation. This situation arises when a business experiences a loss, because including the dilutive shares in the calculation would reduce the loss per share.

In addition to these three adjustments to the denominator, apply all of the adjustments to the denominator already noted for basic earnings per share.

Tip: The rules related to diluted earnings per share appear complex, but they are founded upon one principle – that you are trying to establish the absolute worst-case scenario to arrive at the smallest possible amount of earnings per share. If you are faced with an unusual situation involving the calculation of diluted earnings per share and are not sure what to do, that rule will likely apply.

If there is a share issuance that is contingent upon certain conditions being satisfied, and those conditions were met by the end of the reporting period, include them in the calculation as of the beginning of the period. However, if the conditions were not met by the end of the period, then include in the calculation, as of the beginning of the period, any shares that would be issuable if:

- The end of the reporting period were the end of the contingency period; and
- The result would be dilutive.

If the number of contingent shares issued is based on a certain amount of earnings, and the company achieved those earnings during the reporting period, include the contingent shares in the calculation; but only if the effect is dilutive.

In addition to the issues just noted, here are a number of additional situations that could impact the calculation of diluted earnings per share:

- *Most advantageous exercise price.* When you calculate the number of potential shares that could be issued, do so using the most advantageous conversion rate from the perspective of the person or entity holding the security to be converted.
- *Settlement assumption.* If there is an open contract that could be settled in common stock or cash, assume that it will be settled in common stock, but only if the effect is dilutive.
- *Effects of convertible instruments.* If there are convertible instruments outstanding, include their dilutive effect if they dilute earnings per share. Consider convertible preferred stock to be anti-dilutive when the dividend on any converted shares is greater than basic earnings per share. Similarly, convertible debt is considered anti-dilutive when the interest expense on any converted shares exceeds basic earnings per share. The following example illustrates the concept.

EXAMPLE

Milagro Corporation earns a net profit of $2 million, and it has 5 million common shares outstanding. In addition, there is a $1 million convertible loan that has an eight percent interest rate. The loan may potentially convert into 500,000 of Milagro's common shares. Milagro's incremental tax rate is 35 percent.

Milagro's basic earnings per share is $2,000,000 ÷ 5,000,000 shares, or $0.40/share. The following calculation shows the compilation of Milagro's diluted earnings per share:

Net profit	$2,000,000
+ Interest saved on $1,000,000 loan at 8%	80,000
- Reduced tax savings on foregone interest expense	-28,000
= Adjusted net earnings	$2,052,000
Common shares outstanding	5,000,000
+ Potential converted shares	500,000
= Adjusted shares outstanding	5,500,000
Diluted earnings per share ($2,052,000 ÷ 5,500,000)	**$0.37/share**

- *Option exercise.* If there are any dilutive options and warrants, assume that they are exercised at their exercise price. Then, convert the proceeds into the total number of shares that the holders would have purchased, using the average market price during the reporting period. Then use in the diluted earnings per share calculation the difference between the number of shares assumed to have been issued and the number of shares assumed to have been purchased. The following example illustrates the concept.

EXAMPLE

Milagro Corporation earns a net profit of $200,000, and it has 5,000,000 common shares outstanding that sell on the open market for an average of $12 per share. In addition, there are 300,000 options outstanding that can be converted to Milagro's common stock at $10 each.

Milagro's basic earnings per share is $200,000 ÷ 5,000,000 common shares, or $0.04 per share.

Milagro's controller wants to calculate the amount of diluted earnings per share. To do so, he follows these steps:

1. *Calculate the number of shares that would have been issued at the market price.* Thus, he multiplies the 300,000 options by the average exercise price of $10 to arrive at a total of $3,000,000 paid to exercise the options by their holders.
2. *Divide the amount paid to exercise the options by the market price to determine the number of shares that could be purchased.* Thus, he divides the $3,000,000 paid to exercise the options by the $12 average market price to arrive at 250,000 shares that could have been purchased with the proceeds from the options.
3. *Subtract the number of shares that could have been purchased from the number of options exercised.* Thus, he subtracts the 250,000 shares potentially purchased from the 300,000 options to arrive at a difference of 50,000 shares.

4. *Add the incremental number of shares to the shares already outstanding*. Thus, he adds the 50,000 incremental shares to the existing 5,000,000 to arrive at 5,050,000 diluted shares.

Based on this information, the controller arrives at diluted earnings per share of $0.0396, for which the calculation is:

$200,000 net profit ÷ 5,050,000 common shares

- *Put options*. If there are purchased put options, only include them in the diluted earnings per share calculation if the exercise price is higher than the average market price during the reporting period.
- *Call options*. If there are purchased call options, only include them in the diluted earnings per share calculation if the exercise price is lower than the market price.

> **Tip:** There is only a dilutive effect on the diluted earnings per share calculation when the average market price is greater than the exercise prices of any options or warrants.

- *Compensation in shares*. If company employees are awarded shares that have not vested or stock options as forms of compensation, treat these grants as options when calculating diluted earnings per share. Consider these grants to be outstanding on the grant date, rather than any later vesting date.
- *Repurchase agreements*. If there is a contract that requires a business to reacquire its own shares, *and* the repurchase price is higher than the average market price during the past period, *and* there is a dilutive effect, include them in the calculation of diluted earnings per share. To do so, assume that a sufficient number of shares were issued at the beginning of the reporting period to raise the funds needed to repurchase the shares. Then include the difference between the number of shares issued to raise funds and the number of shares retired in the calculation of diluted earnings per share.
- *Dilutive shares*. If there is potential dilutive common stock, add all of it to the denominator of the diluted earnings per share calculation. Unless there is more specific information available, assume that these shares are issued at the beginning of the reporting period.

Always calculate the number of potential dilutive common shares independently for each reporting period presented in the financial statements.

Presentation of Earnings per Share

You normally list the basic and diluted earnings per share information at the bottom of the income statement, and should do so for every period included in the income statement. Also, if you report diluted earnings per share in *any* of the periods included in the company's income statement, you must report it for *all* of the periods included in the statement. The following sample illustrates the concept.

Sample Presentation of Earnings per Share

Earnings per Share	20x3	20x2	20x1
From continuing operations			
Basic earnings per share	$1.05	$0.95	$0.85
Diluted earnings per share	1.00	0.90	0.80
From discontinued operations			
Basic earnings per share	$0.20	$0.17	$0.14
Diluted earnings per share	0.15	0.08	0.07
From total operations			
Basic earnings per share	$1.25	$1.12	$0.99
Diluted earnings per share	1.15	0.98	0.87

The Public Company Closing Process

A publicly-held company is required by the Securities and Exchange Commission (SEC) to file a large report concerning its financial condition at the end of each quarter. These are the Form 10-Q (for quarterly filings) and Form 10-K (for annual filings). The contents of both reports are discussed in the following sections.

The additional steps needed to close the books for a publicly-held company include all of the following:

1. *Auditor investigation.* The company's outside auditors must conduct a review of the company's financial statements and disclosures for its quarterly results, and a full audit of its annual results. This is the most time-consuming of the public company requirements. The company can reduce the amount of time required for a review or audit by providing full staff support to the audit team, as well as by having all requested information available as of the beginning of the audit or review work.
2. *Legal review.* It would be extremely unwise to issue the financial statement package without first having legal counsel review the statements and (especially) the disclosures to ensure that all required disclosures have been made, and to verify that all statements made are correct and fully supportable. This review is usually completed near or after the end of the work done by the auditors, but can be scheduled slightly sooner if you believe the disclosures to be substantially complete at that time.
3. *Officer certification.* Depending upon what type of Form is being issued, different company officers are required to certify that the information in the financial statements presents fairly the financial condition and results of

operations of the business. Since there are substantial penalties and jail time involved if an officer were to make a false certification, it should be no surprise that the signing officers will want to spend time reviewing the complete set of financial statements and disclosures. This review can be done before the auditors have completed their work, so officer certification does not usually increase the duration of the closing process.

4. *Audit committee and board approvals.* The audit committee must approve every Form 10-Q, and the board of directors must approve every Form 10-K. Given the number of people involved, schedule review and approval meetings well in advance, to be conducted a few days prior to the required filing date of the applicable Form. Scheduling the review slightly early gives you time to make adjustments, in case anyone expresses concerns during the review, and wants changes to be made prior to filing.

   Issue the complete set of financial statements and disclosures to the audit committee or board member at least one full day in advance of a review and approval meeting, so that they have sufficient time to examine the material.
5. *EDGARize and file.* Once the Form 10-Q or Form 10-K is complete and fully approved, you must file it with the SEC. The filing is done using the Electronic Data Gathering, Analysis, and Retrieval (EDGAR) system that is operated by the SEC. This information can be submitted in various formats, but you will almost certainly have to convert it from the format in which the documents were originally prepared. This means hiring someone to convert the reports to the applicable format, which is a process known as *EDGARizing*. Not only is the conversion specialist responsible for converting the financial statements, but this person also files the statements with the SEC on behalf of the company. The conversion process usually takes one or two days, but factor in additional time for the auditors to review the converted format – the auditors must give their approval before you can file with the SEC.

The closing process described here is very slow, so be sure to have the financial statements prepared as soon as possible after the end of the applicable reporting period. Doing so should leave enough time to prepare the statements for filing by the designated due date.

The Form 10-Q

A publicly-held company is required to issue the Form 10-Q to report the results of its first, second, and third fiscal quarters. The Form 10-Q includes not just the financial statements, but also a number of disclosures. The following table itemizes the more common disclosures.

Selection of Form 10-Q Disclosures

Item Header	Description
Item 1A. Risk factors	This is a thorough listing of all risks that the company may experience. It warns investors of what could reduce the value of their investments in the company.
Item 3. Legal proceedings	Describe any legal proceedings currently involving the company, and its estimate of the likely outcome of those proceedings.
Item 4. Submission of matters to a vote of security holders	Describe matters submitted to the shareholders for a vote during the most recent quarter of the fiscal year.
Item 7. Management's discussion and analysis (MD&A)	Describe opportunities, challenges, risks, trends, future plans, and key performance indicators, as well as changes in revenues, the cost of goods sold, other expenses, assets, and liabilities.
Item 7A. Quantitative and qualitative disclosures about market risk	Quantify the market risk at the end of the last fiscal year for the company's market risk-sensitive instruments.
Item 8. Financial statements and supplementary data	Make all disclosures required by GAAP, including descriptions of: • Accrued liabilities • Acquisitions • Discontinued operations • Fixed assets • Income taxes • Related party transactions • Segment information • Stock options
Item 9A. Controls and procedures	Generally describe the system of internal controls, testing of controls, changes in controls, and management's conclusions regarding the effectiveness of those controls.
Item 15. Exhibits and financial statement schedules	Item 601 of Regulation S-K requires that a business attach a number of exhibits to the Form 10-K, including (but not limited to): • Code of ethics • Material contracts • Articles of incorporation • Bylaws • Acquisition purchase agreements

Before filing, the Form 10-Q must be signed by an authorized officer, as well as the principal financial or chief accounting officer.

You must file the Form 10-Q within 40 days of the end of the fiscal quarter if the company is either a large accelerated filer or an accelerated filer. If that is not the case, file the Form within 45 days of the end of the fiscal quarter. A large accelerated filer is a company having an aggregate market value owned by investors who are not affiliated with the company of a minimum of $700 million. This measurement is as of the last business day of the most recent second fiscal quarter. An accelerated filer is a company having an aggregate market value owned by investors who are not affiliated with the company of less than $700 million, but more than $75 million. This measurement is as of the last business day of the most recent second fiscal quarter.

The Form 10-K

A publicly-held company is required to issue the Form 10-K to report the results of its fiscal year. The Form 10-K includes not just the financial statements, but also a number of additional disclosures. The following table itemizes the more common disclosures.

Selection of Form 10-K Disclosures

Item Header	Description
Item 1. Business	Provide a description of the company's purpose, history, operating segments, customers, suppliers, sales and marketing operations, customer support, intellectual property, competition, and employees. It should tell readers what the company does and describe its business environment.
Item 1A. Risk factors	This is a thorough listing of all risks that the company may experience. It warns investors of what could reduce the value of their investments in the company.
Item 1B. Unresolved staff comments	Disclose all unresolved comments received from the SEC if they are material. (only applies to written comments from the SEC received at least 180 days before the fiscal year-end by an accelerated or large accelerated filer)
Item 2. Properties	Describe the leased or owned facilities of the business, including square footage, lease termination dates, and lease amounts paid per month.
Item 3. Legal proceedings	Describe any legal proceedings currently involving the company, and its estimate of the likely outcome of those proceedings.
Item 4. Submission of matters to a vote of security holders	Describe matters submitted to the shareholders for a vote during the fourth quarter of the fiscal year.
Item 5. Market for company stock	Describe where the company's stock trades and the number of holders of record, as well as the high and low closing prices per share, by quarter.

Item Header	Description
Item 6. Selected financial data	For the last five years, state selected information from the company's income statement and balance sheet (should be in tabular comparative format).
Item 7. Management's discussion and analysis (MD&A)	Describe opportunities, challenges, risks, trends, future plans, and key performance indicators, as well as changes in revenues, the cost of goods sold, other expenses, assets, and liabilities.
Item 7A. Quantitative and qualitative disclosures about market risk	Quantify the market risk at the end of the last fiscal year for the company's market risk-sensitive instruments.
Item 8. Financial statements and supplementary data	Make all disclosures required by GAAP, including descriptions of: • Accrued liabilities • Acquisitions • Discontinued operations • Fixed assets • Income taxes • Related party transactions • Segment information • Stock options
Item 9. Changes in and disagreements with accountants on accounting and financial disclosure	Describe any disagreements with the auditors when management elects to account for or disclose transactions in a manner different from what the auditors want.
Item 9A. Controls and procedures	Generally describe the system of internal controls, testing of controls, changes in controls, and management's conclusions regarding the effectiveness of those controls.
Item 10. Directors, executive officers and corporate governance	Identify the executive officers, directors, promoters, and individuals classified as control persons.
Item 11. Executive compensation	Itemize the types of compensation paid to company executives.
Item 12. Security ownership of certain beneficial owners and management and related stockholder matters	State the number of shares of all types owned or controlled by certain individuals classified as beneficial owners and/or members of management.

Item Header	Description
Item 13. Certain relationships and related transactions, and director independence	If there were transactions with related parties during the past fiscal year, and the amounts involved exceeded $120,000, describe the transactions.
Item 14. Principal accountant fees and services	State the aggregate amount of any fees billed in each of the last two fiscal years for professional services rendered by the company's auditors for: • Reviews and audits; • Audit-related activities; • Taxation work; and • All other fees.
Item 15. Exhibits and financial statement schedules	Item 601 of Regulation S-K requires that a business attach a number of exhibits to the Form 10-K, including (but not limited to): • Code of ethics • Material contracts • Articles of incorporation • Bylaws • Acquisition purchase agreements

Before filing, the Form 10-K must be signed by *all* of the following:

- Principal executive officer
- Principal financial officer
- Controller
- A majority of the board of directors

You must file the Form 10-K within 60 days of the end of the fiscal year if the company is a large accelerated filer or an accelerated filer, or within 75 days of the end of the fiscal year if the company is an accelerated filer. If the company does not have either designation, file it within 90 days of the end of the fiscal year.

The Form 8-K

The Form 8-K is by far the most commonly-issued SEC filing. A public company uses it to disclose a broad range of material events that impact the business. The following table itemizes the types of disclosures that can appear in a Form 8-K.

Types of Form 8-K Disclosures

Item Header	Description
Item 1.101. Entry into a material definitive agreement	Refers to an agreement not made in the ordinary course of business. Disclose the agreement date, the names of the parties, and the general terms of the agreement.
Item 1.102. Termination of a material definitive agreement	Refers to the non-standard termination of an agreement not made in the ordinary course of business. Disclose the termination date, the general terms of the agreement, the circumstances of the termination, and any termination penalties.
Item 1.103. Bankruptcy or receivership	If the business enters bankruptcy or receivership, identify the proceeding, the name of the court, the date when jurisdiction was assumed, and the identity of the receiver. There are additional disclosures regarding reorganization plans.
Item 2.01. Completion of acquisition or disposition of assets	Disclose the date of asset acquisition or disposition, describe the assets, and identify the counterparty. Also note the nature and amount of consideration involved. Further, note the source of funds for an acquisition, if there is a material relationship between the company and the source of funds.
Item 2.02. Results of operations and financial condition	Disclose material non-public information regarding the company's results of operations or financial condition if it was publicly announced or released by someone acting on behalf of the company.
Item 2.03. Creation of a direct financial obligation	If the company enters into a material, direct financial obligation, disclose the date when the obligation began, describe the transaction, note the amount and terms of the obligation, and other material issues. If the company becomes directly or contingently liable for a material amount under an off-balance sheet arrangement, disclose the same information, as well as the material terms whereby it may become a direct obligation, the nature of any recourse provisions, and the undiscounted maximum amount of any future payments.
Item 2.04. Triggering events that accelerate or increase a direct financial obligation	If there was a triggering event that altered a direct financial obligation and the effect is material, disclose the date of the event, describe it, note the amount of the obligation, and the payment terms.
Item 2.05. Costs associated with exit or disposal activities	If the company commits to an exit or disposal plan, disclose the date of the commitment, describe the course of action, and estimate the range of costs for each major type of cost and in total.
Item 2.06. Material impairments	If the company concludes that there is a material impairment charge, disclose the date of this conclusion, describe the impaired assets, and the facts and circumstances leading to the conclusion. Also note the estimated amount of the impairment charge.

Item Header	Description
Item 3.01. Notice of delisting or failure to satisfy a continued listing rule	If the company has received notice that it does not satisfy a rule for continued listing on an exchange, disclose the date when any notice was received, the applicable rule not being satisfied, and actions the company will take in response to the notice. If the company has submitted an application to delist from an exchange, disclose the action taken and the date of the action.
Item 3.02. Unregistered sales of equity securities	If the company sells unregistered securities, state the date of sale and the title and amount of the securities sold. Also name the principal underwriters and the names of the persons to whom the securities were sold. Also note the aggregate offering price and the amount of any discounts or commissions paid. Also describe any terms under which the securities are convertible into company stock.
Item 3.03. Material modifications to rights of security holders	If there has been a material modification to the rights of security holders, disclose the modification date, the name of the affected class of securities, and the effect on the rights of the security holders.
Item 4.01. Changes in registrant's certifying accountant	Disclose whether the company's existing independent accountant has resigned or been dismissed. Also disclose whether a new independent accountant has been engaged.
Item 4.02. Non-reliance on previously issued financial statements or a related audit report or completed interim review	If the company concludes that previously issued financial statements contain errors and so should not be relied upon, disclose the date when this conclusion was reached and identify the financial statements and periods that cannot be relied upon. Also note the facts underlying this conclusion, and state whether the issue has been discussed with the company's independent accountant.
Item 5.01. Changes in control of registrant	If there is a change in control of the company, disclose the identity of the persons who acquired control, the date of the change in control, the basis of the control, the amount of consideration used by the acquiring person, the sources of funds used, the identity of the persons from whom control was assumed, and any arrangements between the old and new control groups.
Item 5.02. Departure of directors or certain officers; election of directors; appointment of certain officers; compensatory arrangements of certain officers	If a director has resigned or will not stand for re-election due to a disagreement with the company, disclose the date of the resignation or refusal to stand for election, the positions held by the director, and describe the circumstances. If the director has sent written correspondence to the company concerning this matter, attach it to the 8-K. If a senior manager of the company resigns from the company or is terminated, disclose the date of the event. If a new senior manager is hired, disclose the person's name, position, and date of appointment, and compensation arrangements.

Item Header	Description
Item 5.03. Amendments to articles of incorporation or bylaws; change in fiscal year	If the company amends its articles of incorporation or bylaws, disclose the effective date of the amendment, and describe the alteration. If the company changes its fiscal year, disclose the change date, and the date of the new fiscal year end.
Item 5.04. Temporary suspension of trading under registrant's employee benefit plans	When a director or officer of the company is subject to a blackout period for an equity security, disclose the reasons for the blackout period, a description of those transactions to be suspended, the class of securities subject to the blackout, and the expected beginning and ending dates of the blackout period.
Item 5.05. Amendments to the registrant's code of ethics, or waiver of a provision of the code of ethics	If there has been an amendment to or waiver of the company's code of ethics, disclose the date and nature of the event. If a waiver is involved, also state the name of the person to whom the waiver was granted.
Item 5.06. Change in shell company status	If the company was a shell company (see the Initial Public Offering chapter), and has ceased being classified as a shell, disclose the material terms of the transaction.
Item 5.07. Submission of matters to a vote of security holders	If any matters have been submitted to shareholders for a vote, disclose the date of the meeting, whether it was a special or annual meeting, the names of directors elected, and a summarization of each matter voted upon at the meeting. Also state the number of votes cast for, against, and withheld on each voting matter, as well as by individual director (if there is a director election).
Item 5.08. Shareholder director nominations	If the company did not hold an annual meeting in the preceding year, or if the date of this year's meeting is more than 30 days from the date of the preceding year's meeting, disclose the date by which a nominating shareholder must submit notice on Schedule 14N, so that the company can include any director nominations by shareholders in its proxy materials.
Item 6.01. ABS informational and computational material	Disclose any informational and computational material for asset-backed securities.
Item 6.02. Change of servicer or trustee	If a servicer or trustee has resigned or been replaced, or if a new servicer has been appointed, disclose the date and nature of the event. For a new servicer, describe the material terms of the agreement and the servicer's duties.
Item 6.03. Change in credit enhancement or other external report	If the depositor becomes aware of any material enhancement or support that was previously applicable for any class of asset-backed securities, and which has been terminated other than by contract expiration or the completion by all parties of their obligations, disclose the date of termination, the identity of the parties providing enhancement or support, the terms and conditions of the enhancement or support, the circumstances of

Item Header	Description
	the termination, and any early termination penalties.
Item 6.04. Failure to make a required distribution	If distributions are not made to the holders of asset-backed securities by the required date, disclose the nature of the failure.
Item 6.05. Securities Act updating procedure	If any material pool characteristic of an offering of asset-backed securities differs by more than five percent from the prospectus description at the time of issuance, disclose the characteristics of the actual asset pool.
Item 7.01. Regulation FD disclosure	The company may disclose any information that it elects to disclose under the provisions of Regulation FD (see the Regulation FD chapter).
Item 8.01. Other events	The company can, at its option, disclose any information that is not specifically identified elsewhere in the Form 8-K. This is typically only done if the company believes that the information will be of importance to the holders of its securities.
Item 9.01. Financial statements and exhibits	Attach the financial statements, pro forma financial information, and any other exhibits filed along with the Form 8-K.

Every Form 8-K must be filed within four business days of the event being disclosed. When a reportable event occurs on a weekend or holiday, the four-day rule begins on the next business day.

The Disclosure of Non-GAAP Information

Some publicly-held companies want to present the best possible version of their results to the investment community, and do so by selectively disclosing only the better portions of their actual financial results. The result can be misleading, when compared to GAAP. To mitigate the effects of this misleading information, the SEC's Regulation G requires certain additional disclosures. The following text is taken from the Regulation:

a. Whenever a registrant … publicly discloses material information that includes a non-GAAP financial measure, the registrant must accompany that non-GAAP financial measure with:

   1. A presentation of the most directly comparable financial measure calculated and presented in accordance with GAAP; and
   2. A reconciliation … of the differences between the non-GAAP financial measure disclosed or released with the most comparable financial measure or measures calculated and presented in accordance with GAAP.

b. A registrant, or a person acting on its behalf, shall not make public a non-GAAP financial measure that, taken together with the information accompanying that measure and any other accompanying discussion of that measure, contains an untrue statement of a material fact or omits to state a material fact necessary in order to make the presentation of the non-GAAP financial measure, in light of the circumstances under which it is presented, not misleading.

Regulation G also contains limited exemptions for certain foreign issuers of securities or in relation to proposed business combinations.

Tip: To avoid the reconciliation requirements of Regulation G, it is easiest to adopt a policy of never issuing non-GAAP financial measures without the written approval of the company's disclosure committee.

An example of how Regulation G may be used to construct an information release is noted in the following example.

EXAMPLE

The reported net loss of Hegemony Toy Company was strongly impacted by the recognition of a $500,000 impairment charge against our goodwill asset. We believe that an adjusted net income measure more closely represents our actual performance, because it excludes the one-time, non-cash impairment charge. We define adjusted net income as the net income or loss of the company, less the impact of impairment charges.

Adjusted net income is not a financial performance measurement under GAAP. Adjusted net income has material limitations and should not be used as an alternative to such GAAP measurements as net income, cash flows from operations, investing, or financing activities, or other financial statement data contained within the financial statements. Because the adjusted net income figure is not defined by GAAP, and can be compiled in many ways, it may not be comparable to other similarly titled performance measurements issued by other companies.

The following table presents a reconciliation of Hegemony's adjusted net income to our net loss during fiscal year 201X.

	For the Year Ended December 31, 201X
Adjusted net income	$400,000
Impairment charge	(500,000)
Net loss	$(100,000)

In summary, the SEC requires that any non-GAAP information disclosed by a company must be accompanied by a reconciliation to a financial measurement that has been calculated using GAAP, and it should not be misleading. This means that non-GAAP information can still be released; it is up to the reader of the presented information to examine the accompanying reconciliation and decide if the non-GAAP information is relevant to his or her investing needs.

Summary

For the controller of a publicly-held company, it may sometimes appear as though the *only* responsibility involves the filing of the Forms 10-Q and 10-K, because they take so much time to prepare. Never underestimate the workload associated with public company financial reporting – it is downright oppressive. We recommend that you conduct a thorough review of the time required to prepare the necessary filings, including a discussion of any concerns the auditors may have about the timeliness of work completion and errors found, and present these findings to senior management along with a request for additional resources. Otherwise, you may find that you do not have sufficient time to engage in all of the other responsibilities of the controller position.

Chapter 14
Management Reports

Introduction

The controller may be responsible for the issuance of a startling number of management reports that address not only financial issues, but also possibly operational ones. In this chapter, we address not only the types of reports that you may want to issue, but also their contents and ongoing maintenance. Ideally, the result should be a small core group of reports that are continually adjusted to match the needs of the business.

Related Podcast Episode: Episodes 148, 186, 222, and 234 of the Accounting Best Practices Podcast discuss best practices for accounting reports, inventory variances, data presentation, and how to find the right metrics, respectively. You can listen to them at: **accountingtools.com/podcasts**

Controller Responsibilities

Basically, the controller is responsible for issuing a variety of reports to management and others within the company. However, you also have to ensure that the information provided is useful for the recipients, and that generating reports is not excessively costly. These issues lead to the following responsibilities:

- Provide reports to management as requested
- Review existing reports to ascertain whether they are still needed or should be modified
- Generate and issue reports in the most cost-effective manner

The Duration of a Report

Before you delve into the array of management reports that are available, first consider the effort required to create and distribute each one, as well as the extent to which the reports will be used. What you will likely find is that only a few line items on a report are truly useful to the recipients, and also that the level of report usefulness declines over time.

These issues mean that every report issued by the accounting department should be examined on a regular basis to see if they should be modified or possibly discontinued entirely. It should be a rare report that continues unchanged for more than a year.

By continually examining the usage level of reports and adjusting the reports accordingly, you may reduce the workload of the accounting staff. Also, this should increase the cost-benefit of the reports – that is, the effort that goes into a report is paid for by being highly applicable to the recipient.

Responsibility Reporting

Responsibility reporting is the concept that every revenue item and cost in a business can be traced to one person within the organization, so that person should receive reports about the specific items for which he or she is responsible. Here are several examples of responsibility reporting:

- *Raw materials cost.* Report it to the purchasing manager.
- *Rent expense.* Report it to the person who negotiated and signed the building lease.
- *Wages.* Report it to the person supervising the employee earning the wages.
- *Warranty expense.* Report it to the engineering manager.

Further, responsibility reporting requires different levels of information aggregation, depending on the position of the recipient within the business. Thus, the president receives the income statement for the entire business, while the production manager only sees the cost incurred by the production department, and a machine operator may be limited to seeing the excess scrap produced by his machine.

This concept is terrific from the perspective of the company president, since it means that everyone in the company is aware of the revenues and expenses for which they are responsible. The controller may have a somewhat less enthusiastic viewpoint, since this calls for a virtual blizzard of reports. To avoid becoming overwhelmed by reports, the accounting staff should create a customized report template for each report recipient, and then set up the templates to automatically run at fixed intervals throughout the month. This approach completely automates report creation, though it also means that the reports will probably not be tweaked at regular intervals to meet the needs of recipients, since there are so many reports.

The Flash Report

The single most crucial report that the controller should issue is the flash report. This is the ultimate in short-term information, for it is designed to inform management of issues that are occurring either right now or in the immediate past. The intent of the flash report is to warn management of problems in areas necessary for the short-term survival of the company. Thus, the report should not contain any information on which managers are unlikely to take action. Examples of items that might appear in a flash report are:

Related to Cash

- *Cash balance.* This is a perennial favorite for the flash report, since an impending cash shortage can shut down any business.

- *Debt remaining.* It is more important to know how much untapped debt is remaining on the company's line of credit than the amount of debt that the company already has, because the latter information is already available on the balance sheet. This line item is closely associated with the cash balance, since it reveals the company's available liquidity.
- *Receivables 90+ days.* This is the amount of accounts receivables more than 90 days old, and shows the amount of cash that is most at risk of not being collected. It may be necessary to provide an accompanying detail of who is not paying, and the amount unpaid by each customer.
- *Obsolete inventory.* This is the disposal value of any inventory designated as obsolete. You do not need to report the original cost of this inventory, since the intent of this line item is to state the amount of cash that can be gleaned from selling the inventory. A large balance could trigger fast action by management to convert the designated inventory to cash.

Related to Sales

- *Backlog.* This is the order backlog that has not yet been shipped. You might consider listing this item first on the flash report, since it is the key indicator for the generation of sales to support the business.
- *Contribution margin.* The size of the backlog is not sufficient information for management if the sales staff is buying sales by offering low prices. Hence the need for this line item, which is revenues minus the direct costs of selling products. This information may only be available on a monthly basis, so include the latest information when available. This information is not listed on the income statement, since that document is organized to report the gross margin, which also includes a number of fixed costs.

Related to Bottlenecks

- *Bottleneck utilization.* This is the percentage of theoretically available time during which the bottleneck operation ran during the reporting period. The company needs to maximize this percentage in order to earn a profit.

Related to Customer Service

- *Percent order line items shipped on time.* Customers respond well to receiving goods on time, so track the percentage shipped by the promise date.

Tip: Do not include too many line items in the flash report, since managers do not want to wade through too much information. Instead, present just the top ten metrics that really matter to company operations.

A sample flash report is shown below. Note that the information is listed on a trend line, so that managers can see where there may be a potential problem in comparison to the results of prior periods.

EXAMPLE

After much discussion with management, the controller of Milagro Corporation unveils the following flash report:

	This Week	Last Week	2 Weeks Ago	3 Weeks Ago
Cash Issues				
Cash balance	$150,000	$180,000	$190,000	$200,000
Debt remaining	310,000	325,000	350,000	400,000
Receivables 90+ days	89,000	62,000	35,000	15,000
Obsolete inventory	5,000	6,000	8,000	10,000
Sales Issues				
Backlog	520,000	590,000	620,000	650,000
Contribution margin	42%	41%	55%	58%
Bottleneck Issues				
Bottleneck utilization	86%	88%	91%	93%
Customer Service Issues				
Percent orders shipped on time	82%	85%	90%	96%

The controller includes a commentary with the flash report, pointing out a variety of problems. The company is losing its order backlog, has a growing amount of unpaid accounts receivable, and is rapidly losing contribution margin on its sales. Further, the company is suffering from a rapid decline in its percentage of order line items shipped on time. In short, this flash report reveals a company in significant disarray.

Tip: Note the complete absence of ratios in the flash report. Ratios are useful for investigating the long-term performance of a business, but the flash report is all about short-term performance that management can act upon – and ratios are not useful for that purpose.

You will likely need to evaluate the flash report at regular intervals and alter its contents to match the changing circumstances of the business. For example, if the company enters a new market, there may be a need for metrics related to that market. Or, if the bottleneck operation has shifted, discontinue reporting on the old bottleneck and switch to the new one.

Expense Reporting

The accounting department is continually being asked to provide reports concerning expenses incurred in various parts of the business. When you issue this information, do not simply state the expense incurred in the previous period (which is the usual request), since it provides little useful information. You could provide the information in comparison to the budgeted expense for the period, but the budgeted amount could be exceedingly unrealistic, so the comparison is less than useful. A better approach is to present the information alongside the same expenses incurred in previous periods. Doing so provides a solid basis of comparison, and reveals whether the most recent expenses are in accordance with historical trends. The following sample report shows the concept:

Sample Expense Report Format

	September	October	November	December
Wages	$45,000	$46,500	$47,250	$53,000
Payroll taxes	3,150	3,250	3,300	3,700
Rent	3,500	3,500	3,750	3,750
Office expenses	1,200	1,350	1,400	1,650
Travel and entertainment	800	950	800	4,000
Utilities	620	600	700	750
Other expenses	450	425	470	510
Totals	$54,720	$56,575	$57,670	$67,360

The sample shows the expenses incurred by a typical department. Compensation expenses are listed near the top of the report, since this expense is frequently the largest one incurred by many departments, with other expenses listed in declining order by the amounts usually incurred. Thus, the reader's attention is drawn to the top of the report, where most of the expenses are located. Also, the presentation of side-by-side results by month makes it easy for the report recipient to skim through the report and make note of anything that rises above or falls below the long-term average.

Expenses are similar to Newton's first law of motion. That first law states:

> The velocity of a body remains constant unless the body is acted upon by an external force.

You can change a few words to arrive at Bragg's first law of accounting, which is:

> Expense levels remain constant unless the business is acted upon by a supplier or manager.

Suppliers tend to raise prices, while managers take steps to reduce expenses. These opposing forces appear in the expense reports as changes in expense levels. A good controller can take advantage of the first law by reporting expenses only by exception. Thus, the preceding sample expense report might trigger a controller statement that the change in office rent in November was triggered by a new lease, while the surge in the travel and entertainment expense in December was caused by the company Christmas party. This additional level of reporting centers the attention of management on the key expense exceptions, while ignoring all of the other expenses that are not changing.

An exceptional controller will go one step further and make recommendations regarding how to make changes to expenses. Here are examples of controller-provided commentary:

- "The rent expense is 20% above the rents for similar buildings within one mile of the company facility; recommend negotiating with the landlord to drop the lease rate in exchange for extending the term of the lease."
- "Telephone expenses can be reduced by 15% if the company adopts a single cell phone carrier for all employees."
- "Travel expenses can be reduced by 5% if the company adopts a common travel agent for all company travel."

However, the level of controller-provided commentary noted here is extremely time-consuming, so even the best controller will probably only be able to make an occasional recommendation that includes a sufficient level of detail to convince management to act upon it.

Tip: Proactive controller commentary should be welcome for office and administration expenses, since this is the key area in which the accounting staff should have some expertise. However, the controller's advice may not be so welcome in other areas; consequently, be much more circumspect in making recommendations regarding the cost of materials, product designs, marketing campaigns, and so forth.

Margin Reporting

Management will likely make inquiries about the earnings that the company is achieving in such areas as customers, products, product lines, stores, and operating units. If the chart of accounts has been constructed to accumulate information for any of these categories, the accounting department should be able to provide the requested information. However, here are several issues to consider regarding the construction of margin reports:

- *Information sources*. For many margin analyses, such as margins by customer, it requires a considerable amount of manual analysis to obtain the required information. If so, push back if the requesting person wants this information on a continuing basis, since it will take up too much staff time to create.
- *Cost allocations*. It is rarely advisable to allocate overhead costs in a margin report. By doing so, you are artificially reducing the reported margin on

every line item in the report, which may lead to management shutting down products, product lines, stores, or divisions that actually have adequate profit margins.

- *Automation.* If a margin report proves to be valuable, take all possible steps to automate it. For example, if management wants to see a margin report by product, create standard costs for the direct costs associated with each product, include those standard costs in the margin report, and set up a process for routinely reviewing how closely the standard costs match actual costs.

Perhaps the most common of all margin reports is one that details the margin for individual products during a particular time period. When creating this report, only include those costs that vary directly with changes in unit volume; this usually means that only the cost of materials is included in the report, since manufacturing overhead and direct labor costs do not vary at the unit level. A sample product margin report is shown below.

Sample Product Margin Report

	Revenue	Units Sold	×	Standard Cost of Materials	=	Total Cost of Materials	Margin $
French press	$180,000	900		$90.00		$81,000	$99,000
Moka pot	62,000	380		73.25		27,835	34,165
Percolator pro	220,000	1,500		66.00		99,000	121,000
Roaster home edition	470,000	3,760		56.50		212,440	257,560
Roaster junior	100,000	1,100		40.90		44,990	55,010
Roaster pro	250,000	800		140.00		112,000	138,000
Vacuum coffee maker	123,000	300		184.50		55,350	67,650
Totals	$1,405,000	8,740				$632,615	$772,385

Another possible addition to the product margin report is the cost of commissions (if any), since they usually vary directly with unit sales.

If a company has a number of similar products that are aggregated into a product line, there may be a request to determine the margin associated with the entire product line. When constructing this report, you can include more expenses than just the cost of materials, since other expense types may be directly associated with the product line. The following expenses might be included:

- *Advertising.* This is the cost of any advertising or other marketing expenses related to the product line in question.
- *Engineering.* There may be a dedicated team of engineers involved with the design of only those products included in the product line. Only include those engineering compensation and other costs that would disappear if the product line were to be cancelled.

- *Manufacturing overhead.* There may be a significant amount of overhead cost associated with a product line, such as a production manager, equipment maintenance, and utilities. Only include those costs that would disappear if the product line were to be cancelled.
- *Selling expenses.* There may be a dedicated sales force that only sells the product line. Their compensation, payroll taxes, and travel and entertainment expenses should be included.

A sample product line margin report that includes the preceding expense elements is shown below.

Sample Product Line Margin Report

Product Line	Revenue	Direct Materials	Engineering	Overhead	Sales and Marketing	Margin
Home products	$800,000	$320,000	$65,000	$165,000	$130,000	$120,000
Restaurant products	390,000	156,000	82,000	80,000	40,000	32,000
School products	640,000	320,000	39,000	128,000	90,000	63,000
Totals	$1,830,000	$796,000	$186,000	$373,000	$260,000	$215,000

The same format just shown for a product line works well for a margin report constructed for a retail location, though the engineering, overhead, and sales and marketing costs should be replaced with expenses that would terminate if the store were closed, such as:

- *Wages and payroll taxes.* This is the compensation and related payroll taxes that would disappear if the store were closed. Thus, you would not include an apportionment of the cost of a regional store manager.
- *Advertising.* There may be advertising expenses related to a specific location. Do not include advertising if the expenditures are for a group of stores.
- *Rent.* This is the rent that would be eliminated if the store were closed. Do not include it if the company must still pay the rent even if the store closes.
- *Utilities.* There are usually some electrical and heating costs that would be eliminated as a result of a store closure.

A sample store margin report that includes the preceding expense elements is shown next.

Sample Store Margin Report

Store Location	Revenue	Direct Materials	Wages	Advertising	Other Expenses	Margin
Evanston	$900,000	$360,000	$270,000	$25,000	$200,000	$45,000
Freeport	1,050,000	420,000	270,000	25,000	230,000	105,000
Muncie	820,000	328,000	270,000	20,000	190,000	12,000
Totals	$2,770,000	$1,108,000	$810,000	$70,000	$620,000	$162,000

If you are asked to create a margin report for customers, be extremely careful about adding any expenses to the report. The reason is that most expenses related to the servicing of customers are incurred for *many* customers, not just one. For example, it would be unwise to include in a margin report the labor cost associated with the customer service or field service calls related to a specific customer, because those costs are likely to still exist even if the customer were to be terminated. However, it is acceptable to include other costs in a customer margin analysis, such as:

- *Commissions*. Salesperson commissions are almost certainly related to specific sales, so you can include them in the analysis.
- *Deductions*. Some customers claim an inordinate number of deductions when paying their invoices, which should certainly be included in the analysis.

A sample customer margin report that includes the preceding expense elements is shown below.

Sample Customer Margin Report

Customer Name	Revenue	Direct Materials	Commissions	Deductions	Margin
Gadzooks Coffee	$95,000	$48,000	$4,000	$13,000	$30,000
Kona Distributors	130,000	70,000	5,000	32,000	23,000
Marlowe Coffee	247,000	136,000	10,000	20,000	81,000
Peaberry Coffee	86,000	41,000	3,000	1,000	41,000
Totals	$558,000	$295,000	$22,000	$66,000	$175,000

The preceding customer margin report reveals a common issue that triggers the request to develop the report – there are substantial differences in the amount of payment deductions taken by customers. In the sample, the second-largest customer, Kona Distributors, takes such large deductions that it is the least profitable of the customers listed in the report.

As you can see from the various sample margin reports presented here, be careful to *only* include those expenses in the analysis that would be eliminated if the subject of the report were to be terminated. All other expenses are irrelevant, and so should not be included.

Variance Reporting

If you have a standard costing system, consider setting up a variance reporting system. A variance is the difference between the actual cost incurred and the standard cost against which it is measured. A variance can also be used to measure the difference between actual and expected sales. Thus, variance analysis can be used to review the performance of both revenue and expenses.

There are two basic types of variances from a standard that can arise, which are the rate variance and the volume variance. Here is more information about both types of variances:

- *Rate variance*. A rate variance (which is also known as a *price* variance) is the difference between the actual price paid for something and the expected price, multiplied by the actual quantity purchased. The "rate" variance designation is most commonly applied to the labor rate variance, which involves the actual cost of direct labor in comparison to the standard cost of direct labor. The rate variance uses a different designation when applied to the purchase of materials, and may be called the *purchase price variance* or the *material price variance*.
- *Volume variance*. A volume variance is the difference between the actual quantity sold or consumed and the budgeted amount, multiplied by the standard price or cost per unit. If the variance relates to the sale of goods, it is called the *sales volume variance*. If it relates to the use of direct materials, it is called the *material yield variance*. If the variance relates to the use of direct labor, it is called the *labor efficiency variance*. Finally, if the variance relates to the application of overhead, it is called the *overhead efficiency variance*.

Thus, variances are based on either changes in cost from the expected amount, or changes in the quantity from the expected amount. The most common variances that a controller elects to report on are subdivided within the rate and volume variance categories for direct materials, direct labor, and overhead. It is also possible to report these variances for revenue. Thus, the primary variances are:

	Rate Variance	Volume Variance
Materials	Purchase price variance	Material yield variance
Direct labor	Labor rate variance	Labor efficiency variance
Fixed overhead	Fixed overhead spending variance	Not applicable
Variable overhead	Variable overhead spending variance	Variable overhead efficiency variance
Revenue	Selling price variance	Sales volume variance

All of the variances noted in the preceding table are explained below, including examples to demonstrate how they are applied.

The Purchase Price Variance

The purchase price variance is the difference between the actual price paid to buy an item and its standard price, multiplied by the actual number of units purchased. The formula is:

(Actual price - Standard price) × Actual quantity = Purchase price variance

A positive variance means that actual costs have increased, and a negative variance means that actual costs have declined.

The standard price is the price that your engineers believe the company should pay for an item, given a certain quality level, purchasing quantity, and speed of delivery. Thus, the variance is really based on a standard price that was the collective opinion of several employees based on a number of assumptions that may no longer match a company's current purchasing situation.

EXAMPLE

During the development of its annual budget, the engineers and purchasing staff of Milagro Corporation decide that the standard cost of a green widget should be set at $5.00, which is based on a purchasing volume of 10,000 for the upcoming year. During the subsequent year, Milagro only buys 8,000 units, and so cannot take advantage of purchasing discounts, and ends up paying $5.50 per widget. This creates a purchase price variance of $0.50 per widget, and a variance of $4,000 for all of the 8,000 widgets that Milagro purchased.

There are a number of possible causes of a purchase price variance. For example:

- *Layering issue*. The actual cost may have been taken from an inventory layering system, such as a first-in first-out system, where the actual cost varies from the current market price by a substantial margin.
- *Materials shortage*. There is an industry shortage of a commodity item, which is driving up the cost.
- *New supplier*. The company has changed suppliers for any number of reasons, resulting in a new cost structure that is not yet reflected in the standard.
- *Rush basis*. The company incurred excessive shipping charges to obtain materials on short notice from suppliers.
- *Volume assumption*. The standard cost of an item was derived based on a different purchasing volume than the amount at which the company now buys.

Material Yield Variance

The material yield variance is the difference between the actual amount of material used and the standard amount expected to be used, multiplied by the standard cost of the materials. The formula is:

(Actual unit usage - Standard unit usage) × Standard cost per unit

= Material yield variance

An unfavorable variance means that the unit usage was greater than anticipated.

The standard unit usage is developed by the engineering staff, and is based on expected scrap rates in a production process, the quality of raw materials, losses during equipment setup, and related factors.

EXAMPLE

The engineering staff of Milagro Corporation estimates that 8 ounces of rubber will be required to produce a green widget. During the most recent month, the production process used 315,000 ounces of rubber to create 35,000 green widgets, which is 9 ounces per product. Each ounce of rubber has a standard cost of $0.50. Its material yield variance for the month is:

(315,000 Actual unit usage - 280,000 Standard unit usage) × $0.50 Standard cost/unit

= $17,500 Material yield variance

There are a number of possible causes of a material yield variance. For example:

- *Scrap*. Unusual amounts of scrap may be generated by changes in machine setups, or because changes in acceptable tolerance levels are altering the amount of scrap produced. A change in the pattern of quality inspections can also alter the amount of scrap.
- *Material quality*. If the material quality level changes, this can alter the amount of quality rejections. If an entirely different material is substituted, this can also alter the amount of rejections.
- *Spoilage*. The amount of spoilage may change in concert with alterations in inventory handling and storage.

Labor Rate Variance

The labor rate variance is the difference between the actual labor rate paid and the standard rate, multiplied by the number of actual hours worked. The formula is:

(Actual rate - Standard rate) × Actual hours worked = Labor rate variance

An unfavorable variance means that the cost of labor was more expensive than anticipated.

The standard labor rate is developed by the human resources and engineering employees, and is based on such factors as the expected mix of pay levels among the production staff, the amount of overtime likely to be incurred, the amount of new hiring at different pay rates, the number of promotions into higher pay levels, and the outcome of contract negotiations with any unions representing the production staff.

EXAMPLE

The human resources manager of Milagro Corporation estimates that the average labor rate for the coming year for Milagro's production staff will be $25/hour. This estimate is based on a standard mix of personnel at different pay rates, as well as a reasonable proportion of overtime hours worked.

During the first month of the new year, Milagro has difficulty hiring a sufficient number of new employees, and so must have its higher-paid existing staff work overtime to complete a number of jobs. The result is an actual labor rate of $30/hour. Milagro's production staff worked 10,000 hours during the month. Its labor rate variance for the month is:

($30/hour Actual rate - $25/hour Standard rate) × 10,000 hours

= $50,000 Labor rate variance

There are a number of possible causes of a labor rate variance. For example:

- *Incorrect standards.* The labor standard may not reflect recent changes in the rates paid to employees (which tend to occur in bulk for all staff).
- *Pay premiums.* The actual amounts paid may include extra payments for shift differentials or overtime.
- *Staffing variances.* A labor standard may assume that a certain job classification will perform a designated task, when in fact a different position with a different pay rate may be performing the work.

Labor Efficiency Variance

The labor efficiency variance is the difference between the actual labor hours used to produce an item and the standard amount that should have been used, multiplied by the standard labor rate. The formula is:

(Actual hours - Standard hours) × Standard rate = Labor efficiency variance

An unfavorable variance means that labor efficiency has worsened, and a favorable variance means that labor efficiency has increased.

The standard number of hours represents the best estimate of your industrial engineers regarding the optimal speed at which the production staff can manufacture goods. This figure can vary considerably, based on assumptions regarding the setup time of a production run, the availability of materials and machine capacity, employee skill levels, the duration of a production run, and other factors. Thus, the multitude of variables involved makes it especially difficult to create a standard that you can meaningfully compare to actual results.

EXAMPLE

During the development of its annual budget, the industrial engineers of Milagro Corporation decide that the standard amount of time required to produce a green widget should be 30 minutes, which is based on certain assumptions about the efficiency of Milagro's production staff, the availability of materials, capacity availability, and so forth. During the month, widget materials were in short supply, so Milagro had to pay production staff even when there was no material to work on, resulting in an average production time per unit of 45 minutes. The company produced 1,000 widgets during the month. The standard cost per labor hour is $20, so the calculation of its labor efficiency variance is:

(750 Actual hours - 500 Standard hours) × $20 Standard rate

= $5,000 Labor efficiency variance

There are a number of possible causes of a labor efficiency variance. For example:

- *Instructions*. The employees may not have received written work instructions.
- *Mix*. The standard assumes a certain mix of employees involving different skill levels, which does not match the actual staffing.
- *Training*. The standard may be based on an assumption of a minimum amount of training that employees have not received.
- *Work station configuration*. A work center may have been reconfigured since the standard was created, so the standard is now incorrect.

Variable Overhead Spending Variance

The variable overhead spending variance is the difference between the actual and budgeted rates of spending on variable overhead. The formula is:

Actual hours worked × (Actual overhead rate - Standard overhead rate)

= Variable overhead spending variance

A favorable variance means that the actual variable overhead expenses incurred per labor hour were less than expected.

The variable overhead spending variance is a compilation of production expense information submitted by the production department, and the projected labor hours to be worked, as estimated by the industrial engineering and production scheduling staffs, based on historical and projected efficiency and equipment capacity levels.

EXAMPLE

The controller of Milagro Corporation calculates, based on historical and projected cost patterns, that the company should experience a variable overhead rate of $20 per labor hour worked, and builds this figure into the budget. In April, the actual variable overhead rate turns out to be $22 per labor hour. During that month, production employees work 18,000 hours. The variable overhead spending variance is:

18,000 Actual hours worked × ($22 Actual variable overhead rate - $20 Standard overhead rate)

= $36,000 Variable overhead spending variance

There are a number of possible causes of a variable overhead spending variance. For example:

- *Account misclassification.* The variable overhead category includes a number of accounts, some of which may have been incorrectly classified and so do not appear as part of variable overhead (or vice versa).
- *Outsourcing.* Some activities that had been sourced in-house have now been shifted to a supplier, or vice versa.
- *Supplier pricing.* Suppliers have changed their prices, which have not yet been reflected in updated standards.

Variable Overhead Efficiency Variance

The variable overhead efficiency variance is the difference between the actual and budgeted hours worked, which are then applied to the standard variable overhead rate per hour. The formula is:

Standard overhead rate × (Actual hours - Standard hours)

= Variable overhead efficiency variance

A favorable variance means that the actual hours worked were less than the budgeted hours, resulting in the application of the standard overhead rate across fewer hours, resulting in less expense incurred.

The variable overhead efficiency variance is a compilation of production expense information submitted by the production department, and the projected labor hours to be worked, as estimated by the industrial engineering and production scheduling staffs, based on historical and projected efficiency and equipment capacity levels.

EXAMPLE

The controller of Milagro Corporation calculates, based on historical and projected labor patterns, that the company's production staff should work 20,000 hours per month and incur $400,000 of variable overhead costs per month, so it establishes a variable overhead rate of $20 per hour. In May, Milagro installs a new materials handling system that significantly improves production efficiency and drops the hours worked during the month to 19,000. The variable overhead efficiency variance is:

$20 Standard overhead rate/hour × (19,000 Hours worked - 20,000 Standard hours)

= $20,000 Variable overhead efficiency variance

Fixed Overhead Spending Variance

The fixed overhead spending variance is the difference between the actual fixed overhead expense incurred and the budgeted fixed overhead expense. An unfavorable variance means that actual overhead expenditures were greater than planned. The formula is:

Actual fixed overhead - Budgeted fixed overhead = Fixed overhead spending variance

The amount of expense related to fixed overhead should (as the name implies) be relatively fixed, and so the fixed overhead spending variance should not theoretically vary much from the budget. However, if the manufacturing process reaches a step cost trigger point, where a whole new expense must be incurred, then this can cause a significant unfavorable variance. Also, there may be some seasonality in fixed overhead expenditures, which may cause both favorable and unfavorable variances in individual months of a year, but which cancel each other out over the full year.

EXAMPLE

The production manager of Milagro Corporation estimates that the fixed overhead should be $700,000 during the upcoming year. However, since a production manager left the company and was not replaced for several months, actual expenses were lower than expected, at $672,000. This created the following favorable fixed overhead spending variance:

($672,000 Actual fixed overhead - $700,000 Budgeted fixed overhead)

= $(28,000) Fixed overhead spending variance

There are a number of possible causes of a fixed overhead spending variance. For example:

- *Account misclassification.* The fixed overhead category includes a number of accounts, some of which may have been incorrectly classified and so do not appear as part of fixed overhead (or vice versa).
- *Outsourcing.* Some activities that had been sourced in-house have now been shifted to a supplier, or vice versa.
- *Supplier pricing.* Suppliers have changed their prices, which have not yet been reflected in updated standards.

Selling Price Variance

The selling price variance is the difference between the actual and expected revenue that is caused by a change in the price of a product or service. The formula is:

(Actual price - Budgeted price) × Actual unit sales = Selling price variance

An unfavorable variance means that the actual price was lower than the budgeted price.

The budgeted price for each unit of product or sales is developed by the sales and marketing managers, and is based on their estimation of future demand for these products and services, which in turn is affected by general economic conditions and the actions of competitors. If the actual price is lower than the budgeted price, the result may actually be favorable to the company, as long as the price decline spurs demand to such an extent that the company generates an incremental profit as a result of the price decline.

EXAMPLE

The marketing manager of Milagro Corporation estimates that the company can sell a green widget for $80 per unit during the upcoming year. This estimate is based on the historical demand for green widgets.

During the first half of the new year, the price of the green widget comes under extreme pressure as a new supplier in Ireland floods the market with a lower-priced green widget. Milagro must drop its price to $70 in order to compete, and sells 20,000 units during that period. Its selling price variance during the first half of the year is:

($70 Actual price - $80 Budgeted price) × 20,000 units = $(200,000) Selling price variance

---

There are a number of possible causes of a selling price variance. For example:

- *Discounts.* The company has granted various discounts to customers to induce them to buy products.

- *Marketing allowances*. The company is allowing customers to deduct marketing allowances from their payments to reimburse them for marketing activities involving the company's products.
- *Price points*. The price points at which the company is selling are different from the price points stated in its standards.
- *Product options*. Customers are buying different product options than expected, resulting in an average price that differs from the price points stated in the company's standards.

Sales Volume Variance

The sales volume variance is the difference between the actual and expected number of units sold, multiplied by the budgeted price per unit. The formula is:

(Actual units sold - Budgeted units sold) × Budgeted price per unit

= Sales volume variance

An unfavorable variance means that the actual number of units sold was lower than the budgeted number sold.

The budgeted number of units sold is derived by the sales and marketing managers, and is based on their estimation of how the company's product market share, features, price points, expected marketing activities, distribution channels, and sales in new regions will impact future sales. If the product's selling price is lower than the budgeted amount, this may spur sales to such an extent that the sales volume variance is favorable, even though the selling price variance is unfavorable.

EXAMPLE

The marketing manager of Milagro Corporation estimates that the company can sell 25,000 blue widgets for $65 per unit during the upcoming year. This estimate is based on the historical demand for blue widgets, as supported by new advertising campaigns in the first and third quarters of the year.

During the new year, Milagro does not have a first quarter advertising campaign, since it is changing advertising agencies at that time. This results in sales of just 21,000 blue widgets during the year. Its sales volume variance is:

(21,000 Units sold - 25,000 Budgeted units) × $65 Budgeted price per unit

= $260,000 Unfavorable sales volume variance

There are a number of possible causes of a sales volume variance. For example:

- *Cannibalization*. The company may have released another product that competes with the product in question. Thus, sales of one product cannibalize sales of the other product.
- *Competition*. Competitors may have released new products that are more attractive to customers.
- *Price*. The company may have altered the product price, which in turn drives a change in unit sales volume.
- *Trade restrictions*. A foreign country may have altered its barriers to competition.

Problems with Variance Analysis

There are several problems with the various types of variances just described in this chapter, which are:

- *The use of standards*. A central issue is the use of standards as the basis for calculating variances. What is the motivation for creating a standard? Standard creation can be a political process where the amount agreed upon is designed to make a department look good, rather than setting a target that will improve the company. If standards are politically created, variance analysis becomes useless from the perspective of controlling the company.
- *Feedback loop*. The accounting department does not calculate variances until after it has closed the books and created financial statements, so there is a gap of potentially an entire month from when a variance arises and when it is reported to management. A faster feedback loop would be to eliminate variance reporting and instead create a reporting process that provides for feedback within moments of the occurrence of a triggering event.
- *Information drill down*. Many of the issues that cause variances are not stored within the accounting database. For example, the reason for excessive material usage may be a machine setup error, while excessive labor usage may be caused by the use of an excessive amount of employee overtime. In neither case will the accounting staff discover these issues by examining their transactional data. Thus, a variance report only highlights the general areas within which problems occurred, but does not necessarily tell anyone the nature of the underlying problems.

The preceding issues do not always keep controllers from calculating complete sets of variances for management consumption, but they do bring the question of whether the work required to calculate variances is a good use of the accounting staff's time.

Which Variances to Report

A lot of variances have been described in this section. Do you really need to report them all to management? Not necessarily. If management agrees with a reduced reporting structure, you can report on just those variances over which management has some ability to reduce costs, and which contain sufficiently large variances to be worth reporting on. The following table provides commentary on the characteristics of the variances.

Name of Variance	Commentary
Materials	
Purchase price variance	Material costs are controllable to some extent, and comprise a large part of the cost of goods sold; possibly the most important variance
Material yield variance	Can contain large potential cost reductions driven by quality issues, production layouts, and process flow; a good opportunity for cost reductions
Labor	
Labor rate variance	Labor rates are difficult to change; do not track unless you can shift work into lower pay grades
Labor efficiency variance	Can drive contrary behavior in favor of long production runs, when less labor efficiency in a just-in-time environment results in greater overall cost reductions; not recommended
Overhead	
Variable overhead spending variance	Caused by changes in the actual costs in the overhead cost pool, and so should be reviewed
Variable overhead efficiency variance	Caused by a change in the basis of allocation, which has no real impact on underlying costs; not recommended
Fixed overhead spending variance	Since fixed overhead costs should not vary much, a variance here is worth careful review; however, most components of fixed overhead are long-term costs that cannot be easily changed in the short term
Revenue	
Selling price variance	Caused by a change in the product price, which is under management control, and therefore should be brought to their attention
Sales volume variance	Caused by a change in the unit volume sold, which is not under direct management control, though this can be impacted by altering the product price

The preceding table shows that the variances most worthy of management's attention are the purchase price variance, variable overhead spending variance, fixed overhead spending variance, and selling price variance. Reducing the number of reported variances is well worth the controller's time, since reporting the entire suite of variances calls for a great deal of investigative time to track down variance causes and then configure the information into a report suitable for management consumption.

How to Report Variances

A variance is a simple number, such as an unfavorable purchase price variance of $15,000. It tells management very little, since there is not enough information on which to base any corrective action. Consequently, the controller needs to dig down into the underlying data to determine the actual causes of each variance, and then report the causes. Doing so is one of the most important value-added activities of the accounting department, since it leads directly to specific cost reductions. The following table is an example of the level of variance detail to report to management.

Variance Item	Amount*	Variance Cause
Purchase Price		
Order quantity	$500	Bought wrappers at half usual volume, and lost purchase discount
Substitute material	1,500	Used more expensive PVC piping; out of stock on regular item
Variable Overhead		
Rush order	300	Overnight charge to bring in grease for bearings
Utility surcharge	2,400	Charged extra for power usage during peak hours
Fixed Overhead		
Property taxes	3,000	Tax levy increased by 8%
Rent override	8,000	Landlord charge for proportional share of full-year expenses
Selling Price		
Marketing discounts	4,000	Customers took discounts for advertising pass-through
Sales returns	11,000	450 units returned with broken spring assembly

* Note: All amounts are unfavorable variances

The preceding table can be expanded to include the names of the managers responsible for correcting each item noted.

Summary

The controller is probably responsible for the issuance of more management reports than everyone else in a business, combined. This means that there is a considerable responsibility to not issue erroneous or misleading information that might lead to serious missteps by management. Thus, you should withhold the distribution of any reports that initially appear to contain unusual results, to verify that the information is correct (or not). Also, do not issue reports that may be misleading. This is a particular concern when issuing margin reports, since allocated expenses can artificially create a low margin that might incorrectly lead management to terminate a product, product line, or store, or drop a customer. Finally, do not overwhelm the company with reports. As noted in the Variance Reporting section, just because there is a variance does not mean that you must report it. Instead, only issue reports containing meaningful information that management should act upon. All other reports are simply wasting their time, and make it more difficult to find the relevant information that they need to run the business.

Chapter 15
Ratio Analysis

Introduction

The controller is usually expected to provide some analysis alongside the financial statements, as well as of other financial aspects of the business. The starting point of this analysis is typically a standard set of ratios. When a ratio indicates a problem, the controller then investigates the underlying reasons in more detail, and reports any actionable findings back to management. In this chapter, we describe a selection of the more useful ratios that can form the foundation of a controller's analysis responsibilities. We address ratios and calculations for sales and earnings performance, liquidity, return on equity, the size of various asset groups, and the performance of the sales department.

Related Podcast Episodes: Episodes 26, 27, 28, 29, 30, 31, and 35 of the Accounting Best Practices Podcast discuss ratios for payroll, inventory, liquidity, cash flow, asset utilization, operating performance, and the accounting department, respectively. You can listen to them at: **accountingtools.com/podcasts** or **iTunes**

Controller Responsibilities

The controller is responsible for establishing a set of key ratios that are consistently compiled and reported to management. The resulting ratio analysis has a strong orientation on the financial performance and liquidity of the business. The controller should also periodically examine the existing set of ratios to see if they are still needed, or if a more appropriate configuration of ratios would be of more use to management. These issues result in the following responsibilities:

- Provide a standard set of ratios to management on a recurring basis
- Provide additional analysis with the ratios to show the reasons for the reported results
- Review existing ratios to ascertain whether they are still needed or should be modified

Deflated Sales Growth

In an inflationary environment, it is relatively easy for a company to report continually increasing sales, for it can routinely ratchet up its prices. It is possible to factor out this inflationary increase by deflating the reported sales level by the amount of the consumer price index, or some similar measure of inflation. To calculate deflated sales growth, follow these steps:

1. Determine which inflation index to use for the deflation calculation. The consumer price index is most commonly used.
2. Divide the price index for the preceding year by the price index for this year, and multiply the result by the net sales of the business for the current year. This yields the deflated sales for the current year.
3. Subtract the net sales for the preceding year from the deflated sales for the current year, and divide by the net sales for the preceding year.

The main issue with the measurement of deflated sales growth is to apply the same type of inflation index to the measurement from year to year, so that ongoing measurements are comparable.

EXAMPLE

Viking Fitness has opened a chain of health clubs in a country that is experiencing a high rate of inflation. In the preceding year, the country had a consumer price index of 132. In the current year, the index increased to 158. In the preceding year, Viking reported sales of 58,000,000 pesos. In the current year, the company reported sales of 73,000,000 pesos, with no additional health clubs having been opened. Based on this information, Viking's deflated sales growth is:

$$\frac{(73{,}000{,}000 \text{ Pesos} \times (132 \text{ CPI} \div 158 \text{ CPI})) - 58{,}000{,}000 \text{ Pesos}}{58{,}000{,}000 \text{ Pesos}}$$

$$= 5.2\% \text{ Deflated sales growth}$$

Thus, despite the high inflation rate, the company did indeed succeed in increasing its same-location sales by 5.2% during the current year.

Deflated Profit Growth

When a business operates in a highly inflationary environment, a decline in the value of its home currency can cause the business to report unusually high profits in comparison to prior periods. To gain a better understanding of the underlying profit growth of the business, it is necessary to deflate the profits for the current period and then compare them to the profits reported for the prior period. To calculate deflated profit growth, follow these steps:

1. Divide the price index for the prior reporting period by the price index for the current reporting period.
2. Multiply the result by the net profit figure reported for the current reporting period.
3. Subtract the net profits for the prior reporting period from the result.
4. Divide the result by the net profit figure for the prior reporting period.

The formula is:

$$\frac{\text{Current period net profit} \times \dfrac{\text{Price index for prior period}}{\text{Price index for current period}} - \text{Prior period net profit}}{\text{Prior period net profit}}$$

The use of price indexes only approximates the true impact of inflation on a business. A price index is based on the changes in prices for a mix of common goods and services, which a company may not use in the same proportions built into the index. For example, a price index may have increased primarily because of a jump in the price of oil, but a company may have minimum expenditures for oil. Consequently, there can be differences between the deflated profit growth calculation and the actual impact of inflation on a business.

EXAMPLE

Aphelion Corporation operates telescopes in the Atacama Desert in northern Chile, and uses the Chilean peso as its home currency. The company reported profits of 5,000,000 pesos in the most recent year, and 4,500,000 pesos in the immediately preceding year. The price index for the current year was 127, as opposed to 106 for the preceding year. Based on this information, the deflated profit growth of the company is:

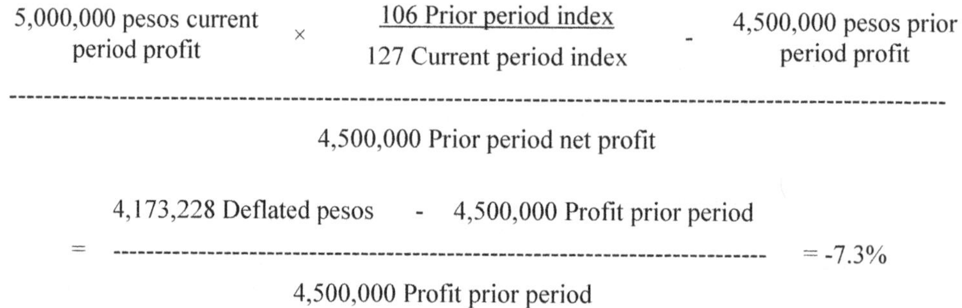

$$\frac{\text{5,000,000 pesos current period profit} \times \dfrac{\text{106 Prior period index}}{\text{127 Current period index}} - \text{4,500,000 pesos prior period profit}}{\text{4,500,000 Prior period net profit}}$$

$$= \frac{\text{4,173,228 Deflated pesos} - \text{4,500,000 Profit prior period}}{\text{4,500,000 Profit prior period}} = -7.3\%$$

Thus, when adjusted for inflation, the profits of Aphelion declined by 7.3% in the current reporting period.

Core Earnings Ratio

There are many ways in which the net profit ratio of a business can be skewed by events that have little to do with the core operating capabilities of a business. To get to the root of the issue and concentrate on only the essential operations of a business, Standard & Poor's has promulgated the concept of core earnings, which strips away all non-operational transactions from a company's reported results.

There are a multitude of unrelated transactions that can be eliminated from net profits, some of which are so specific to certain industries that Standard & Poor's probably never thought of them. The most common of these unrelated transactions are:

- Asset impairment charges
- Costs related to merger activities
- Costs related to the issuance of bonds and other forms of financing
- Gains or losses on hedging activities that have not yet been realized
- Gains or losses on the sale of assets
- Gains or losses related to the outcome of litigation
- Profits or losses from pension income
- Recognized cost of stock options issued to employees
- Recognized cost of warrants issued to third parties
- The accrued cost of restructuring operations that have not yet occurred

Many of these special adjustments only occur at long intervals, so a company may find that its core earnings ratio is quite close to its net profit ratio in one year, and substantially different in the next year. The difference tends to be much larger when a company adds complexity to the nature of its operations, so that more factors can impact net profits.

The calculation of the core earnings ratio is to adjust reported net income for as many of the preceding items as are present, and divide by net sales. The formula is:

$$\frac{\text{Net profits} - \text{Core earnings adjustments}}{\text{Net sales}}$$

EXAMPLE

Subterranean Access, maker of drilling equipment, has reported a fabulous year, with profits of $10,000,000 on sales of $50,000,000. A credit analyst that rates the company's bonds is suspicious of this good fortune, and digs through the company's annual report to derive the core earnings ratio of the business.
She uncovers the following items:

Profit from favorable settlement of a lawsuit	$8,000,000
Profit on earnings from pension fund	500,000
Gain on sale of a subsidiary	3,500,000
Impairment charge on acquired intangible assets	-1,000,000
Total	$11,000,000

When these adjustments are factored out of the company's net profits, it turns out that the core earnings figure is actually a $1,000,000 loss, which results in a core earnings ratio of -2%. Based on this information, the analyst issues a downgrade on the company's debt, on the assumption that the multitude of favorable adjustments will not continue.

Margin of Safety

The margin of safety is the reduction in sales that can occur before the breakeven point of a business is reached. The amount of this buffer is expressed as a percentage. The concept is especially useful when a significant proportion of sales are at risk of decline or elimination, as may be the case when a sales contract is coming to an end. By knowing the amount of the margin of safety, management can gain a better understanding of the risk of loss to which a business is subjected by changes in sales. The opposite situation may also arise, where the margin is so large that a business is well-protected from sales variations.

The margin of safety concept does not work well when sales are strongly seasonal, since some months will yield catastrophically low results. In such cases, annualize the information in order to integrate all seasonal fluctuations into the outcome.

To calculate the margin of safety, subtract the current breakeven point from sales, and divide by sales. The formula is:

$$\frac{\text{Current sales level} - \text{Breakeven point}}{\text{Current sales level}}$$

Here are two alternative versions of the margin of safety:

1. *Budget based.* A company may want to project its margin of safety under a budget for a future period. If so, replace the current sales level in the formula with the budgeted sales level.
2. *Unit based.* If you want to translate the margin of safety into the number of units sold, then use the following formula instead (though note that this version works best if a company only sells one product):

$$\frac{\text{Current sales level} - \text{Breakeven point}}{\text{Selling price per unit}}$$

EXAMPLE

Lowry Locomotion is considering the purchase of new equipment to expand the production capacity of its toy tractor product line. The addition will increase Lowry's operating costs by \$100,000 per year, though sales will also be increased. Relevant information is noted in the following table:

	Before Machinery Purchase	After Machinery Purchase
Sales	$4,000,000	$4,200,000
Gross margin percentage	48%	48%
Fixed expenses	$1,800,000	$1,900,000
Breakeven point	$3,750,000	$3,958,000
Profits	$120,000	$116,000
Margin of safety	6.3%	5.8%

The table reveals that both the margin of safety and profits worsen slightly as a result of the equipment purchase, so expanding production capacity is probably not a good idea.

Interest Coverage Ratio

The interest coverage ratio measures the ability of a company to pay the interest on its outstanding debt. A high ratio indicates that a business can pay for its interest expense several times over, while a low ratio is a strong indicator that an organization may default on its loan payments.

It is useful to track the interest coverage ratio on a trend line, in order to spot situations where a company's results or debt burden are yielding a downward trend in the ratio. An investor would want to sell the equity holdings in a company showing such a downward trend, especially if the ratio drops below 1.5:1, since this indicates a likely problem with meeting debt obligations.

To calculate the interest coverage ratio, divide earnings before interest and taxes (EBIT) by the interest expense for the measurement period. The formula is:

$$\frac{\text{Earnings before interest and taxes}}{\text{Interest expense}}$$

EXAMPLE

Carpenter Holdings generates $5,000,000 of earnings before interest and taxes in its most recent reporting period. Its interest expense in that period is $2,500,000. Therefore, the company's interest coverage ratio is calculated as:

$$\frac{\$5,000,000 \text{ EBIT}}{\$2,500,000 \text{ Interest expense}}$$

$$= 2:1 \text{ Interest coverage ratio}$$

The ratio indicates that Carpenter's earnings should be sufficient to enable it to pay the interest expense.

A company may be accruing an interest expense that is not actually due for payment yet, so the ratio can indicate a debt default that will not really occur, or at least until such time as the interest is due for payment.

Return on Equity

The return on equity (ROE) ratio reveals the amount of return earned by investors on their investments in a business. It is one of the metrics most closely watched by investors. Given the intense focus on ROE, it is frequently used as the basis for bonus compensation for senior managers.

ROE is essentially net income divided by shareholders' equity. ROE performance can be enhanced by focusing on improvements to three underlying measurements, all of which roll up into ROE. These sub-level measurements are:

- *Profit margin*. Calculated as net income divided by sales. Can be improved by trimming expenses, increasing prices, or altering the mix of products or services sold.
- *Asset turnover*. Calculated as sales divided by assets. Can be improved by reducing receivable balances, inventory levels, and/or the investment in fixed assets, as well as by lengthening payables payment terms.
- *Financial leverage*. Calculated as assets divided by shareholders' equity. Can be improved by buying back shares, paying dividends, or using more debt to fund operations.

Or, stated as a formula, the return on equity is as follows:

$$\text{Return on Equity} = \frac{\text{Net income}}{\text{Sales}} \times \frac{\text{Sales}}{\text{Assets}} \times \frac{\text{Assets}}{\text{Shareholders' equity}}$$

EXAMPLE

Hammer Industries manufactures construction equipment. The company's return on equity has declined from a high of 25% five years ago to a current level of 10%. The CFO wants to know what is causing the problem, and assigns the task to a financial analyst, Wendy. She reviews the components of ROE for both periods, and derives the following information:

	ROE		Profit Margin		Asset Turnover		Financial Leverage
Five Years Ago	25%	=	12%	×	1.2x	×	1.75x
Today	10%	=	10%	×	0.6x	×	1.70x

The information in the table reveals that the primary culprit causing the decline is a sharp reduction in the company's asset turnover. This has been caused by a large buildup in the company's inventory levels, which have been caused by management's insistence on stocking larger amounts of finished goods in order to increase the speed of order fulfillment.

The multiple components of the ROE calculation present an opportunity for a business to generate a high ROE in several ways. For example, a grocery store has low profits on a per-unit basis, but turns over its assets at a rapid rate, so that it earns a profit on many sale transactions over the course of a year. Conversely, a manufacturer of custom goods realizes large profits on each sale, but also maintains a significant amount of component parts that reduce asset turnover. The following illustration shows how both entities can earn an identical ROE, despite having such a different emphasis on profits and asset turnover. In the illustration, we ignore the effects of financial leverage.

Comparison of Returns on Equity

	ROE		Profit Margin		Asset Turnover
Grocery Store	20%	=	2%	×	10x
Custom manufacturer	20%	=	40%	×	0.5x

Usually, a successful business is able to focus on either a robust profit margin *or* a high rate of asset turnover. If it were able to generate both, its return on equity would be so high that the company would likely attract competitors who want to emulate the underlying business model. If so, the increased level of competition usually drives down the overall return on equity in the market to a more reasonable level.

A high level of financial leverage can increase the return on equity, because it means a business is using the minimum possible amount of equity, instead relying on debt to fund its operations. By doing so, the amount of equity in the denominator of the return on equity equation is minimized. If any profits are generated by funding activities with debt, these changes are added to the numerator in the equation, thereby increasing the return on equity.

The trouble with employing financial leverage is that it imposes a new fixed expense in the form of interest payments. If sales decline, this added cost of debt could trigger a steep decline in profits that could end in bankruptcy. Thus, a business that relies too much on debt to enhance its shareholder returns may find itself in significant financial trouble. A more prudent path is to employ a modest amount of additional debt that a company can comfortably handle even through a business downturn.

EXAMPLE

The president of Finchley Fireworks has been granted a bonus plan that is triggered by an increase in the return on equity. Finchley has $2,000,000 of equity, of which the president plans to buy back $600,000 with the proceeds of a loan that has a 6% after-tax interest rate. The following table models this plan:

	Before Buyback	After Buyback
Sales	$10,000,000	$10,000,000
Expenses	9,700,000	9,700,000
Debt interest expense	---	36,000
Profits	300,000	264,000
Equity	2,000,000	1,400,000
Return on equity	15%	19%

The model indicates that this strategy will work. Expenses will be increased by the new amount of interest expense, but the offset is a steep decline in equity, which increases the return on equity. An additional issue to be investigated is whether the company's cash flows are stable enough to support this extra level of debt.

A business that has a significant asset base (and therefore a low asset turnover rate) is more likely to engage in a larger amount of financial leverage. This situation arises because the large asset base can be used as collateral for loans. Conversely, if a company has high asset turnover, the amount of assets on hand at any point in time is relatively low, giving a lender few assets to designate as collateral for a loan.

Tip: A highly successful company that spins off large amounts of cash may generate a low return on equity, because it chooses to retain a large part of the cash. Cash retention increases assets and so results in a low asset turnover rate, which in turn drives down the return on equity. Actual ROE can be derived by stripping the excess amount of cash from the ROE equation.

Return on equity is one of the primary tools used to measure the performance of a business, particularly in regard to how well management is enhancing shareholder value. As noted in this section, there are multiple ways to enhance ROE. However, we must warn against the excessive use of financial leverage to improve ROE, since the use of debt can turn into a major burden if cash flows decline.

A case can be made that ROE should be ignored, since an excessive focus on it may drive management to pare back on a number of discretionary expenses that are needed to build the long-term value of a company. For example, the senior management team may cut back on expenditures for research and development, training, and marketing in order to boost profits in the short term and elevate ROE. However, doing so impairs the ability of the business to build its brand and compete effectively over the long term. Some management teams will even buy their companies back from investors, so that they are not faced with the ongoing pressure to enhance ROE. In a buyback situation, managers see that a lower ROE combined with a proper level of reinvestment in the business is a better path to long-term value.

Days Sales Outstanding

When evaluating the amount of accounts receivable outstanding, it is best to judge based on the proportion of receivables to sales. This proportion can be expressed as the average number of days over which receivables are outstanding before they are paid, which is called days sales outstanding, or DSO. DSO is the most popular of all collection measurements.

Days sales outstanding is most useful when compared to the standard number of days that customers are allowed before payment is due. Thus, a DSO figure of 40 days might initially appear excellent, until you realize that the standard payment terms are only five days. A combination of prudent credit granting and robust collections activity is the likely cause when the DSO figure is only a few days longer than the standard payment terms. From a management perspective, it is easiest to spot collection problems at a gross level by tracking DSO on a trend line, and watching for a sudden spike in the measurement in comparison to what was reported in prior periods.

To calculate DSO, divide 365 days into the amount of annual credit sales to arrive at credit sales per day, and then divide this figure into the average accounts receivable for the measurement period. Thus, the formula is:

$$\frac{\text{Average accounts receivable}}{\text{Annual sales} \div 365 \text{ days}}$$

EXAMPLE

The controller of Oberlin Acoustics, maker of the famous Rhino brand of electric guitars, wants to derive the days sales outstanding for the company for the April reporting period. In April, the beginning and ending accounts receivable balances were $420,000 and $540,000 respectively. The total credit sales for the 12 months ended April 30 were $4,000,000. The controller derives the following DSO calculation from this information:

$$\frac{(\$420{,}000 \text{ Beginning receivables} + \$540{,}000 \text{ Ending receivables}) \div 2}{\$4{,}000{,}000 \text{ Credit sales} \div 365 \text{ Days}}$$

$$=$$

$$\frac{\$480{,}000 \text{ Average accounts receivable}}{\$10{,}959 \text{ Credit sales per day}}$$

$$= 43.8 \text{ Days}$$

The correlation between the annual sales figure used in the calculation and the average accounts receivable figure may not be close, resulting in a misleading DSO number. For example, if a company has seasonal sales, the average receivable figure may be unusually high or low on the measurement date, depending on where the company is in its seasonal billings. Thus, if receivables are unusually low when the measurement is taken, the DSO days will appear unusually low, and vice versa if the receivables are unusually high. There are two ways to eliminate this problem:

- *Annualize receivables.* Generate an average accounts receivable figure that spans the entire, full-year measurement period.
- *Measure a shorter period.* Adopt a rolling quarterly DSO calculation, so that sales for the past three months are compared to average receivables for the past three months. This approach is most useful when sales are highly variable throughout the year.

Whatever measurement methodology is adopted for DSO, be sure to use it consistently from period to period, so that the results will be comparable on a trend line.

Tip: If DSO is increasing, the problem may be that the processing of credit memos has been delayed. If there is a processing backlog, at least have the largest ones processed first, which may reduce the amount of receivables outstanding by a noticeable amount.

Best Possible DSO

After running the DSO calculation, it may be useful to establish a benchmark against which to compare the DSO. This benchmark is the best possible DSO, which is the best collection performance that you can expect, given the existing payment terms given to customers. The calculation is:

$$\frac{\text{Current receivables}}{\text{Annual credit sales}} \times 365$$

The key element in this formula is the *current* receivables. The calculation is essentially designed to show the best possible level of receivables, based on the assumption that DSO is only based on current receivables (i.e., there are no delinquent invoices present in the calculation).

EXAMPLE

The collections manager of the Red Herring Fish Company has established that the company's DSO is 22 days. Since the company requires short payment terms on its short-lived products, the question arises – is 22 days good or bad? At the end of the current period, Red Herring's current receivables were $30,000, and its trailing 12-month credit sales were $1,000,000. Based on this information, the best possible DSO is:

$$\frac{\$30{,}000 \text{ Current receivables}}{\$1{,}000{,}000 \text{ Credit sales}} \times 365$$

$$= 11 \text{ Days}$$

In short, actual DSO is running at a rate double that of the company's best possible DSO, and so should be considered an opportunity for improvement.

Inventory Turnover

The turnover of inventory is the rate at which inventory is used over a measurement period. This is an important measurement, for many businesses are burdened by an excessively large investment in inventory, which can consume the bulk of available cash. When there is a low rate of inventory turnover, this implies that a business may have a flawed purchasing system that bought too many goods, or that stocks were increased in anticipation of sales that did not occur. In both cases, there is a high risk of inventory aging, in which case it becomes obsolete and has reduced resale value.

When there is a high rate of inventory turnover, this implies that the purchasing function is tightly managed. However, it may also mean that a business does not have the cash reserves to maintain normal inventory levels, and so is turning away prospective sales. The latter scenario is most likely when the amount of debt is high and there are minimal cash reserves.

To calculate inventory turnover, divide the ending inventory figure into the annualized cost of sales. If the ending inventory figure is not a representative number, then use an average figure instead. The formula is:

$$\frac{\text{Annual cost of goods sold}}{\text{Inventory}}$$

You can also divide the result of this calculation into 365 days to arrive at days of inventory on hand. Thus, a turnover rate of 4.0 becomes 91 days of inventory.

EXAMPLE

An analyst is reviewing the inventory situation of the Hegemony Toy Company. The business incurred $8,150,000 of cost of goods sold in the past year, and has ending inventory of $1,630,000. Total inventory turnover is calculated as:

$$\frac{\$8{,}150{,}000 \text{ Cost of goods sold}}{\$1{,}630{,}000 \text{ Inventory}}$$

$$= 5 \text{ Turns per year}$$

The five turns figure is then divided into 365 days to arrive at 73 days of inventory on hand.

Sales Productivity

Sales productivity is the ability of the sales staff to generate profitable sales. A profitable sale is considered to be one that has a high throughput, where throughput is sales minus all totally variable expenses. We do not measure the sales generated by the sales staff, since there may be little throughput associated with those sales.

To calculate sales productivity, divide the total estimated throughput booked by the sales staff by the total sales department expense incurred. The formula is:

$$\frac{\text{Total sales booked} - \text{All variable expenses associated with sales booked}}{\text{Total sales department expenses}}$$

EXAMPLE

The president of Armadillo Security Armor is concerned that the sales department is not being overly productive in booking new sales. He has the company controller accumulate the following information:

	January	February	March
Bookings	\$4,200,000	\$4,315,000	\$4,520,000
Related variable expenses	\$1,470,000	\$1,726,000	\$2,034,000
Throughput percentage	65%	60%	55%
Sales expenses	\$250,000	\$260,000	\$265,000
Sales productivity	10.9x	10.0x	9.4x

The analysis reveals that the sales staff is increasing sales, but giving away margin in order to do so. The result is an ongoing decline in the department's sales productivity. It would be better to book fewer sales at higher margins, thereby generating more profit for the company.

Sales productivity should be judged over multiple periods, since some sales can take several reporting periods to finalize, and so might yield a measurement that spikes and slumps from month to month. Also, the measurement correlates with the experience level of the sales staff, so expect it to decline immediately after new sales employees are hired.

Sales Backlog Ratio

The sales backlog ratio provides an indicator of the ability of a business to maintain its current level of sales. When noted on a trend line, the measurement clearly indicates changes that will likely translate into future variations in sales volume. For example, if the ratio exhibits an ongoing trend of declines, this is a strong indicator that a business is rapidly working through its backlog, and may soon begin to report sales reductions. The opposite trend of an increasing sales backlog does not necessarily translate into improved future sales, if a company has a bottleneck that prevents it from accelerating the rate at which it converts customer orders into sales.

To calculate the sales backlog ratio, divide the total dollar value of booked customer orders by the net sales figure for the past quarter. Only quarterly sales are used, rather than sales for the past year, in order to more properly reflect a company's short-term revenue-generating capability. The formula is:

$$\frac{\text{Total order backlog}}{\text{Quarterly sales}}$$

A different way of deriving the same information is to calculate for the number of days sales that can be derived from the existing order backlog. This figure is derived by dividing the average sales per day into the total backlog. The formula is:

$$\frac{\text{Total order backlog}}{\text{Quarterly sales} \div 90 \text{ days}}$$

The customer order information needed for this ratio cannot be entirely derived from a company's financial statements. Instead, it must be derived from internal reports that aggregate customer order information.

The ratio is of less use in the following situations:

- A retail environment, where there is no backlog
- A seasonal business, where the intent of the business model is to build order volume until the prime selling season, and then fulfill all orders
- A just-in-time "pull" model, where the intent is to fulfill orders as soon after receipt as possible

---

EXAMPLE

Henderson Mills reports the following sales and backlog information:

	April	May	June
Rolling 3-month sales	$9,000,000	$9,500,000	$9,600,000
Month-end backlog	5,000,000	4,000,000	3,500,000
Sales backlog ratio	0.55:1	0.42:1	0.36:1

The table indicates that Henderson is increasing its sales by chewing through its order backlog, which the company has been unable to replace. The result is likely to be the complete elimination of the order backlog in the near future, after which sales can be expected to plummet, unless steps are taken to book more customer orders.

Measurement Consistency

When a measurement is being presented for multiple periods, the calculation should be identical for all periods presented. For example, the inclusion of sales in a return on sales figure should always be net sales, not gross sales in one period and net sales in others. Otherwise, results will be so unreliable that managers will learn not to rely upon the presented information. There are several steps that can be taken to ensure a high degree of measurement consistency. Consider the following:

- *Audits.* Have the company's internal auditors occasionally review the measurements to ensure that they are being consistently calculated, and report to a senior manager if this is not the case.
- *Standards sheet.* Create a report on which are listed the calculations for all measurements. This standards sheet can be distributed to all recipients of measurement reports, as well as anyone whose performance is being monitored through the measurements. By doing so, everyone is aware of exactly how measurements are being developed.
- *Measurement locks.* Ideally, measurements should be included in the financial statements report writer, and then locked down with password access. By doing so, it is very difficult for anyone to adjust the calculations without proper authorization.

An issue with the use of a standards sheet is that the person responsible for reporting measurements will be pressured by those employees whose performance is being monitored through the measurements. This pressure will take the form of requests to use alternative calculations that cast the employees' performance in a better light. To counteract this pressure, require the controller to seek the approval of a senior manager (such as the president) before any measurement calculation changes are allowed.

Measurements and the Soft Close

A soft close refers to closing the books at the end of a reporting period without the use of many normal closing steps, such as the use of adjusting entries. A soft close is used to reduce the amount of effort required to close the books, and is considered acceptable when the resulting financial statements are not being issued outside of the company. The soft close is not used for more formal financial statement issuances, such as the year-end financials, because the results may not be entirely accurate.

When the accounting department employs a soft close, any measurements derived from the financial statements may be somewhat suspect. The results are more likely to be inaccurate if either the numerator or denominator of a ratio includes information that would normally have been adjusted with a journal entry as part of the closing process. For example, the absence of a wage accrual in the income statement would artificially increase the amount of net profit reported, and therefore alter the results of any ratio involving the net profit figure.

There are several approaches to consider when deriving measurements from soft close information:

- *Skip selected measurements.* If the results are sufficiently inaccurate, skip certain measurements entirely, and only calculate them in periods when a full set of closing activities have been completed.
- *Skip all measurements.* The main point behind a soft close is to avoid the effort required for a full close – which includes the preparation of a set of performance metrics. Management might agree to avoid all measurements as part of a soft close.
- *Determine variability of results.* It is entirely possible that the adjusting entries not being made in a soft close will result in only minor changes to measurements. This can be tested by comparing the results of measurements from soft close periods and normal close periods. If so, the results can still be released, perhaps along with a cautionary message to recipients.
- *Lengthen measurement period.* The size of adjusting entries tends to decline over lengthy measurement periods in relation to the reported results. This means that a measurement covering a quarterly soft close period is more likely to be accurate than a measurement spanning just one month for which a soft close was employed. If testing proves that this is correct, consider using measurements that cover a trailing three-month period.

Summary

Ratio analysis is a simple way to review the financial results and position of a business, especially when the information is tracked on a trend line. However, do not confine ratio analysis to the contents of the financial statements. Ratios can also provide insights into the operations of *every* department. For example, the controller could create an expanded analysis that is used to review such issues as the proportion of customer warranty claims, the amount of time required to fulfill customer orders, the effectiveness of marketing campaigns, and the rate at which customers are turning over. These additional areas of analysis can provide early warning about problems that might not appear in the financial statements for many months to come. For more information about the full range of available ratios, see the author's *Business Ratios Guidebook*.

Chapter 16
Budgeting

Introduction

Only in the smallest company can a budget be contained within a single page or spreadsheet. In most cases, the level of complexity of the business demands a much more segmented approach, so that key elements of the budget are modularized and then aggregated into a master budget. In this chapter, we show the complete system of budgets, describe how to create each element of the budget, and show how they are linked together to form a complete budget.

Related Podcast Episodes: Episodes 71, 76, 130, and 131 of the Accounting Best Practices Podcast discuss budget model improvement, budgeting controls, the problems with budgets, and operating without a budget, respectively. You can listen to them at: **accountingtools.com/podcasts** or **iTunes**

Controller Responsibilities

The controller is almost always directly responsible for the creation of the annual budget. This does not mean *creating* each element of the budget, but rather *managing* the process whereby budget information is assembled from throughout the company and consolidated into a master budget. Key responsibilities include:

- Manage the overall budget creation process.
- Inform management of issues related to inconsistencies between budget elements, constraints, pacing issues, and cash flow restrictions.
- Store the approved master budget.
- Use the budget as a basis for measuring company performance.

The System of Budgets

The key driver of any budget is the amount of revenue that is expected during the budget period. Revenue is usually compiled in a separate revenue budget. The information in this budget is derived from estimates of which products or services will sell, and the prices at which they can be sold. Forecasted revenue for this budget cannot be derived just from the sales staff, since this would limit the information to the extrapolation of historical sales figures into the future. The chief executive officer provides additional strategic information, while the marketing manager addresses new-product introductions and the purchasing staff provides input on the availability of raw materials that may restrict sales. Thus, a group effort from many parts of a company is needed to create the revenue budget.

Once the revenue budget is in place, a number of additional budgets are derived from it that relate to the production capabilities of the company. The following components are included in this cluster of budgets:

- *Ending inventory budget.* As its name implies, this budget sets the inventory level as of the end of each accounting period listed in the budget. Management uses this budget to force changes in the inventory level, which is usually driven by a policy to have more or less finished goods inventory on hand. Having more inventory presumably improves the speed with which a company can ship goods to customers, at the cost of an increased investment in working capital. A forced reduction in inventory may delay some shipments to customers due to stockout conditions, but requires less working capital to maintain. The ending inventory budget is used as an input to the production budget.
- *Production budget.* This budget shows expected production at an aggregated level. The production budget is based primarily on the sales estimates in the revenue budget, but it must also take into consideration existing inventory levels and the desired amount of ending inventory as stated in the ending inventory budget. If management wants to increase inventory levels in order to provide more rapid shipments to customers, the required increase in production may trigger a need for more production equipment and direct labor staff. The production budget is needed in order to derive the direct labor budget, manufacturing overhead budget, and direct materials budget.
- *Direct labor budget.* This budget calculates the amount of direct labor staffing expected during the budget period, based on the production levels itemized in the production budget. This information can only be generally estimated, given the vagaries of short-term changes in actual production scheduling. However, direct labor usually involves specific staffing levels to crew production lines, so the estimated amount of direct labor should not vary excessively over time, within certain production volume parameters. This budget should incorporate any planned changes in the cost of labor, which may be easy to do if there is a union contract that specifies pay increases as of specific dates. It provides rough estimates of the number of employees needed, and is of particular interest to the human resources staff in developing hiring plans. It is a key source document for the cost of goods sold budget.
- *Manufacturing overhead budget.* This budget includes all of the overhead costs expected to be incurred in the manufacturing area during the budget period. It is usually based on historical cost information, but can be adjusted for step cost situations, where a change in the structure or capacity level of a production facility strips away or adds large amounts of expenses at one time. Even if there are no changes in structure or capacity, the manufacturing overhead budget may change somewhat in the maintenance cost area if management plans to alter these expenditures as machines age or are replaced. This budget is a source document for the cost of goods sold budget.

- *Direct materials budget.* This budget is derived from a combination of the manufacturing unit totals in the production budget and the bills of material for those units, and is used in the cost of goods sold budget. If a company produces a large variety of products, this can become an excessively detailed and burdensome budget to create and maintain. Consequently, it is customary to estimate material costs in aggregate, such as at the product line level.
- *Cost of goods sold budget.* This budget contains a summarization of the expenses detailed in the direct material budget, manufacturing overhead budget, and direct materials budget. This budget usually contains such additional information as line items for revenue, the gross margin, and key production statistics. It is heavily used during budget iterations, since management can consult it to view the impact of various assumptions on gross margins and other aspects of the production process.

Once the revenue and production-related budgets have been completed, there are still several other budgets to assemble that relate to other functions of the company. They are:

- *Sales and marketing budget.* This budget is comprised of the compensation of the sales and marketing staff, sales travel costs, and expenditures related to various marketing programs. It is closely linked to the revenue budget, since the number of sales staff (in some industries) is the prime determinant of additional sales. Further, marketing campaigns can impact the timing of the sales shown in the revenue budget.
- *Administration budget.* This budget includes the expenses of the executive, accounting, treasury, human resources, and other administrative staff. These expenses are primarily comprised of compensation, followed by office expenses. A large proportion of these expenses are fixed, with some headcount changes driven by total revenues or other types of activity elsewhere in the company.

A budget that is not directly impacted by the revenue budget is the research and development budget. This budget is authorized by senior management, and is set at an amount that is deemed appropriate, given the projected level of new product introductions that management wants to achieve, and the company's competitive posture within the industry. The size of this budget is also influenced by the amount of available funding and an estimate of how many potentially profitable projects can be pursued.

Once these budgets have been completed, it is possible to determine the capital budgeting requirements of the company, as well as its financing needs. These two topics are addressed in the capital budget and the financing budget:

- *Capital budget.* This budget shows the cash flows associated with the acquisition of fixed assets during the budget period. Larger fixed assets are noted individually, while smaller purchases are noted in aggregate. The information in this budget is used to develop the budgeted balance sheet, depreciation expense, and the cash requirements needed for the financing budget. The capital budget is addressed separately in the Capital Budgeting chapter.

- *Financing budget.* This budget is the last of the component budgets developed, because it needs the cash inflow and outflow information from the other budgets. With this information in hand, the financing budget addresses how funds will be invested (if there are excess cash inflows) or obtained through debt or equity financing (if there is a need for additional cash). This budget also incorporates any additional cash usage information that is typically addressed by the board of directors, including dividends, stock repurchases, and repositioning of the company's debt to equity ratio. The interest expense or interest income resulting from this budget is incorporated into the budgeted income statement.

Once the capital budget and financing budget have been created, the information in all of the budgets is summarized into a master budget. This master budget is essentially an income statement. A more complex budget also includes a balance sheet that itemizes the major categories of assets, liabilities, and equity. There may also be a statement of cash flows that itemizes the sources and uses of funds.

The complete system of budgets is shown in the following exhibit.

Exhibit: The System of Budgets

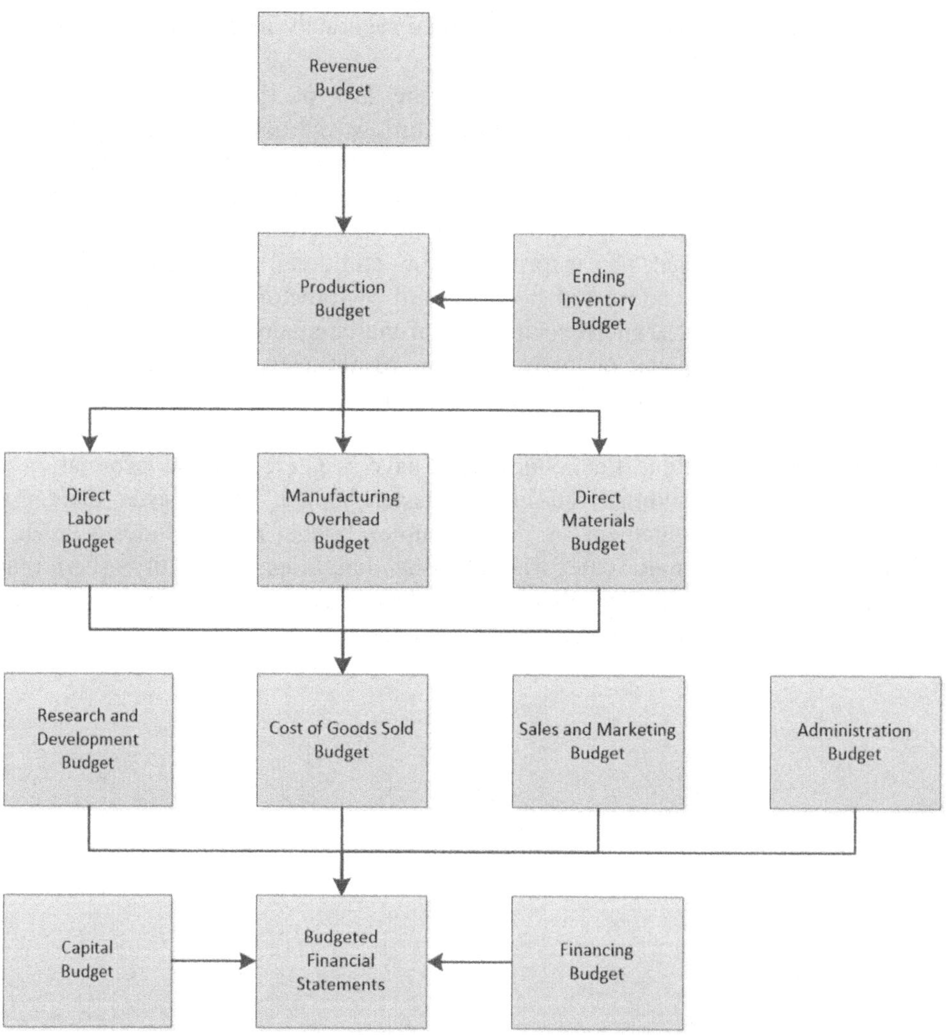

It may be useful to append a ratios page to the budget. These ratios are most useful when compared to historical trends, to see if the results generated by the budget model appear reasonable. Typical ratios to consider for this page are revenue per person, inventory turnover, accounts receivable turnover, and working capital as a percentage of sales.

In summary, the system of budgets ultimately depends upon the revenue budget and the amount of planned ending inventory. These two budgets directly or indirectly influence the amounts budgeted in many other parts of the corporate budget.

The Reasons for Budget Iterations

There are several very good reasons why the first version of a corporate budget is sent back for additional work. These issues are:

- *Constraints*. If there are bottlenecks within the company that interfere with its ability to generate additional sales, then does the budget provide sufficient funding to impact these bottlenecks? If not, the company can budget whatever results it wants, but it has virtually no chance of achieving them. For example, a machine in the production area may be a bottleneck that keeps a company from producing any more products – if you do not deal with the bottleneck, sales will not increase, irrespective of improvements anywhere else in the company.
- *Pacing*. If a company intends to expand operations in new geographical areas, or to open new distribution channels, or to offer entirely new products, it should build into the budget an adequate amount of time to ramp up each operation. This issue of pacing should include consideration of the sales cycle of customers, which may be extremely long. For example, expanding the customer base to include municipal governments may be an excellent idea, but may require a sales cycle of greater than a year, given the advance notice needed by governments to budget for purchases.
- *Financing*. If a company has a hard cap on the amount of funding that it will have available during the budget period, then the requirements of the budget must not exceed that funding limitation. This is one of the more common reasons for budget iterations, especially in small companies, where it may be difficult to obtain new funding.
- *Historical metrics*. If a company has been unable to achieve certain performance benchmarks in the past, what has changed to allow it to do so now? The chances are good that the company will still have trouble improving beyond its historical ability to do so, which means that the budget should be adjusted to meet its historical metrics. For example, if a business has historically been unable to generate more than $1 million of sales per salesperson, the preliminary budget should continue to support a similar proportion of sales to salespeople. Similarly, a historical tendency for accounts receivable to be an average of 45 days old prior to payment should probably be reflected in the preliminary budget, rather than a more aggressive collection assumption.

This section has highlighted the need to conduct a close examination of preliminary versions of a budget to see if it meets a number of reasonableness criteria. This usually calls for adjustments to the budget, which typically begins with excessively optimistic assumptions, followed by a certain amount of retrenching.

We now turn to an examination of the various components of the corporate budget.

Overview of the Revenue Budget

The basic revenue budget contains an itemization of a company's sales expectations for the budget period, which may be in both units and dollars. If a company has a large number of products, it usually aggregates its expected sales into a smaller number of product categories; otherwise, the revenue budget becomes too unwieldy.

The projected unit sales information in the sales budget feeds directly into the production budget, from which the direct materials and direct labor budgets are created. The revenue budget is also used to give managers a general sense of the scale of operations, for when they create the manufacturing overhead budget, the sales and marketing budget, and the administration budget. The total net sales dollars listed in the revenue budget are carried forward into the revenue line item in the master budget.

Most companies sell a large number of products and services, and must find a way to aggregate them into a revenue budget that strikes a balance between revealing a reasonable level of detail and not overwhelming the reader with a massive list of line-item projections. There are several ways to aggregate information to meet this goal.

One approach is to summarize revenue information by sales territory, as shown below. This approach is most useful when the primary source of information for the revenue budget is the sales managers of the various territories, and is particularly important if the company is planning to close down or open up new sales territories; changes at the territory level may be the primary drivers of changes in sales. In the example, the Central Plains sales territory is expected to be launched midway through the budget year and to contribute modestly to total sales volume by year end.

Sample Revenue Budget by Territory

Territory	Quarter 1	Quarter 2	Quarter 3	Quarter 4	Total
Northeast	$135,000	$141,000	$145,000	$132,000	$553,000
Mid-Atlantic	200,000	210,000	208,000	195,000	813,000
Southeast	400,000	425,000	425,000	395,000	$1,645,000
Central plains	0	0	100,000	175,000	275,000
Rocky mountain	225,000	235,000	242,000	230,000	932,000
West coast	500,000	560,000	585,000	525,000	2,170,000
Totals	$1,460,000	$1,571,000	$1,705,000	$1,652,000	$6,388,000

If you aggregate revenue information by sales territory, then the various territory managers are expected to maintain additional detail regarding sales in their territories, which is kept separate from the formal budget document.

Another approach is to summarize revenue information by contract, as shown below. This is realistically the only viable way to structure the revenue budget in situations where a company is heavily dependent upon a set of contracts that have definite ending dates. In this situation, you can divide the budget into existing and projected contracts, with subtotals for each type of contract, in order to separately show firm revenues and less-likely revenues. This type of revenue budget is commonly used when a company is engaged in services or government work.

Sample Revenue Budget by Contract

Contract	Quarter 1	Quarter 2	Quarter 3	Quarter 4	Total
Existing Contracts:					
Air Force #01327	$175,000	$175,000	$25,000	$--	$375,000
Coast Guard #AC124	460,000	460,000	460,000	25,000	1,405,000
Marines #BG0047	260,000	280,000	280,000	260,000	1,080,000
Subtotal	$895,000	$915,000	$765,000	$285,000	$2,860,000
Projected Contracts:					
Air Force resupply	$--	$--	$150,000	$300,000	$450,000
Army training	--	210,000	600,000	550,000	1,360,000
Marines software	10,000	80,000	80,000	100,000	270,000
Subtotal	$10,000	$290,000	$830,000	$950,000	$2,080,000
Totals	$905,000	$1,205,000	$1,595,000	$1,235,000	$4,940,000

Yet another approach for a company having a large number of products is to aggregate them into product lines, and then create a summary-level budget at the product line level. This approach is shown below. However, if you create a revenue budget for product lines, also consider creating a supporting schedule of projected sales for each of the products within that product line, in order to properly account for the timing and revenue volumes associated with the ongoing introduction of new products and cancellation of old ones. An example of such a supporting schedule is also shown below, itemizing the "Alpha" line item in the product line revenue budget. Note that this schedule provides detail about the launch of a new product (the Alpha Windmill) and the termination of another product (the Alpha Methane Converter) that are crucial to the formulation of the total revenue figure for the product line.

Sample Revenue Budget by Product Line

Product Line	Quarter 1	Quarter 2	Quarter 3	Quarter 4	Total
Product line alpha	$450,000	$500,000	$625,000	$525,000	$2,100,000
Product line beta	100,000	110,000	150,000	125,000	485,000
Product line charlie	250,000	250,000	300,000	300,000	1,100,000
Product line delta	80,000	60,000	40,000	20,000	200,000
Totals	$880,000	$920,000	$1,115,000	$970,000	$3,885,000

Sample Supporting Schedule for the Revenue Budget by Product Line

	Quarter 1	Quarter 2	Quarter 3	Quarter 4	Total
Alpha product line detail:					
Alpha Flywheel	$25,000	$35,000	$40,000	$20,000	$120,000
Alpha Generator	175,000	225,000	210,000	180,000	790,000
Alpha Windmill	--	--	200,000	250,000	450,000
Alpha Methane Converter	150,000	140,000	25,000	--	315,000
Alpha Nuclear Converter	100,000	100,000	150,000	75,000	425,000
Totals	$450,000	$500,000	$625,000	$525,000	$2,100,000

A danger in constructing a supporting schedule for a product line revenue budget is that you delve too deeply into all of the various manifestations of a product, resulting in an inordinately large and detailed schedule. This situation might arise when a product comes in many colors or options. In such cases, engage in as much aggregation at the individual product level as necessary to yield a schedule that is not *excessively* detailed. Also, it is nearly impossible to forecast sales at the level of the color or specific option mix associated with a product, so it makes little sense to create a schedule at that level of detail.

In summary, the layout of the revenue budget is highly dependent upon the type of revenue that a company generates. We have described different formats for companies that are structured around products, contract-based services, and sales territories. If a company engages in more than one of these activities, one should still create the revenue-specific formats shown in this section in order to provide insights into the sources of revenues, and then carry forward the totals of those schedules to a master revenue budget that lists the totals in separate line items. Users of this master revenue budget can then drill down to the underlying revenue budget schedules to obtain additional information. An example of a master revenue budget that is derived from the last two example revenue budgets is shown below.

Sample Master Revenue Budget

	Quarter 1	Quarter 2	Quarter 3	Quarter 4	Total
Contract revenue	$905,000	$1,205,000	$1,595,000	$1,235,000	$4,940,000
Product revenue	880,000	920,000	1,115,000	970,000	3,885,000
Totals	$1,785,000	$2,125,000	$2,710,000	$2,205,000	$8,825,000

The Ending Finished Goods Inventory Budget

The ending finished goods inventory budget states the number of units of finished goods inventory at the end of each budget period. It also calculates the cost of finished goods inventory. The amount of this inventory tends to be similar from period to period, assuming that the production department manufactures to meet demand levels in each budget period. However, there are a variety of reasons why you may want to alter the amount of ending finished goods inventory, such as:

- *Customer service.* If management wants to improve customer service, one way to do so is to increase the amount of ending inventory, which allows the company to fulfill customer orders more quickly and avoid backorder situations.
- *Inventory record accuracy.* If the inventory record keeping system is inaccurate, then it is necessary to maintain additional amounts of inventory on hand, both of raw materials and finished goods, to ensure that customer orders are fulfilled on time.
- *Manufacturing planning.* If you are using a manufacturing resources planning (MRP) system, then the company is producing in accordance with a sales and production plan, which requires a certain amount of both raw materials and finished goods inventory. If you change to the just-in-time (JIT) manufacturing planning system, then you are only producing as required by customers, which tends to reduce the need for inventory.
- *Product life cycles.* If there are certain products or even entire product lines that a company is planning to terminate, then factor the related inventory reductions into the amount of planned ending inventory.
- *Product versions.* If the sales and marketing staff want to offer a product in a number of versions, you may need to keep a certain amount of each type of inventory in stock. Thus, an increase in the number of product versions equates to an increase in ending inventory.
- *Supply chain duration.* If you are planning to switch to a supplier located far away from the company, be aware that this calls for having a larger safety stock of finished goods on hand, so that deliveries to customers will not be impacted if there is a problem in receiving goods on time from the supplier.
- *Working capital reduction.* If you want to increase the amount of inventory turnover, this reduces the amount of cash invested in working capital, but also has the offsetting effect of leaving less inventory in reserve to cover sudden surges in customer orders.

If you do plan to alter the ending amount of inventory, it is useful to create separate layers of ending inventory in the budget that reflect each of the decisions made, so that readers of the budget can see the numerical impact of operational decisions.

In the following example, we assume that changes made in the immediately preceding budget period will continue to have the same impact on inventory in the *next* budget period, so that the adjusted ending inventory in the last period will be the starting point for our adjustments in the next period. We can then make the following adjustments to the unadjusted ending inventory level to arrive at an adjusted ending inventory:

- *Internal systems changes.* Shows the impact of altering the manufacturing system, such as changing from an MRP to a JIT system.

- *Financing changes*. Shows the impact of altering inventory levels in order to influence the amount of working capital used.
- *Product changes*. Shows the impact of product withdrawals and product introductions.
- *Seasonal changes*. Shows the impact of building inventory for seasonal sales, followed by a decline after the selling season has concluded.
- *Service changes*. Shows the impact of changing inventory levels in order to alter order fulfillment rates.

If management is attempting to reduce the company's investment in inventory, it may mandate such a large drop in ending inventory that the company will not realistically be able to operate without significant production and shipping interruptions. You can spot these situations by including the budgeted inventory turnover level in each budget period, as well as the actual amount of turnover in the corresponding period in the preceding year. This is shown in the following example as the historical actual days of inventory, followed by the planned days of inventory for the budget period. Comparing the two measurements may reveal large period-to-period changes, which management should examine to see if it is really possible to reduce inventory levels to such an extent.

EXAMPLE

Milagro Corporation has a division that sells portable coffee machines for campers. Milagro wants to incorporate the following changes into its calculation of the ending finished goods inventory:

1. Switch from the MRP to the JIT manufacturing system in the second quarter, which will decrease inventory by 250 units.
2. Reduce inventory by 500 units in the first quarter to reduce working capital requirements.
3. Add 500 units to inventory in the third quarter as part of the rollout of a new product.
4. Build inventory in the first three quarters by 100 units per quarter in anticipation of seasonal sales in the fourth quarter.
5. Increase on-hand inventory by 400 units in the second quarter to improve the speed of customer order fulfillment for a specific product.

The ending finished goods inventory unit and cost calculation follows:

(units)	Quarter 1	Quarter 2	Quarter 3	Quarter 4
Unadjusted ending inventory level	2,000	1,600	1,850	2,450
+/- Internal system changes	0	-250	0	0
+/- Financing changes	-500	0	0	0
+/- Product changes	0	0	500	0
+/- Seasonal changes	100	100	100	-300
+/- Service changes	0	400	0	0
Adjusted ending inventory	1,600	1,850	2,450	2,150
× Standard cost per unit	$45	$45	$45	$45
Total ending inventory cost	$72,000	$83,250	$110,250	$96,750
Historical actual days of inventory	100	108	135	127
Planned days of inventory	92	106	130	114

The days of inventory calculation at the bottom of the table shows few differences from actual experience in the second and third quarters, but the differences are greater in the first and fourth quarters. Management should review its ability to achieve the indicated inventory reductions in those quarters.

The ending finished goods inventory budget shown in the preceding example is quite simplistic, for it assumes that you want to apply the same inventory policies and systems to a company's *entire* inventory. For example, this means that you want to increase inventory levels for all types of inventory in order to increase customer order fulfillment speeds, when in fact you may only want to do so for a relatively small part of the inventory.

If you want to adjust inventory levels at a finer level of detail, then consider creating a budget that sets inventory levels by business unit or product line. It is generally too time-consuming to set inventory levels at the individual product level, especially if demand at this level is difficult to predict.

The Production Budget

The production budget calculates the number of units of products that must be manufactured, and is derived from a combination of the sales forecast and the planned amount of finished goods inventory to have on hand. The production budget is typically presented in either a monthly or quarterly format. The basic calculation used by the production budget is:

+ Forecasted unit sales
+ Planned finished goods ending inventory balance
= Total production required

- Beginning finished goods inventory
= Units to be manufactured

It can be very difficult to create a comprehensive production budget that incorporates a forecast for every variation on a product that a company sells, so it is customary to aggregate the forecast information into broad categories of products that have similar characteristics. The calculation of the production budget is illustrated in the following example.

EXAMPLE

Milagro Corporation plans to produce an array of plastic coffee cups for the upcoming budget year. Its production needs are as follows:

	Quarter 1	Quarter 2	Quarter 3	Quarter 4
Forecast unit sales	5,500	6,000	7,000	8,000
+ Planned ending inventory units	500	500	500	500
= Total production required	6,000	6,500	7,500	8,500
- Beginning finished goods inventory	-1,000	-500	-500	-500
= Units to be manufactured	5,000	6,000	7,000	8,000

The planned ending finished goods inventory at the end of each quarter declines from an initial 1,000 units to 500 units, since the materials manager believes that the company is maintaining too much finished goods inventory. Consequently, the plan calls for a decline from 1,000 units of ending finished goods inventory at the end of the first quarter to 500 units by the end of the second quarter, despite a projection for rising sales. This may be a risky forecast, since the amount of safety stock on hand is being cut while production volume increases by over 30 percent. Given the size of the projected inventory decline, there is a fair chance that Milagro will be forced to increase the amount of ending finished goods inventory later in the year.

The production budget deals entirely with unit volumes; it does not translate its production requirements into dollars. Instead, the unit requirements of the budget are shifted into other parts of the budget, such as the direct labor budget and the direct materials budget, which are then translated into dollars.

When formulating the production budget, it is useful to consider the impact of proposed production on the capacity of any bottleneck operations in the production area. It is entirely possible that some production requirements will not be possible given the production constraints, so you will either have to scale back on production requirements, invest in more fixed assets, or outsource the work. The following example illustrates the issue.

EXAMPLE

Milagro Corporation revises the production budget described in the preceding example to incorporate the usage of a bottleneck machine in its manufacturing area. The revised format follows, beginning with the last row of information from the preceding example:

	Quarter 1	Quarter 2	Quarter 3	Quarter 4
Units to be manufactured	5,000	6,000	7,000	8,000
× Minutes of bottleneck time/unit	15	15	15	15
= Planned bottleneck usage (minutes)	75,000	90,000	105,000	120,000
- Available bottleneck time (minutes)*	110,160	110,160	110,160	110,160
= Remaining available time (minutes)	35,160	20,160	5,160	-9,840

* Calculated as 90 days × 24 hours × 60 minutes × 85% up time = 110,160 minutes

The table reveals that there is not enough bottleneck time available to meet the planned production level in the fourth quarter. However, Milagro can increase production in earlier quarters to make up the shortfall, since there is adequate capacity available at the bottleneck in the earlier periods.

Note in the preceding example that the amount of available bottleneck time was set at 85 percent of the maximum possible amount of time available. We make such assumptions because of the inevitable amount of downtime associated with equipment maintenance, unavailable raw materials, scrapped production, and so forth. The 85 percent figure is only an example – the real amount may be somewhat higher or substantially lower.

Another issue impacting the production budget is the need to incur step costs when production exceeds a certain volume level. For example, a company may need to open a new production facility, production line, or work shift to accommodate any additional increase in production past a certain amount of volume. It may be possible to adjust the production schedule to accelerate production in slow periods in order to stockpile inventory and avoid such step costs in later periods.

Production Budgeting for Multiple Products

The production budget shown thus far has centered on the manufacture of a single product. How do you create a production budget if you have multiple products? The worst solution is to attempt to re-create in the budget a variation on the production schedule for the entire budget period – the level of detail required to do so would be inordinately high. Instead, consider one of the following alternatives:

- *Bottleneck focus*. Rather than focusing on the production of a variety of products, only budget for the amount of time that they require at the bottleneck operation. For example, rather than focusing on the need to manufacture every aspect of 20 different products, you could focus on the time that each product needs at a single production operation. If you have multiple production lines or facilities, then only budget for usage of the bottleneck at each location.
- *Product line focus*. In many cases, there are only modest differences in the production activities needed to create any product within a product line. If there are such production commonalities, consider treating the entire production line as a single product with common production requirements.
- *80/20 rule*. It is likely that only a small number of products comprise most of a company's production volume. If this is case, consider detailed budgeting for the production of the 20 percent of all products that typically comprise 80 percent of all sales, and a vastly reduced (and aggregated) amount of budgeting for the remaining products.
- *MRP II planning*. If a company uses a manufacturing requirements planning (MRP II) system, the software may contain a planning module that allows you to input estimates of production requirements, and generate detailed requirements for machine usage, direct labor, and direct materials. If so, you can input the totals from this module into the budget without also copying in all of the supporting details.

The Direct Materials Budget (Roll up Method)

The direct materials budget calculates the materials that must be purchased, by time period, in order to fulfill the requirements of the production budget. The basic calculation for the roll up method is to multiply the estimated amount of sales (in units) in each reporting period by the standard cost of each item to arrive at the standard amount of direct materials cost expected for each product. Standard costs are derived from the bill of materials for each product. A bill of materials is the record of the materials used to construct a product. A sample calculation is noted on the next page.

Sample Calculation of the Cost of Direct Materials

	Quarter 1	Quarter 2	Quarter 3	Quarter 4
Product A				
Units	100	120	110	90
Standard cost/each	$14.25	$14.25	$14.25	$14.25
Total cost	$1,425	$1,710	$1,568	$1,283
Product B				
Units	300	350	375	360
Standard cost/each	$8.40	$8.40	$8.40	$8.40
Total cost	$2,520	$2,940	$3,150	$3,024
Grand total cost	$3,945	$4,650	$4,718	$4,307

Note that the preceding example only addressed the direct materials *expense* during the budget period. It did not address the amount of materials that should be purchased during the period; doing so requires that you also factor in the planned amounts of beginning and ending inventory. The calculation used for direct material purchases is:

+ Raw materials required for production
+ Planned ending inventory balance
= Total raw materials required

- Beginning raw materials inventory
= Raw materials to be purchased

The presence or absence of a beginning inventory can have a major impact on the amount of direct materials needed during a budget period – in some cases, there may be so much inventory already on hand that a company does not need to purchase *any* additional direct materials. In other cases, and especially where management wants to build the amount of ending inventory (as arises when a company is preparing for a seasonal sales surge), it may be necessary to purchase far more direct materials than are indicated by sales requirements in just a single budget period. The following example illustrates how beginning and ending inventory levels can alter direct material requirements.

EXAMPLE

Milagro Corporation plans to produce a variety of large-capacity coffee dispensers for camping, and 98% of the raw materials required for this production involve plastic resin. Thus, there is only one key commodity to be concerned with. The production needs of Milagro for the resin commodity are shown in the following direct materials budget:

	Quarter 1	Quarter 2	Quarter 3	Quarter 4
Product A (units to produce)	5,000	6,000	7,000	8,000
× Resin/unit (lbs)	2	2	2	2
= Total resin needed (lbs)	10,000	12,000	14,000	16,000
+ Planned ending inventory	2,000	2,400	2,800	3,200
= Total resin required	12,000	14,400	16,800	19,200
- Beginning inventory	1,600	2,000	2,400	2,800
= Resin to be purchased	10,400	12,400	14,400	16,400
Resin cost per pound	$0.50	$0.50	$0.55	$0.55
Total resin cost to purchase	$5,200	$6,200	$7,920	$9,020

The planned ending inventory at the end of each quarter is planned to be 20% of the amount of resin used during that month, so the ending inventory varies over time, gradually increasing as production requirements increase. The reason for the planned increase is that Milagro has some difficulty receiving resin in a timely manner from its supplier, so it maintains a safety stock of inventory on hand.

The purchasing department expects that global demand will drive up the price of resin, so it incorporates a slight price increase into the third quarter, which carries forward into the fourth quarter.

If you use the roll up method, you are basing the unit volume of materials on the quantities listed in the bill of materials for each item. It is essential that the information in bills of material be as accurate as possible, since the materials management department relies on this information to purchase materials and schedule production. However, what if the bill of materials information is incorrect, even if only by a small amount? Then, under the roll up method, that incorrect amount will be multiplied by the number of units to be produced in the budget period, which can result in quite a large error in the amount of materials used in the budget.

The Direct Materials Budget (Historical Method)

In a typical business environment, there may be a multitude of factors that impact the amount of direct materials as a percentage of sales, including scrap, spoilage, rework, purchasing quantities, and volatility in commodity prices. Many companies are unable to accurately capture these factors in their bills of material, which makes it nearly impossible for them to create a reliable direct materials budget using the roll up method that was just described.

In such cases, an alternative budget calculation is the historical method, under which you assume that the historical amount of direct materials, as a percentage of revenues, will continue to be the case during the budget period. This approach means that you copy forward the historical percentage of direct material costs, with additional line items to account for any budgeted changes in key assumptions.

Under the historical method, adjust the projected amount of sales for any increase or decrease in production that is required for planned changes in the amount of ending inventory, and express the result as adjusted revenue. You can then multiply the adjusted revenue figure by the historical percentage of direct materials to arrive at the total direct materials cost required to achieve the production budget. Despite the need for these adjustments, it is much easier to create a direct materials budget using the historical method than by using the roll up method.

EXAMPLE

Milagro Corporation finds that its last direct materials budget, which was created using the roll up method, did not come anywhere near actual results. This year, Milagro wants to use the historical method instead, using the historical direct materials rate of 32% of revenues as the basis for the budget. To avoid having the company become complacent and not work toward lower direct material costs, the budget also includes several adjustment factors that are expected from a number of improvement projects. There is also an adjustment factor that addresses a likely change in the mix of products to be sold during the budget period. The budget model is:

	Quarter 1	Quarter 2	Quarter 3	Quarter 4
Projected revenue	$4,200,000	$5,000,000	$5,750,000	$8,000,000
+/- planned ending inventory change	-400,000	+100,000	+250,000	-350,000
Adjusted revenue	$3,800,000	$5,100,000	$6,000,000	$7,650,000
Historical direct materials percentage	27.1%	27.1%	27.1%	27.1%
+ / - Adjustment for product mix	+3.4%	+4.0%	+1.8%	-0.9%
- Adjustment for scrap reduction	0.0%	0.0%	-0.2%	-0.2%
- Adjustment for rework reduction	0.0%	-0.1%	-0.1%	-0.1%
= Adjusted direct materials percentage	30.5%	31.0%	28.6%	25.9%
Total direct materials cost	$1,159,000	$1,581,000	$1,716,000	$1,981,350

The problem with the historical method is that it is based on a certain mix of products that were sold in the past, each possibly with a different proportion of direct materials to sales. It is unlikely that the same mix of products will continue to be sold through the budget period; thus, applying an historical percentage to a future period may yield an incorrect direct materials cost. You can mitigate this issue by including an adjustment factor in the budget (as was shown in the preceding example), which modifies the historical percentage for what is expected to be the future mix of product sales.

The Direct Labor Budget

The cost of direct labor is rarely variable. Instead, the production manager must retain experienced employees, which calls for paying them irrespective of the vagaries of the production schedule. Also, a production operation usually calls for a certain minimum number of employees in order to crew the production lines or work cells – it is not possible to operate the equipment with fewer people. Because of this crewing requirement, a company must spend a certain minimum amount for direct labor personnel, irrespective of the actual quantity of items manufactured. The resulting direct labor budget, known as the *crewing method*, is quite simple. Just budget for the number of people needed to staff the production area, which tends to remain fixed within a certain range of production volumes. The following example illustrates the concept.

EXAMPLE

Milagro Corporation determines the fixed labor cost needed to crew an entire production line, and then makes adjustments to the budget for those periods in which they expect production volumes to require the use of staff overtime. It uses this method with its titanium coffee grinder production line. This production line is staffed by eight people, and can produce 1,000 grinders per quarter with no overtime. The company expects to require additional production during the second quarter that will require the addition of two temporary workers to the production line. There are also plans for a 6% pay raise at the beginning of the fourth quarter. The direct labor budget for this production line is:

	Quarter 1	Quarter 2	Quarter 3	Quarter 4
Coffee grinder line:				
Staffing headcount	8	10	8	8
× Quarterly pay per person	$10,400	$10,400	$10,400	$11,024
= Total direct labor cost	$83,200	$104,000	$83,200	$88,192

The Manufacturing Overhead Budget

The manufacturing overhead budget contains all manufacturing costs other than the costs of direct materials and direct labor. Expenses normally considered part of manufacturing overhead include:

- Depreciation
- Facilities maintenance
- Factory rent
- Factory utilities
- Indirect materials, such as supplies
- Insurance on the factory and inventory
- Materials management staff compensation
- Personal property taxes on manufacturing equipment

- Production employee fringe benefits
- Production employee payroll taxes
- Production supervisor compensation
- Quality assurance staff compensation

The information in the manufacturing overhead budget becomes part of the cost of goods sold line item in the master budget.

EXAMPLE

Milagro Corporation owns a division that produces coffee beanery equipment for third world countries. Milagro budgets all raw materials and direct labor in the direct materials budget and direct labor budget, respectively. Its manufacturing overhead costs are stated in the manufacturing overhead budget as follows:

	Quarter 1	Quarter 2	Quarter 3	Quarter 4
Production management salaries	$142,000	$143,000	$144,000	$145,000
Management payroll taxes	10,000	10,000	11,000	11,000
Depreciation	27,000	27,000	29,000	29,000
Facility maintenance	8,000	7,000	10,000	9,000
Rent	32,000	32,000	32,000	34,000
Personal property taxes	6,000	5,000	7,000	6,000
Quality assurance expenses	3,000	3,000	3,000	3,000
Utilities	10,000	10,000	10,000	12,000
Total manufacturing overhead	$238,000	$237,000	$236,000	$237,000

The production management salaries line item contains the wages paid to the manufacturing supervisors, the purchasing staff, and production planning staff, and gradually increases over time to reflect changes in pay rates. The depreciation expense is relatively fixed, though there is an increase in the third quarter that reflects the purchase of new equipment. Both the freight and supplies expenses are closely linked to actual production volume, and so their amounts fluctuate in conjunction with planned production levels. The rent expense is a fixed cost, but does increase in the fourth quarter to reflect a scheduled rent increase.

A step cost is a cost that does not change steadily, but rather at discrete points. Thus, it is a fixed cost within certain boundaries, outside of which it will change. Several of the larger expense line items in the manufacturing overhead budget are step costs, so they tend to be incurred when a certain production volume is reached, and then stay approximately the same until production volumes change to a significant extent. This means that some line items can be safely copied from the actual expenditures in the preceding year with only minor changes. For example, if the current production level requires a second shift, and a production supervisor for that shift, then the manufacturing overhead budget for the next year should include the salary of that supervisor as long as there is going to be a second shift. Examples of situations giving rise to step costs are:

- *Additional production line.* If an entire production line is added, expect to incur step costs for all supporting staff, including materials management, supervision, and quality assurance personnel. There will also likely be an increase in the cost of utilities.
- *Additional shift.* If the facility is to be kept open for a second or third shift, expect to incur step costs for additional supervisors, as well as for a jump in the cost of utilities needed to power the facility during the extra time period.

Other expenses in this budget will require more analysis than the step costs just described. In particular, expenditures for the maintenance of machines and buildings can vary over time, depending upon the age of the assets being maintained and the need for large maintenance overhauls from time to time. For example, the expenditure for machinery maintenance may have been $100,000 in the preceding year, but can now be dropped to $50,000 in the new budget period because the company has replaced much of the equipment that had been requiring the bulk of the maintenance.

It is very difficult to run a facility at close to 100% of capacity. In this situation, equipment tends to break down more frequently, so a high utilization level requires additional overhead expenditures for parts, supplies, and maintenance labor.

The Sales and Marketing Budget

Selling expenses are those costs incurred to demonstrate products to customers and obtain orders from them, while marketing expenses involve the positioning, placement, and advertising of a company's products and services. More specifically, the following expenses fall within the general category of sales and marketing expenses:

- *Sales compensation.* This is the cost of paying base salaries, wages, bonuses, and commissions to the sales staff.
- *Other compensation.* This is the cost of the salaries and wages paid primarily to the marketing staff.
- *Order entry compensation.* This is the wages paid to the order entry staff and its management.
- *Advertising and promotions.* This is the set of activities managed by the marketing staff, and may include print advertising, Internet advertising, radio and television advertisements, billboards, coupons, catalogs, direct mail solicitations, one-time promotions, samples, and so forth.
- *Research.* This covers the expenses incurred by the marketing department to discover the optimal ways to promote products and services.
- *Office expenses.* These are the usual expenses incurred to run an office, including rent, utilities, and supplies.

Depending on the size of the department, it may be necessary to further subdivide the preceding expenses by functional area within the department. Specifically, consider separately tracking the performance of the following areas:

- Direct selling to customers
- Sales promotions
- Market research
- Customer service
- Customer warranties
- Selling activities by region

The most common type of sales and marketing budget is one that itemizes expenses by type. This is a simple design that shows budgeted compensation, promotions, travel, office expenses, and so forth. An example of this budget format follows:

Sales and Marketing Budget by Expense Type

Expense Type	Quarter 1	Quarter 2	Quarter 3	Quarter 4	Total
Salaries and wages	$270,000	$275,000	$320,000	$380,000	$1,245,000
Commissions	10,000	70,000	120,000	140,000	340,000
Payroll taxes	22,000	27,000	35,000	41,000	125,000
Promotions	0	50,000	85,000	42,000	177,000
Advertising	20,000	22,000	22,000	28,000	92,000
Research	0	0	35,000	0	35,000
Travel and entertainment	40,000	20,000	80,000	70,000	210,000
Office expenses	15,000	15,000	21,000	21,000	72,000
Other	5,000	5,000	5,000	5,000	20,000
Totals	$382,000	$484,000	$723,000	$727,000	$2,316,000

Though the budget format by expense type is the most common, it also tends to hide what may be very important information at the sales region and customer level. Ideally, your primary sales and marketing budget should be by expense type, with additional budgeting at the territory and customer levels if you feel that the additional amount of budgeting investigation creates valuable information.

If a company is organized by sales territory, then certainly recast the sales and marketing budget to determine the projected level of expenditures by territory. This is particularly important if most of the sales staff is assigned to specific territories, since this means that most of the cost structure of the company is oriented toward the territory format. You can then match territory gross margins with territory sales and marketing costs to determine earnings by territory. A typical format for such a budget is:

Sales and Marketing Budget by Territory

Sales Territory	Quarter 1	Quarter 2	Quarter 3	Quarter 4	Total
Department overhead	$250,000	$255,000	$255,000	$260,000	$1,020,000
Northeast region					
Compensation	400,000	410,000	430,000	450,000	1,690,000
Promotions	65,000	0	75,000	0	140,000
Travel	23,000	23,000	25,000	25,000	96,000
Other	18,000	19,000	19,000	19,000	75,000
Subtotal	$506,000	$452,000	$549,000	$494,000	$2,001,000
North central region					
Compensation	450,000	600,000	620,000	630,000	2,300,000
Promotions	75,000	0	80,000	0	155,000
Travel	31,000	33,000	35,000	39,000	138,000
Other	20,000	24,000	26,000	26,000	96,000
Subtotal	$576,000	$657,000	$761,000	$695,000	$2,689,000
Totals	$1,332,000	$1,364,000	$1,565,000	$1,449,000	$5,710,000

Diminishing Returns Analysis

A company will find that, after it achieves a certain amount of sales volume, the cost of generating additional sales goes up. This is caused by a variety of factors, such as having to offer more product features, ship products into more distant sales regions, increase warranty coverage, and so forth. Thus, the cost of obtaining each incremental sale will eventually reach the point where there is no further profit to be gained.

The concept of diminishing returns analysis is a useful one for the sales manager, since he or she should realize that it requires a gradual proportional increase in the sales and marketing budget over time in order to continue to increase sales. You cannot simply assume that the costs incurred in the preceding year to generate a certain sales volume can be applied to the next tranche of projected sales growth.

The concept of diminishing returns is difficult to calculate precisely, since it can appear in varying degrees throughout the budget. Here are some areas to be aware of:

- *Incremental sales staff.* If you add a sales person to an existing sales territory, it is likely that the existing sales staff is already handling the easiest sales, which means that the new hire will have to work harder to gain a smaller amount of sales than the average salesperson. You can estimate this reduced amount and build it into the budget.

- *Incremental advertising.* If you launch a new advertising campaign designed to bring in new customers, does the campaign target a smaller group than had been the case with previous campaigns, or is the targeted group one with less income to spend? Has research shown that increasing amounts of advertising result in incrementally fewer sales? If so, is there an optimal advertising expenditure level beyond which the return on funds expended declines?
- *Incremental region.* When you add a new geographic area, consider how the new region varies from the company's existing sales territories. If it has a less dense population, then it may be more expensive to contact them regarding a sale. If there is entrenched competition, expect a lower market share than normal. If products must be converted for use in a different language, how does the cost of doing so alter the product profit?
- *Incremental product.* If you add a product to an existing product line, will the new addition cannibalize the sales of other products in the product line?
- *Incremental sales channel.* When you add a new sales channel, does it cannibalize the sales of an existing channel? What is the cost of the infrastructure required to maintain the new channel? Will the new channel damage the company's relations with distributors or retailers?

This discussion does not mean that the sales manager should not push for continual sales growth, only that a detailed analysis is needed to clarify the diminishing returns that will be generated from the increased sales, and to ensure that those returns are noted in the budget.

The Research and Development Budget

The amount of funds to allocate to the research and development (R&D) budget can be an extraordinarily difficult discussion, for there is no correct answer – a small amount carefully invested can have an enormous payback, while a large investment can be frittered away among a variety of ho-hum projects. Still, there are several ways to generate a general estimate of how much funding to assign to R&D. They are:

- *Historical.* If a certain funding level has worked for the company in the past, then consider using it again – adjusted for inflation.
- *Industry benchmark.* If the industry as a whole spends a certain proportion of sales on R&D, this at least gives an indication of the level of spending required to compete over the long term. Better yet, isolate the same metric for just the top-performing competitors, since their level of R&D spending is more likely to be your target.
- *Best in class benchmark.* Look outside of the industry for companies that do a very good job on their R&D, and match their spending level as a proportion of sales. This is a particularly important approach when your company

is in a moribund industry where R&D spending is minimal, and you want to take a different approach.

- *Percent of cash flow.* Management may be willing to spend a certain proportion of its available cash on R&D on an ongoing basis, irrespective of what competitors are spending. This is a much better approach than apportioning a percentage of net income to R&D, since net income does not necessarily equate to cash flow, and a commitment to spend a certain proportion of net income could lead to a cash shortage.

No matter what method is used to derive the appropriate funding level, senior management should settle upon the *minimum* R&D funding level that must be maintained over the long term in order to remain competitive in the industry, and be sure never to drop below that figure.

The R&D budget is typically comprised of the following expense categories:

- *Compensation and benefits.* Compensation tends to be the largest R&D expenditure.
- *Contract services.* It is common to shift some research work to independent laboratories that specialize in particular types of work. In some cases, virtually all R&D work may be contracted out, in which case this becomes the largest R&D expenditure category.
- *Consumable supplies.* In some types of R&D, the staff may use (or destroy) a significant amount of supplies as part of its work. Depending on the situation, this can be quite a significant expense.
- *Office expenses.* These are the standard operational costs of running a department, such as utilities and office rent.
- *Depreciation on equipment.* There will be recurring depreciation charges for any fixed assets used by the R&D staff.
- *Amortization of acquired intangible assets.* If a company has acquired a patent or other intangible asset from another entity, it will likely have to amortize the asset over its useful life.

There are three general formats you can use to construct an R&D budget. They are:

- *Integrated into engineering department.* If the amount of funds expended on R&D is minor, do not budget for it separately. Instead, include it within the budget for the engineering department, either aggregated into a single line item or spread among the various expense line items attributable to that department.
- *Treated as a separate department.* If the expenditures associated with specific projects are relatively minor, and the R&D staff may be occupied with several projects at the same time, it may be sufficient to simply aggregate all expenses into a department-level budget for R&D, and not attempt to further assign expenses to specific projects.

- *Treated as projects within a department.* If there are significant expenditures that can be traced to individual projects, consider creating an R&D budget that clearly shows which projects are expected to consume funds.

The following two examples show the budget reporting format for treating R&D as a separate department with no further subdivision by project, and for revealing projects within the department.

Sample R&D Budget at the Department Level

	Quarter 1	Quarter 2	Quarter 3	Quarter 4	Total
Compensation	$150,000	$150,000	$160,000	$165,000	$625,000
Contract services	320,000	180,000	450,000	250,000	1,200,000
Consumable supplies	25,000	25,000	25,000	25,000	100,000
Office expenses	8,000	8,000	9,000	9,000	34,000
Depreciation	10,000	10,000	10,000	10,000	40,000
Amortization	15,000	15,000	15,000	15,000	60,000
Totals	$528,000	$388,000	$669,000	$474,000	$2,059,000

Sample R&D Budget at the Project Level

	Quarter 1	Quarter 2	Quarter 3	Quarter 4	Total
Department overhead	$23,000	$24,000	$24,000	$26,000	$97,000
Project Alpha					
Compensation	82,000	82,000	84,000	84,000	332,000
Contract services	65,000	65,000	75,000	70,000	275,000
Other	15,000	18,000	18,000	20,000	71,000
Project subtotal	162,000	165,000	177,000	174,000	678,000
Project Beta					
Compensation	40,000	60,000	60,000	60,000	220,000
Contract services	35,000	30,000	30,000	30,000	125,000
Other	5,000	7,000	7,000	10,000	29,000
Project subtotal	80,000	97,000	97,000	100,000	374,000
Totals	$265,000	$286,000	$298,000	$300,000	$1,149,000

Note in the second example that not all expenses could be assigned to a specific project, so they were instead listed separately from the projects under the "department overhead" designation.

The Administration Budget

The administration budget contains all of the expenses that are not directly involved in the provision of products or services to customers, or their sale to customers. This usually means that the following departments are included in the administration budget:

Accounting	Human resources	Public relations
Corporate	Information technology	Risk management (insurance)
Facilities	Internal auditing	Treasury
	Legal	

In a larger company, there may be individual budgets for each of these departments, rather than an administration department.

The expense line items included in the administration budget generally include the following:

Audit fees	Director fees	Payroll taxes
Bank fees	Dues and subscriptions	Property taxes
Charitable contributions	Employee benefits	Rent
Compensation	Insurance	Supplies
Consulting fees	Legal fees	Travel and entertainment
Depreciation		Utilities

The information in the administration budget is not directly derived from any other budgets. Instead, managers use the general level of corporate activity to determine the appropriate amount of expenditure. When creating this budget, consider the following issues:

- *Compensation*. The largest item in this budget is usually employee compensation, so pay particular attention to the formulation of this amount and test it for reasonableness.
- *Historical basis*. The amounts in this budget are frequently carried forward from actual results in the preceding year. This may be reasonable, but some costs may disappear due to the termination of a contract, or increase due to contractually scheduled price increases.
- *Step costs*. Determine when any step costs may be incurred, such as additional staff to support reporting requirements when a company goes public, and incorporate them into the budget.
- *Zero base analysis*. It may be useful to occasionally re-create the administration budget from the ground up, justifying the need for each expense. This is a time-consuming process, but may uncover a few expense items that can be eliminated.

The following example illustrates the basic layout of an administration budget.

EXAMPLE

Milagro Corporation compiles the following administration budget, which is organized by expense line item:

	Quarter 1	Quarter 2	Quarter 3	Quarter 4
Audit fees	$35,000	$0	$0	$0
Bank fees	500	500	500	500
Insurance	5,000	5,500	6,000	6,000
Payroll taxes	10,000	10,500	10,500	11,000
Property taxes	0	25,000	0	0
Rent	11,000	11,000	11,000	14,000
Salaries	140,000	142,000	144,000	146,000
Supplies	2,000	2,000	2,000	2,000
Travel and entertainment	4,500	8,000	4,000	4,000
Utilities	2,500	3,000	3,000	4,000
Other expenses	1,500	1,500	1,500	2,000
Total expenses	$212,000	$209,000	$182,500	$189,500

The CEO of Milagro likes to restate the administration budget by department, so that he can assign responsibility for expenditures to the managers of those departments. This results in the following variation on the same budget:

	Quarter 1	Quarter 2	Quarter 3	Quarter 4
Accounting department	$130,500	$102,500	$102,000	$108,000
Corporate department	30,000	30,000	30,000	30,000
Human resources department	19,500	19,500	18,000	19,000
IT department	25,000	25,000	25,000	25,000
Treasury department	7,000	7,000	7,500	7,500
Unassigned expenses	0	25,000	0	0
Total expenses	$212,000	$209,000	$182,500	$189,500

The reconfigured administration budget contains an "unassigned expenses" line item for property taxes, since management does not believe that expense is specifically controllable by any of the administrative departments.

The preceding example reveals a common characteristic of most line items in the administration budget, which is that most costs are fixed over the short term, and so only vary slightly from period to period. The exceptions are pay increases and scheduled events, such as audits. Otherwise, the main reason for a sudden change in an administrative expense is a step cost, such as increasing the headcount. This type of minimal cost variability is typical for the administration budget.

The Compensation Budget

The key goals of a compensation budget are to itemize the pay rates of all employees, the dates on which you expect to alter their pay, and all associated payroll taxes. This budget is usually contained within the various departmental budgets. We describe it separately here, because it involves several unique budgeting issues.

The compensation budget in the following example separates the calculation of compensation, social security taxes, Medicare taxes, and federal unemployment taxes. The separate calculation of these items is the only way to achieve a reasonable level of accuracy in the calculation of payroll taxes, since there are different tax rates and wage caps associated with each of the taxes. The pertinent information related to each of the indicated payroll taxes is:

Tax Type	Tax Rate	2017 Wage Cap
Social security	6.20%	\$127,200
Medicare	1.45%	No cap
Federal unemployment	0.80%	\$7,000

In a lower-wage environment, there may be few employees whose pay exceeds the social security wage cap, which makes the social security tax budget quite simple to calculate. However, in situations where compensation levels are quite high, expect to meet social security wage caps within the first two or three quarters of the year. Given the size of the social security match paid by employers, it is especially important to budget for the correct amount of tax; otherwise, the compensation budget could be inaccurate by a significant amount.

The simplest of the tax calculations is for the Medicare tax, since there is no wage cap for it. We have presented its calculation in the example as a table in which we calculate it for each individual employee. However, given the lack of a wage cap, you can more easily create a budget for it with a single line item that multiplies total compensation in every budget period by the Medicare tax rate.

Given the size of the social security and Medicare expenses, the paltry amount of the federal unemployment tax may seem like an afterthought. However, since it is based on a very low wage cap, nearly all of the expense is incurred in the first calendar quarter of each year, where it represents a modest expense bump. Some companies create a separate budget schedule for this expense, just to ensure that the correct amount is included in the first quarter of each year. Others find the cost to be so insignificant that they do not track it.

These concepts are noted in the following example, where we present separate budgets for base pay, social security, Medicare, and federal unemployment taxes, and then aggregate them into a master compensation budget.

EXAMPLE

Milagro Corporation is starting up a small group that will deal with research concerning the flavor of Kenyan and Ethiopian coffee beans. The company decides to create a separate compensation budget for the group, which includes five employees. The compensation budget is as follows, with quarters in which pay raises are scheduled being highlighted. Note that the annual salary is stated in each calendar quarter.

Base Pay Budget

	Quarter 1	Quarter 2	Quarter 3	Quarter 4
Erskin, Donald	$75,000	$75,000	$79,500	$79,500
Fells, Arnold	45,000	46,250	46,250	46,250
Gainsborough, Amy	88,000	88,000	88,000	91,500
Harmon, Debra	68,500	68,500	70,000	70,000
Illescu, Adriana	125,000	125,000	125,000	125,000
Annual compensation	$401,500	$402,750	$408,750	$412,250
Quarterly compensation	$100,375	$100,688	$102,188	$103,063

Social Security Budget (6.2% tax, $127,200 wage cap)

	Quarter 1	Quarter 2	Quarter 3	Quarter 4
Erskin, Donald	$1,163	$1,163	$1,232	$1,232
Fells, Arnold	698	717	717	717
Gaisborough, Amy	1,364	1,364	1,364	1,418
Harmon, Debra	1,062	1,062	1,085	1,085
Illescu, Adriana	1,938	1,938	1,938	1,938
Totals	$6,225	$6,244	$6,336	$6,390

Medicare Budget (1.45% tax, no wage cap)

	Quarter 1	Quarter 2	Quarter 3	Quarter 4
Erskin, Donald	$272	$272	$288	$288
Fells, Arnold	163	168	168	168
Gaisborough, Amy	319	319	319	332
Harmon, Debra	248	248	254	254
Illescu, Adriana	453	453	453	453
Totals	$1,455	$1,460	$1,482	$1,495

Federal Unemployment Tax Budget (0.8% tax, $7,000 wage cap)

	Quarter 1	Quarter 2	Quarter 3	Quarter 4
Erskin, Donald	$56	$0	$0	$0
Fells, Arnold	56	0	0	0
Gaisborough, Amy	56	0	0	0
Harmon, Debra	56	0	0	0
Illescu, Adriana	56	0	0	0
Totals	$280	$0	$0	$0

Milagro then shifts the summary totals from each of the preceding tables into a master compensation budget, as follows:

Master Compensation Budget

	Quarter 1	Quarter 2	Quarter 3	Quarter 4
Total base pay	$100,375	$100,688	$102,188	$103,063
Total social security	6,225	6,244	6,336	6,390
Total Medicare	1,455	1,460	1,482	1,495
Total unemployment	280	0	0	0
Grand totals	$108,335	$108,392	$110,006	$110,948

In the preceding example, compensation is shown in each quarter on an annualized basis, since it is easier to review the budget for errors when the information is presented in this manner. The information is then stepped down to a quarterly basis, which is used to calculate payroll taxes.

Overtime is difficult to predict at the level of an individual employee, but can be estimated at a more aggregated level. It is easiest to use the historical proportion of overtime hours, adjusted for expectations in the budget period. This means that you can multiply an overtime percentage by the aggregate amount of employee compensation to derive the amount of budgeted overtime pay. The following example illustrates the concept.

EXAMPLE

Milagro Corporation operates a production line for which the sales season is November through January. Milagro prefers to deactivate the production line for the first half of the calendar year and then run it with substantial employee overtime during the third quarter and a portion of the fourth quarter of the year. This results in the following overtime budget, which also assumes that a production crew is still working during the first half of the year – they just happen to be working on other production lines.

	Quarter 1	Quarter 2	Quarter 3	Quarter 4
Total wage expense	$250,000	$255,000	$270,000	$240,000
Overtime percentage	0%	2%	28%	12%
Overtime pay	$0	$5,100	$75,600	$28,800
Social security for overtime pay	$0	$316	$4,687	$1,786
Medicare for overtime pay	0	$74	$1,096	$418
Total overtime compensation	$0	$390	$5,783	$2,204

There is no calculation of the federal unemployment tax in the overtime budget, since that amount has such a low wage cap that the maximum amount would already have been included in the compensation budget.

The trouble with the overtime calculation format just presented is that it does not account for the social security wage cap, which is calculated at the level of the individual employee. It is easiest to simply assume that the wage cap is never reached, which may result in some excess amount of social security tax being budgeted. Realistically, few employees who are paid on an hourly basis will exceed the wage cap, so this should be a minor issue for most companies.

The Budgeted Income Statement

The core of the master budget is the budgeted income statement. It is derived from nearly all of the budgets that we have already discussed, and looks quite a bit like a standard income statement. This is a sufficient summarization of the budget for many companies, because they are primarily concerned with *financial performance*. However, some companies may still have an interest in their projected *financial position* (especially cash), which is contained in the balance sheet. Since the balance sheet is more difficult to derive than the income statement, they may be content to use a rough calculation of ending cash position whose components are mostly derived from information already in the budget. The following sample income statement contains this rough estimation of the ending cash balance in each period.

Sample Budgeted Income Statement

	Quarter 1	Quarter 2	Quarter 3	Quarter 4
Revenue	$2,200,000	$2,425,000	$2,500,000	$2,545,000
Cost of goods sold:				
Direct labor expense	220,000	253,000	253,000	253,000
Direct materials expense	767,000	838,000	831,000	840,000

	Quarter 1	Quarter 2	Quarter 3	Quarter 4
Manufacturing overhead	293,000	293,000	309,000	310,000
Total cost of goods sold	1,280,000	1,384,000	1,393,000	1,403,000
Gross margin	$920,000	$1,041,000	$1,107,000	$1,142,000
Sales and marketing	315,000	351,000	374,000	339,000
Administration	453,500	452,500	435,000	447,000
Research and development	50,000	52,000	54,000	55,500
Profits before taxes	$101,500	$185,500	$244,000	$300,500
Income taxes	35,500	65,000	85,500	105,000
Profits after taxes	$66,000	$120,500	$158,500	$195,500
Cash flow:				
Beginning cash	$50,000	-$52,500	$77,500	$7,000
+ Net profit	66,000	120,500	158,500	195,500
+ Depreciation	19,500	17,500	18,000	18,000
- Capital purchases	-38,000	-8,000	-47,000	-28,000
- Dividends	-150,000	0	-200,000	0
Ending cash	-$52,500	$77,500	$7,000	$192,500

The calculation of ending cash is appended to the budgeted income statement because it is partly derived from the net income figure located directly above it in the budget. Also, if a company does not intend to create a balance sheet, it is practical to include a cash calculation on the same page as the income statement.

The trouble with the ending cash measurement presented in the sample is that it is not complete. It does not incorporate any timing delays for when cash may be received or issued, and it also does not factor in the impact of changes in working capital. Thus, it can present inaccurate estimates of cash flow. For a more detailed derivation of ending cash, we need a balance sheet. The compilation of that document is discussed in the next section.

The Budgeted Balance Sheet

The balance sheet is difficult to derive as part of the budgeting process, because little of the information derived through the budgeting process is designed for it. Instead, you need to make a variety of estimates to approximate the amounts of various asset and liability line items as of the end of each budgeted reporting period. The key elements of the balance sheet that require estimation are accounts receivable, inventory, fixed assets, and accounts payable. We will address the derivation of these items next.

Accounts Receivable

Accounts receivable is the amount of sales made on credit that have not yet been paid by customers. It is closely correlated with sales, with a delay measured using days sales outstanding (DSO). DSO is calculated as:

$$\frac{\text{Accounts receivable}}{\text{Annual sales} \div 365 \text{ days}}$$

You then apply the DSO figure to projected credit sales during the budget period to determine the amount of accounts receivable outstanding at any given time.

EXAMPLE

Milagro Corporation has a division whose annual sales are $10 million. Its accounts receivable balance at the end of the most recent month was $1,400,000. Its DSO is calculated as:

$$\frac{\$1{,}400{,}000 \text{ accounts receivable}}{\$10{,}000{,}000 \text{ annual sales} \div 365 \text{ days}}$$

$$= 51 \text{ days sales outstanding}$$

Thus, it takes an average of 51 days for Milagro to collect an account receivable. In its balance sheet budget, Milagro would record as accounts receivable the current month's sales plus 21/30ths of the sales budgeted in the immediately preceding month. Thus, Milagro's budgeted receivables would be calculated as follows for a four-month sample period:

	December*	January	February	March
Credit sales	$790,000	$810,000	$815,000	$840,000
Receivables for month	--	810,000	815,000	840,000
Receivables from prior month	--	553,000	567,000	571,000
Total receivables in balance sheet	--	$1,363,000	$1,382,000	$1,411,000

* Prior year

An alternative approach for calculating the amount of accounts receivable is to calculate the percentage of credit sales that are collected within the month of sales and then within each of the next 30-day time buckets, and apply these layers of collections to a calculation of the ending accounts receivable in each budget period. The following example illustrates the concept.

EXAMPLE

The controller of Milagro Corporation decides to use an alternative method for deriving the ending accounts receivable balance for the division described in the preceding example. The controller finds that, historically, the following percentages of credit sales are paid within the stated time periods:

	Percent Paid	Percent Unpaid
In month of sale	10%	90%
In following month	65%	25%
In 2nd month	18%	7%
In 3rd month	5%	2%
In 4th month	2%	0%
Total	100%	

The controller then uses the following table to derive the ending accounts receivable balance for the month of January, which is part of the budget period. The information from the preceding three months is needed to derive the ending accounts receivable balance in January.

	October (prior year)	November (prior year)	December (prior year)	January
Credit sales	\$815,000	\$820,000	\$790,000	\$810,000
90% of January sales				729,000
25% of December sales				198,000
7% of November sales				57,000
2% of October sales				16,000
Total ending accounts receivable				\$1,000,000

A truly detailed model would assume an even longer collection period for some receivables, which may extend for twice the number of months shown in the model. If you choose to use this method, the increased accuracy from adding more months to the model does not appreciably improve the accuracy of the ending accounts receivable figure. Thus, restrict the accounts receivable layering to no more than three or four months.

The receivables layering method is clearly more labor intensive than the DSO method, though it may result in slightly more accurate results. In the interests of modeling efficiency, we prefer the DSO method. It requires much less space in the budget model, is easy to understand, and produces reasonably accurate results.

Inventory

There should be a relatively constant relationship between the level of sales and the amount of inventory on hand. Thus, if you can calculate the historical number of days of inventory on hand and then match it against the budgeted amount of cost of goods sold through the budget period, you can estimate the amount of inventory that should be on hand at the end of each budget period. The calculation of the days of inventory on hand is:

$$\frac{\text{Inventory}}{\text{Annual cost of goods sold} \div 365 \text{ days}}$$

The estimation concept is shown in the following example.

EXAMPLE

Milagro Corporation has a division that manufactures industrial-grade coffee bean roasters. It maintains a substantial amount of raw materials and finished goods. The company calculates the days of inventory on hand for the preceding quarter as follows:

$$\frac{\$1,000,000 \text{ ending inventory}}{\$1,875,000 \text{ quarterly cost of goods sold} \div 91 \text{ days}}$$

$$= 49 \text{ days of inventory on hand}$$

Milagro expects that the division will continue to have roughly the same proportion of inventory to sales throughout the budget period, so it uses the same days of inventory on hand calculation to derive the ending inventory for each budget period as follows:

	Quarter 1	Quarter 2	Quarter 3	Quarter 4
Cost of goods sold (quarterly)	$1,875,000	$2,000,000	$2,100,000	$1,900,000
Cost of goods sold (monthly)	625,000	667,000	700,000	633,000
Days of inventory assumption	49 days	49 days	49 days	49 days
Ending inventory*	$1,021,000	$1,089,000	$1,143,000	$1,034,000

* Calculated as monthly cost of goods sold × (49 days ÷ 30 days)

The calculation reduces the quarterly cost of goods sold to a monthly figure, so that it can more easily be compared to the days of inventory on hand.

Fixed Assets

The amount and timing of expenditures for fixed assets come from the capital budgeting process (see the Capital Budgeting chapter), and are easily transferred into a fixed asset table that can be used as a source document for the budgeted balance sheet. Further, it may be useful to include in the schedule a standard amount of capital expenditures for each new employee hired; this typically includes the cost of office furniture and computer equipment. Finally, there will always be unforeseen asset purchases, so be sure to reserve some funds for them.

In addition, you can add to the table a calculation of the depreciation associated with newly-acquired assets. Also include an estimate of the depreciation associated with *existing* assets, which you can easily derive either from the fixed asset tracking spreadsheet or software. This information is used in the budgeted income statement.

The following example illustrates the concepts of scheduling fixed assets and depreciation.

EXAMPLE

Milagro Corporation plans to hire 10 administrative staff into one of its divisions during the budget year, and also plans to buy a variety of fixed assets. The following schedule itemizes the major types of fixed assets and the timing of their acquisition. It also includes a summary of the depreciation for both the existing and to-be-acquired assets.

	Quarter 1	Quarter 2	Quarter 3	Quarter 4
Fixed asset purchases:				
Furniture and fixtures	$28,000	$0	$0	$32,000
Office equipment	0	40,000	0	0
Production equipment	100,000	25,000	80,000	0
Vehicles	32,000	0	32,000	0
Unspecified purchases	15,000	15,000	15,000	15,000
Subtotal	$175,000	$80,000	$127,000	$47,000
Purchases for new hires:				
Headcount additions	3	2	1	4
$6,000 × New hires	$18,000	$12,000	$6,000	$24,000
Total fixed asset purchases	$193,000	$92,000	$133,000	$71,000
Depreciation on new purchases:				
Furniture and fixtures (7 year)	$1,000	$1,000	$1,000	$2,142
Office equipment (5 year)	0	2,000	2,000	2,000
Production equipment (10 year)	2,500	3,125	5,125	5,125
Vehicles (5 year)	1,600	1,600	3,200	3,200
Unspecified purchases (5 year)	750	1,500	2,250	3,000
Subtotal	$5,850	$9,225	$13,575	$15,467
Depreciation on existing assets	108,000	107,500	105,000	99,500
Total depreciation	$113,850	$116,725	$118,575	$114,967

Accounts Payable

You can estimate accounts payable with a reasonable amount of precision, because there is usually a constant relationship between the level of credit purchases from suppliers and the amount of unpaid accounts payable. Thus, if you can calculate the days of accounts payable that are usually on hand, then you can relate it to the estimated amount of credit purchases per accounting period and derive the ending accounts payable balance. The formula for accounts payable days is:

$$\frac{\text{Accounts payable}}{\text{Annual credit purchases} \div 365}$$

The estimation concept is illustrated in the following example.

EXAMPLE

Milagro Corporation has a division whose annual purchases on credit in the past year were $4,250,000. Its average accounts payable balance during that period was $410,000. The calculation of its accounts payable days is:

$$\frac{\$410{,}000 \text{ accounts payable}}{\$4{,}250{,}000 \text{ annual credit purchases} \div 365}$$

$$= 35 \text{ accounts payable days}$$

Milagro expects that the division will continue to have roughly the same proportion of credit terms with its suppliers through the budget period, so it uses the same accounts payable days amount to derive the ending accounts payable for each budget period as follows:

	Quarter 1	Quarter 2	Quarter 3	Quarter 4
Purchases on credit (monthly)	$350,000	$380,000	$390,000	$400,000
Accounts payable days assumption	35 days	35 days	35 days	35 days
Ending accounts payable*	$408,000	$443,000	$455,000	$467,000

* Calculated as monthly purchases on credit × (35 days ÷ 30 days)

The problem with the calculation of accounts payable is where to find the information about credit purchases. To calculate the amount of credit purchases, start with the total expenses for the measurement period and subtract from it all payroll and payroll tax expenses, as well as depreciation and amortization. There are other adjusting factors, such as expense accruals and payments made in cash, but this simple calculation should approximate the amount of purchases on credit.

Additional Estimation Elements

There are a few other line items in the balance sheet that require estimation for the budget period. These items are usually adjusted manually, rather than through the use of any formulas. They are:

- *Prepaid expenses*. This line item includes expenses that were paid in advance, and which therefore may be charged to expense at some point during or after the budget period. Examples of prepaid expenses are prepaid rent and insurance. These items may not change in proportion to the level of general corporate activity, so it is best to track them on a separate spreadsheet and manually determine when there will be additions to and deletions from the account.
- *Other assets*. There are likely to be a smorgasbord of stray assets on a company's books that are aggregated into this account. Examples of other assets are rent deposits, payroll advances, and accounts receivable from company officers. As was the case with prepaid expenses, these items may not change in proportion to the level of corporate activity, so track them separately and manually adjust the budget for any changes in them.
- *Income taxes payable*. If a company is earning a taxable profit, then it must make estimated tax payments on the 15th days of April, June, September, and December. You can either schedule these payments to equal the tax paid in the previous year, or a proportion of the actual tax liability in the budget year. Budgeting for this liability based on the tax paid in the previous year is quite simple. If you choose to instead budget for a liability equal to a proportion of the actual tax liability in the budget year, then use the effective tax rate expected for the entire year.

  If you are budgeting for this liability based on the net income in the budget year, it can be difficult to estimate. You may be using accelerated depreciation for the calculation of taxable income, as well as other deferred tax recognition strategies that cause a difference between taxable and actual net income. If such is the case, track these differences in a supporting budget schedule.
- *Accrued liabilities*. There may be a variety of accrued liabilities, such as unpaid vacation time, unpaid wages, and unpaid property taxes. In some cases, such as property taxes, the liability is unlikely to vary unless the company alters its property ownership, and so can be safely extended through the budget period with no alterations. In other cases, such as unpaid vacation time and unpaid wages, there is a direct correlation between the general level of corporate activity (such as headcount) and the amount of the liability. In these cases, use a formula to adjust the liability based on the appropriate underlying measure of activity.
- *Notes payable*. This can encompass loans and leases. Most of these items are on fixed repayment schedules, so a simple repayment table is usually sufficient for tracking the gradual reduction of notes payable. Also, the amount of each periodic debt repayment should be deducted from the

amount of cash on hand. Additions to the notes payable line are addressed in the financing budget.

- *Equity.* The equity section of the balance sheet is composed of a beginning balance that is rolled forward from the previous period, a retained earnings balance into which you incorporate any gains and losses as the budget period progresses over time, and various equity-related financing issues that are addressed in the financing budget.

The Cash Line Item

After filling in all other parts of the balance sheet, the cash line item becomes the "plug" entry to make the statement balance. Just because you enter an amount in the cash line item does not mean that the company will necessarily generate that amount of cash. An early iteration of a budgeted balance sheet has a strange way of revealing an astonishing surplus of cash! Instead, once you have created the initial version of the balance sheet, test it to see if all of the line items are reasonable. Use the following techniques to do so:

- *Growth impact.* If the company is planning on substantial growth, this means that the investment in accounts receivable and inventory should grow significantly, which will consume cash. Conversely, if the company plans to shrink, it should be converting these same items into cash. Thus, if the proposed balance sheet appears to be retaining a consistent amount of working capital through the budget period, irrespective of the sales level, you probably need to revise the working capital line items.
- *Historical comparison.* Compare all line items in the proposed balance sheet to the same line items in the balance sheet for various periods in the preceding year. Are the numbers about the same, or are they approximately in the same proportions to each other? If not, investigate why there are differences.
- *Turnover analysis.* Compare the amount of accounts receivable, inventory, and accounts payable turnover in the proposed budget to the actual turnover ratios for these items in the preceding year. Unless you are making significant structural changes in the business, it is likely that the same turnover ratios should apply to the budget period.

If you are satisfied that the budgeted balance sheet appears reasonable after these tests, then the cash line item may also be considered achievable.

The Financing Budget

Once a first draft of the budget has been prepared and a preliminary balance sheet constructed, you will have an idea of the cash requirements of the business, and can then construct a financing budget.

This budget addresses the need of a business for *more* cash. You can construct a financing budget that addresses this need in two ways:

- *Obtain a loan.* At a minimum, it is usually possible to obtain an asset-based loan (i.e., one that is backed by a company's accounts receivable and inventory). However, these loans are also limited to a proportion of those assets, and so may not be overly large. Other loans that are not tied to assets usually carry a substantially higher interest rate.
- *Sell stock.* If the existing shareholders are amenable, consider selling stock in the company to current or new investors. Unlike a loan, there is no obligation to pay the money back, so this addition to equity reduces the financial risk of the company. However, investors expect a high return on their investment through an increase in the value of the company or increased dividends.

In addition to these financing solutions, also consider going back into the main budget and making one or more of the following changes, thereby altering the amount of cash needed by the business:

- *Cost reduction.* There may be some parts of the business where expenses can be pruned in order to fund more activities elsewhere. Across-the-board reductions are usually a bad idea, since some parts of the business may already be running at a minimal expenditure level, and further reductions would cut into their performance.
- *Discretionary items.* If there are discretionary expenditures in the budget whose absence will not have an immediate impact on the business, consider reducing or eliminating them or changing the date on which you purchase them.
- *Dividends.* If there are dividends planned that have not yet been authorized by the board of directors, consider either reducing them or delaying the payment date.
- *Sales growth.* If the budgeted level of sales is creating a significant requirement for more working capital and capital expenditures, consider reducing the amount of planned growth to meet the amount of financing that you have available.
- *Sell assets.* If there is a strong need for cash that is driven by an excellent business opportunity, it may be time to sell off assets in lower-performing parts of the business and invest the funds in the new opportunity.

Once you have made all of the preceding adjustments, construct the financing budget. It should contain an itemization of the cash position as stated in the budgeted balance sheet, after which you itemize the various types of financing needed to ensure that the company maintains a positive cash balance at all times. In addition, there should be a section that derives from the balance sheet the total amount that the company can potentially borrow against its assets; this establishes an upper limit on the amount of borrowing. The following example illustrates the concept of the financing budget.

EXAMPLE

Milagro Corporation has completed a first draft of its budget, and finds that there are several cash shortfalls during the budget period. The controller constructs the following financing budget to address the problem.

	Quarter 1	Quarter 2	Quarter 3	Quarter 4
Available asset base:				
Ending inventory	$1,200,000	$1,280,000	$1,310,000	$1,350,000
Ending trade receivables	1,800,000	1,850,000	1,920,000	1,980,000
Allowable inventory (60%)	720,000	768,000	786,000	810,000
Allowable receivables (80%)	1,440,000	1,480,000	1,536,000	1,584,000
Total borrowing base	$2,160,000	$2,248,000	$2,322,000	$2,394,000
Preliminary ending cash balance	-$320,000	-$480,000	-$600,000	-$680,000
Debt Funding:				
Beginning loan balance	$2,000,000			
Available debt*	160,000	88,000	74,000	72,000
Adjusted ending cash balance	-160,000	-$232,000	-$278,000	-$286,000
Equity Funding:				
Stock issuance	$400,000	0	0	0
Final ending cash balance	$240,000	$168,000	$122,000	$114,000

* Calculated as the total borrowing base minus existing debt

The financing budget reveals that Milagro has already used most of the debt available under its loan agreement, and is only able to incrementally borrow in each quarter as the amount of underlying assets gradually increases. To fund the remaining cash shortfall, Milagro plans to sell $400,000 of stock to investors in the first quarter. This not only provides enough cash to cover the projected shortfall, but also leaves a small residual cash buffer.

If the financing budget includes a provision for more debt, you must also include a line item in the budgeted income statement to address the associated incremental increase in interest expense. This means that there is a feedback loop between the financing budget and the balance sheet from which it draws its beginning cash balance; your financing solutions may impact the beginning cash balance upon which the financing budget is based, which in turn may impact the amount of financing needed.

The Compiled Balance Sheet

The budgeted balance sheet is derived from the all of the preceding discussions in this section about the components of the balance sheet. The balance sheet should be compiled in two parts: a detailed compilation that contains a variety of calculations, and a summary-level version that is indistinguishable from a normal balance sheet. The following sample of a detailed balance sheet compilation includes a discussion of each line item. The numbers in the sample are irrelevant – we are only showing how the balance sheet is constructed.

Sample Detailed Balance Sheet Compilation

Line Item	Source	Amount
Assets		
Cash	The amount needed to equalize both sides of the balance sheet	$225,000
Accounts receivable	Based on sales by period and days receivables outstanding	450,000
Inventory	Based on cost of goods sold by period and days of inventory on hand	520,000
Prepaid expenses	Based on beginning balance and adjusted for specific changes	55,000
Fixed assets	Based on beginning balance and changes in the capital budget	1,490,000
Accumulated depreciation	Based on beginning balance and changes in the capital budget	-230,000
Other assets	Based on beginning balance and adjusted for specific changes	38,000
Total assets		$2,548,000
Liabilities		
Accounts payable	Based on credit purchases and days of accounts payable	$182,000
Accrued liabilities	Based on schedule of specific liabilities or based on corporate activity	99,000
Income taxes payable	Based on either the tax paid in the previous year or a proportion of the actual tax liability in the current year	75,000
Notes payable	Based on the beginning balance	720,000
- Debt repayments	Based on a schedule of required repayments	-120,000
+ New debt	From the financing budget	90,000
Total liabilities		$1,046,000

Line Item	Source	Amount
Equity		
Retained earnings	Based on the beginning balance	802,000
- Dividends	As per management instructions	-75,000
- Treasury stock purchases	As per management instructions	-50,000
+ Profit/loss	From the budgeted income statement	475,000
+ Stock sales	From the financing budget	350,000
Total equity		$1,502,000
Total liabilities and equity		$2,548,000

Summary

This chapter has addressed how to compile an annual budget, using a variety of supporting schedules to create a budgeted income statement and balance sheet. When creating this budget, be careful to examine how well the various elements of the budget support each other, and whether the budgeted outcome is a reasonable extension of how well the company has performed in the past. If not, recommend another iteration of the budget to correct these potential problem areas. If senior management instead elects to operate under the current budget version, it is likely that actual results will soon depart from budgeted expectations.

Despite the length of this chapter, it is actually a relatively brief treatment of the budgeting concept. For a more comprehensive view of budgeting, and also a discussion of how to operate without a budget, see the author's *Budgeting* book, which is available on the accountingtools.com website.

Chapter 17
Capital Budgeting

Introduction

Capital budgeting is a series of analysis steps used to evaluate whether a fixed asset should be purchased, usually including an analysis of the costs, related benefits, and impact on capacity levels of the prospective purchase. In this chapter, we will address a broad array of issues to consider when deciding whether to recommend the purchase of a fixed asset, as well as the lease versus buy decision, and post-acquisition auditing.

Related Podcast Episodes: Episodes 45, 144, 145, 147, and 214 of the Accounting Best Practices Podcast discuss throughput capital budgeting, evaluating capital budgeting proposals, capital budgeting with minimal cash, net present value analysis, and discounted cash flows, respectively. You can listen to them at: **accountingtools.com/podcasts** or **iTunes**

Controller Responsibilities

The controller is usually responsible for the budgeting process, of which capital budgeting is a part. If so, the controller may have accounting employees reviewing capital budget proposals, and may also be involved in the decisions to outsource, lease, or buy assets. Thus, the controller's responsibilities are:

- Maintain a capital budgeting review process
- Conduct post-installation reviews of fixed assets
- Participate in the lease or buy decision for fixed assets

Overview of Capital Budgeting

The normal capital budgeting process is for the management team to request proposals to acquire fixed assets from all parts of the company. Managers respond by filling out a standard request form, outlining what they want to buy and how it will benefit the company. The financial analyst or accountant then assists in reviewing these proposals to determine which are worthy of an investment. Any proposals that are accepted are included in the annual budget, and will be purchased during the next budget year. Fixed assets purchased in this manner also require a certain number of approvals, with more approvals required by increasingly senior levels of management if the sums involved are substantial.

These proposals come from all over the company, and so are likely not related to each other in any way. Also, the number of proposals usually far exceeds the amount of funding available. Consequently, management needs a method for ranking the priority of projects, with the possible result that some proposals are not accepted at all. The traditional method for doing so is net present value (NPV) analysis, which focuses on picking proposals with the largest amount of discounted cash flows.

The trouble with NPV analysis is that it does not account for how an investment might impact the profit generated by the entire system of production; instead, it tends to favor the optimization of specific work centers, which may have no particular impact on overall profitability. Also, the results of NPV are based on the future projections of cash flows, which may be wildly inaccurate. Managers may even tweak their cash flow estimates upward in order to gain project approval, when they know that actual cash flows are likely to be lower. Given these issues, we favor constraint analysis over NPV, though NPV is also discussed in this chapter.

A better method for judging capital budget proposals is constraint analysis, which focuses on how to maximize use of the bottleneck operation. The bottleneck operation is the most constricted operation in a company; if you want to improve the overall profitability of the company, then you must concentrate all attention on management of that bottleneck. This has a profound impact on capital budgeting, since a proposal should have some favorable impact on that operation in order to be approved.

There are two scenarios under which certain project proposals may avoid any kind of bottleneck or cash flow analysis. The first is a legal requirement to install an item. The prime example is environmental equipment, such as smokestack scrubbers, that are mandated by the government. In such cases, there may be some analysis to see if costs can be lowered, but the proposal *must* be accepted, so it will sidestep the normal analysis process.

The second scenario is when a company wants to mitigate a high-risk situation that could imperil the company. In this case, the emphasis is not on profitability at all, but rather on the avoidance of a situation. If so, the mandate likely comes from top management, so there is little additional need for analysis, other than a review to ensure that the lowest-cost alternative is selected.

A final scenario is when there is a sudden need for a fixed asset, perhaps due to the catastrophic failure of existing equipment or a strategic shift. These purchases can happen at any time, and so usually fall outside of the capital budget's annual planning cycle. It is generally best to require more than the normal number of approvals for these items, so that management is made fully aware of the situation. Also, if there is time to do so, they are worthy of an unusually intense analysis, to see if they really must be purchased at once, or if they can be delayed until the next capital budgeting approval period arrives.

Once all items are properly approved and inserted into the annual budget, this does not end the capital budgeting process. There is a final review just prior to actually making each purchase, with appropriate approval, to ensure that the company still needs each fixed asset.

The last step in the capital budgeting process is to conduct a post-implementation review, in which you summarize the actual costs and benefits of each fixed asset, and compare these results to the initial projections included in the original application. If the results are worse than expected, this may result in a more in-depth review, with particular attention being paid to avoiding any faulty aspects of the original proposal in future proposals.

Constraint Analysis

Under constraint analysis, the key concept is that an entire company acts as a single system, which generates a profit. Under this concept, capital budgeting revolves around the following logic:

1. Nearly all of the costs of the production system do not vary with individual sales; that is, nearly every cost is an operating expense; therefore,
2. You need to maximize the throughput (revenues minus totally variable costs) of the *entire* system in order to pay for the operating expense; and
3. The only way to increase throughput is to maximize the throughput passing through the bottleneck operation.

Consequently, give primary consideration to those capital budgeting proposals that favorably impact the throughput passing through the bottleneck operation.

From the perspective of constraint management, the only capital investments that should be made in a business are ones that will either increase throughput or reduce operating expenses. When this priority is assigned to capital requests, it is entirely likely that an organization will be able to avoid a number of asset purchases. The following asset requests can be avoided:

1. *Local optimization.* A request may be to increase the efficiency of a workstation that does nothing to increase throughput. If so, the investment is wasted, since the company invests funds and receives no return on its investment.
2. *Sprint capacity increase.* Sprint capacity is excess production capacity positioned upstream from the bottleneck operation. It is needed to ensure that inventory can be rushed to the bottleneck operation to keep it functioning at all times. A request may involve an increase in sprint capacity. If so, review the request to see if the size of the capacity increase is reasonable, based on the company's expectations for the amount of sprint capacity needed.
3. *Constraint capacity increase.* What if a proposed investment *is* designed to increase the capacity of the constraint? If so, compare the projected amount of incremental new capacity to the projected amount of capacity needed to fulfill throughput requirements. It is entirely possible that the investment will create too much capacity, which merely shifts the constraint to a different location in the company. The appropriate response is to scale back the amount of the investment to only build the required amount of additional capacity.
4. *Expense reduction.* If a capital request is not addressed by the preceding review steps, this means the only remaining justification is that the invest-

ment will reduce operating expenses. If so, subject the request to an especially detailed review, with a particular emphasis on the assumptions used to prove that expenses will indeed be reduced. Unless there is a high probability of an adequate expense reduction *and* a low probability of a cost overrun on the investment, reject the request.

The decision to increase the capacity of the constrained resource is a particularly important one. This resource is likely to be the constraint in the system precisely because it is quite expensive to increase the capacity level. Consequently, investments in this area require a considerable amount of investigation. A possible outcome is that these types of investments are delayed until such time as management has accumulated more information about the likelihood of future changes in capacity requirements.

Net Present Value Analysis

Any capital investment involves an initial cash outflow to pay for it, followed by a mix of cash inflows in the form of revenue, or a decline in existing cash flows that are caused by expense reductions. We can lay out this information in a spreadsheet to show all expected cash flows over the useful life of an investment, and then apply a discount rate that reduces the cash flows to what they would be worth at the present date. A discount rate is the interest rate used to discount a stream of future cash flows to their present value. Depending upon the application, typical rates used as the discount rate are a firm's cost of capital or the current market rate. This cash flows calculation is known as *net present value*.

Net present value is the traditional approach to evaluating capital proposals, since it is based on a single factor – cash flows – that can be used to judge any proposal arriving from anywhere in a company. However, the net present value method can be a poor evaluation method if you suspect that the cash flows used to derive an analysis are incorrect.

EXAMPLE

Milagro Corporation is planning to acquire an asset that it expects will yield positive cash flows for the next five years. Its cost of capital is 10%, which it uses as the discount rate to construct the net present value of the project. The following table shows the calculation:

Year	Cash Flow	10% Discount Factor	Present Value
0	-$500,000	1.0000	-$500,000
1	+130,000	0.9091	+118,183
2	+130,000	0.8265	+107,445
3	+130,000	0.7513	+97,669
4	+130,000	0.6830	+88,790
5	+130,000	0.6209	+80,717
		Net Present Value	-$7,196

The net present value of the proposed project is negative at the 10% discount rate, so Milagro should not invest in the project.

In the "10% Discount Factor" column, the factor becomes smaller for periods further in the future, because the discounted value of cash flows are reduced as they progress further from the present day. The discount factor is widely available in textbooks, or can be derived from the following formula:

$$\text{Present value of a future cash flow} = \frac{\text{Future cash flow}}{(1 + \text{Discount rate})^{\text{squared by the number of periods of discounting}}}$$

To use the formula for an example, if we forecast the receipt of $100,000 in one year, and are using a discount rate of 10 percent, then the calculation is:

$$\text{Present value} = \frac{\$100{,}000}{(1+.10)^{1}}$$

Present value = $90,909

A net present value calculation that truly reflects the reality of cash flows will likely be more complex than the one shown in the preceding example. It is best to break down the analysis into a number of sub-categories, so that you can see exactly when cash flows are occurring and with what activities they are associated. Here are the more common contents of a net present value analysis:

- *Asset purchases.* All of the expenditures associated with the purchase, delivery, installation, and testing of the asset being purchased.
- *Asset-linked expenses.* Any ongoing expenses, such as warranty agreements, property taxes, and maintenance, that are associated with the asset.
- *Contribution margin.* Any incremental cash flows resulting from sales that can be attributed to the project.
- *Depreciation effect.* The asset will be depreciated, and this depreciation shelters a portion of any net income from income taxes, so note the income tax reduction caused by depreciation.
- *Expense reductions.* Any incremental expense reductions caused by the project, such as automation that eliminates direct labor hours.
- *Tax credits.* If an asset purchase triggers a tax credit (such as for a purchase of energy-reduction equipment), then note the amount of the credit.
- *Taxes.* Any income tax payments associated with net income expected to be derived from the asset.

- *Working capital changes.* Any net changes in inventory, accounts receivable, or accounts payable associated with the asset. Also, when the asset is eventually sold off, this may trigger a reversal of the initial working capital changes.

By itemizing the preceding factors in a net present value analysis, you can more easily review and revise individual line items.

We have given priority to bottleneck analysis over net present value as the preferred method for analyzing capital proposals, because bottleneck analysis focuses on throughput. The key improvement factor is throughput, since there is no upper limit on the amount of throughput that can be generated, whereas there are only so many operating expenses that can be reduced. This does not mean that net present value should be eliminated as a management tool. It is still quite useful for operating expense reduction analysis, where throughput issues are not involved.

The Payback Method

The most discerning method for evaluating a capital budgeting proposal is its impact on the bottleneck operation, while net present value analysis yields a detailed analysis of cash flows. The simplest and least accurate evaluation technique is the payback method. This approach is still heavily used, because it provides a very fast "back of the envelope" calculation of how soon a company will earn back its investment. This means that it provides a rough measure of how long a company will have its investment at risk before earning back the original amount expended. Thus, it is a rough measure of risk. There are two ways to calculate the payback period, which are:

1. *Simplified.* Divide the total amount of an investment by the average resulting cash flow. This approach can yield an incorrect assessment, because a proposal with cash flows skewed far into the future can yield a payback period that differs substantially from when actual payback occurs.
2. *Manual calculation.* Manually deduct the forecasted positive cash flows from the initial investment amount from Year 1 forward, until the investment is paid back. This method is slower, but ensures a higher degree of accuracy.

EXAMPLE

Milagro Corporation has received a proposal from a manager, asking to spend $1,500,000 on equipment that will result in cash inflows in accordance with the following table:

Year	Cash Flow
1	+$150,000
2	+150,000
3	+200,000
4	+600,000
5	+900,000

The total cash flows over the five-year period are projected to be \$2,000,000, which is an average of \$400,000 per year. When divided into the \$1,500,000 original investment, this results in a payback period of 3.75 years. However, the briefest perusal of the projected cash flows reveals that the flows are heavily weighted toward the far end of the time period, so the results of this calculation cannot be correct.

Instead, the controller runs the calculation year by year, deducting the cash flows in each successive year from the remaining investment. The results of this calculation are:

Year	Cash Flow	Net Invested Cash
0		-\$1,500,000
1	+\$150,000	-1,350,000
2	+150,000	-1,200,000
3	+200,000	-1,000,000
4	+600,000	-400,000
5	+900,000	0

The table indicates that the real payback period is located somewhere between Year 4 and Year 5. There is \$400,000 of investment yet to be paid back at the end of Year 4, and there is \$900,000 of cash flow projected for Year 5. The controller assumes the same monthly amount of cash flow in Year 5, which means that he can estimate final payback as being just short of 4.5 years.

The payback method is not overly accurate, does not provide any estimate of how profitable a project may be, and does not take account of the time value of money. Nonetheless, its extreme simplicity makes it a perennial favorite in many companies.

Capital Budget Proposal Analysis

Reviewing a capital budget proposal does not necessarily mean passing judgment on it exactly as presented. You can attach a variety of suggestions to your analysis of the proposal, which management may incorporate into a revised proposal. Here are some examples:

- *Asset capacity*. Does the asset have more capacity than is actually needed under the circumstances? Is there a history of usage spikes that call for extra capacity? Depending on the answers to these questions, consider using smaller assets with less capacity. If the asset is powered, this may also lead to reductions in utility costs, installation costs, and floor space requirements.
- *Asset commoditization*. Wherever possible, avoid custom-designed machinery in favor of standard models that are readily available. By doing so, it is easier to obtain repair parts, and there may even be an aftermarket for disposing of the asset when the company no longer needs it.

- *Asset features.* Managers have a habit of wanting to buy new assets with all of the latest features. Are all of these features really needed? If an asset is being replaced, then it is useful to compare the characteristics of the old and new assets, and examine any differences between the two to see if they are required. If the asset is the only model offered by the supplier, would the supplier be willing to strip away some features and offer it at a lower price?
- *Asset standardization.* If a company needs a particular asset in large quantities, then adopt a policy of always buying from the same manufacturer, and preferably only buying the same asset every time. By doing so, the maintenance staff becomes extremely familiar with the maintenance requirements of several identical machines, and only has to stock replacement parts for one model.
- *Bottleneck analysis.* As noted earlier in this chapter, assets that improve the amount of throughput in a production operation are usually well worth the investment, while those not impacting the bottleneck require substantially more justification, usually in the direction of reducing operating expenses.
- *Extended useful life.* A manager may be applying for an asset replacement simply because the original asset has reached the end of its recommended useful life. But is it really necessary to replace the asset? Consider conducting a formal review of these assets to see if they can still be used for some additional period of time. There may be additional maintenance costs involved, but this will almost certainly be lower than the cost of replacing the asset.
- *Facility analysis.* If a capital proposal involves the acquisition of additional facility space, consider reviewing any existing space to see if it can be compressed, thereby eliminating the need for more space. For example, shift storage items to less expensive warehouse space, shift from offices to more space-efficient cubicles, and encourage employees to work from home or on a later shift. If none of these ideas work, then at least consider acquiring new facilities through a sublease, which tends to require shorter lease terms than a lease arranged with the primary landlord.
- *Monument elimination.* A company may have a large fixed asset around which the rest of the production area is configured; this is called a monument. If there is a monument, consider adopting a policy of using a larger number of lower-capacity assets. By doing so, you avoid the risk of having a single monument asset go out of service and stopping all production, in favor of having multiple units among which work can be shifted if one unit fails.

The sponsors of capital proposals frequently do *not* appreciate this additional review of their proposals, since it implies that they did not consider these issues themselves. Nonetheless, the savings can be substantial, and so are well worth the aggravation of dealing with annoyed managers.

The Outsourcing Decision

It may be possible to avoid a capital purchase entirely by outsourcing the work to which it is related. By doing so, the company may be able to eliminate all assets related to the area (rather than acquiring more assets), while the burden of maintaining a sufficient asset base now shifts to the supplier. The supplier may even buy the company's assets related to the area being outsourced. This situation is a well-established alternative for high technology manufacturing, as well as for information technology services, but is likely not viable outside of these areas.

If you are in a situation where outsourcing is a possibility, then the likely cash flows resulting from doing so will be highly favorable for the first few years, as capital expenditures vanish. However, the supplier must also earn a profit and pay for its own infrastructure, so the cost over the long term will probably not vary dramatically from what a company would have experienced if it had kept a functional area in-house. There are three exceptions that can bring about a long-term cost reduction. They are:

- *Excess capacity*. A supplier may have such a large amount of excess capacity already that it does not need to invest further for some time, thereby potentially depressing the costs that it would otherwise pass through to its customers. However, this excess capacity pool will eventually dry up, so it tends to be a short-term anomaly.
- *High volume*. There are some outsourcing situations where the supplier is handling such a massive volume of activity from multiple customers that its costs on a per-unit basis decline below the costs that a company could ever achieve on its own. This situation can yield long-term savings to a company.
- *Low costs*. A supplier may locate its facility and work force in low-cost countries or regions within countries. This can yield significant cost reductions in the short term, but as many suppliers use the same technique, it is driving up costs in all parts of the world. Thus, this cost disparity is useful for a period of time, but is gradually declining as a long-term option.

There are risks involved in shifting functions to suppliers. First, a supplier may go out of business, leaving the company scrambling to shift work to a new supplier. Second, a supplier may gradually ramp up prices to the point where the company is substantially worse off than if it had kept the function in-house. Third, the company may have so completely purged the outsourced function from its own operations that it is now completely dependent on the supplier, and has no ability to take it back in-house. Fourth, the supplier's service level may decline to the point where it is impairing the ability of the company to operate. And finally, the company may have entered into a multi-year deal, and cannot escape from the arrangement if the business arrangement does not work out. These are significant issues, and must be weighed as part of the outsourcing decision.

The cautions noted here about outsourcing do not mean that it should be avoided as an option. On the contrary, a rapidly growing company that has minimal access to funds may cheerfully hand off multiple operations to suppliers in order to avoid the up-front costs associated with those operations. Outsourcing is less attractive to stable, well-established companies that have better access to capital.

In summary, outsourcing is an attractive option for rapidly growing companies that do not have sufficient cash to pay for capital expenditures, but also carries with it a variety of risks involving shifting key functions to a supplier over which a company may not have a great deal of control.

The Capital Budgeting Application Form

Most companies require managers to fill out a standardized form for all capital budgeting proposals. The type of information that you include in the form will vary, depending on whether you are basing the approval decision on bottleneck considerations or the results of a net present value analysis. However, the header section of the form will likely be the same in all circumstances. It identifies the project, its sponsor, the date on which it was submitted, and a unique product identification number that is filled in by the recipient. A sample header is:

Sample Application Header

Project name:	*50 ton coffee roaster*		
Project sponsor:	*J. R. Valdez*		
Submission date:	*May 28*	Project number:	*2017-10*

If a proposal is for a legal requirement or a risk mitigation issue, then it is absolved from most analysis, and will likely move to the top of the approved project list. Consequently, the form should contain a separate section for these types of projects, and should involve a different set of approvers. The corporate attorney may be involved, as well as anyone involved in risk management. A sample block in the application form for legal and risk mitigation issues is:

Sample Legal and Risk Mitigation Block

		Required Approvals	
Initial cash flow:	*-$250,000*	All proposals	*Susan Lafferty*
Year 1 cash flow:	*-10,000*		Attorney
Year 2 cash flow:	*-10,000*		
Year 3 cash flow:	*-10,000*	< $100,000	*George Mason*
			Risk Officer
Describe legal or risk mitigation issue:			
Construction of coffee grounds firing facility, per new zoning requirements		$100,000+	*Fred Scurry* President

If you elect to focus on bottleneck considerations for capital budgeting approvals, then include the following block of text in the application form. This block focuses on the changes in cash flow that are associated with a capital expenditure. The block requests an itemization of the cash flows involved in the purchase (primarily for finance planning considerations), followed by requests for information about how the investment will help the company – via an improvement in throughput, a reduction in operating costs, or an increase in the return on investment. In the example, note that the primary improvement used as the basis for the proposal is the improvement in throughput. This also leads to an enhancement of the return on investment. There is an increase in the total net operating cost, which represents a reduction in the positive effect of the throughput, and which is caused by the annual $8,000 maintenance cost associated with the investment.

The approvals for a bottleneck-related investment change from the ones shown previously for a legal or risk mitigation investment. In this case, a process analyst should verify the information included in the block, to ensure that the applicant's claims are correct. The supervisor in whose area of responsibility the investment falls should also sign off, thereby accepting responsibility for the outcome of the investment. A higher-level manager, or even the board of directors, should approve any really large investment proposals.

Sample Bottleneck Approval Block

		Required Approvals	
Initial cash flow:	*-$125,000*	All proposals	*Monica Byers*
Year 1 cash flow:	*-8,000*		Process Analyst
Year 2 cash flow:	*-8,000*		
Year 3 cash flow:	*-8,000*	< $100,000	*Al Rogers*
			Responsible Supervisor
Net throughput change:*	*+$180,000*		
		$100,000+	*Fred Scurry*
Net operating cost change:*	*+$8,000*		President
Change in ROI:*	*+0.08%*		

* On an annual basis

If you do not choose to use a bottleneck-oriented application, then the following block may be useful instead. It is based on the more traditional analysis of net present value. You may also consider using this block as a supplement to the bottleneck block just noted, in case some managers prefer to work with both sets of information.

Sample Net Present Value Approval Block

Year	Cash Out (payments)	Cash In (Revenue)	Incremental Tax Effect	Totals
0	-$1,000,000			-$1,000,000
1	-25,000	+$200,000	+$8,750	+183,750
2	-25,000	+400,000	-61,250	+313,750
3	-25,000	+400,000	-61,250	+313,750
4	-25,000	+400,000	-61,250	+313,750
5	-25,000	+400,000	-61,250	+313,750
Totals	-$1,125,000	+$1,800,000	-$236,250	+$438,750
			Tax Rate:	35%
			Hurdle Rate:	12%
			Net Present Value:	+$13,328

The net present value block requires the presentation of cash flows over a five-year period, as well as the net tax effect resulting from this specific transaction. The tax effect is based on $25,000 of maintenance expenses in every year shown, as well as $200,000 of annual depreciation, and a 35% incremental tax rate. Thus, in Year 2, there is $400,000 of revenue, less $225,000 of depreciation and maintenance expenses, multiplied by 35%, resulting in an incremental tax effect of $61,250.

The block then goes on to state the corporate hurdle rate, which is 12% in the example. We then discount the stream of cash flows from the project at the hurdle rate of 12%, which results in a positive net present value of $13,328. Based on just the net present value analysis, this appears to be an acceptable project.

The text blocks shown here contain much of the key information that management should see before it decides whether to approve a capital investment. In addition, there should be detailed supporting information that precisely describes the nature of the proposed investment, as well as backup information that supports each number included in the form.

The Post Installation Review

It is important to conduct a post installation review of any capital expenditure project, to see if the initial expectations for it were realized. If not, then the results of this review can be used to modify the capital budgeting process to include better information.

Another reason for having a post installation review is that it provides a control over those managers who fill out the initial capital budgeting proposals. If they know there is no post installation review, then they can wildly overstate the forecasted results of their projects with impunity, just to have them approved. Of course, this control is only useful if it is conducted relatively soon after a project is completed. Otherwise, the responsible manager may have moved on in his career, and can no longer be tied back to the results of his work.

It is even better to begin a post installation review while a project is still being implemented, and especially when the implementation period is expected to be long. This initial review gives senior management a good idea of whether the cost of a project is staying close to its initial expectations. If not, management may need to authorize more vigorous management of the project, scale it back, or even cancel it outright.

If the post implementation review results in the suspicion that a project proposal was unduly optimistic, this brings up the question of how to deal with the responsible manager. At a minimum, the proposal reviews can flag any future proposals by this reviewer as suspect, and worthy of especially close attention.

EXAMPLE

Milagro Corporation has just completed a one-year project to increase the amount of production capacity at its primary coffee roasting facility. The original capital budgeting proposal was for an initial expenditure of \$290,000, resulting in additional annual throughput of \$100,000 per year. The actual result is somewhat different. The controller's report includes the following text:

> **Findings:** The proposal only contained the purchase price of the equipment. However, since the machinery was delivered from Columbia, Milagro also incurred \$22,000 of freight charges and \$3,000 in customs fees. Further, the project required the installation of a new concrete pad, a breaker box, and electrical wiring that cost an additional \$10,000. Finally, the equipment proved to be difficult to configure, and required \$20,000 of consulting fees from the manufacturer, as well as \$5,000 for the raw materials scrapped during testing. Thus, the actual cost of the project was \$350,000.
>
> Subsequent operation of the equipment reveals that it cannot operate without an average of 20% downtime for maintenance, as opposed to the 5% downtime that was advertised by the manufacturer. This reduces throughput by 15%, which equates to a drop of \$15,000 in throughput per year, to \$85,000.
>
> **Recommendations:** To incorporate a more comprehensive set of instructions into the capital budgeting proposal process to account for transportation, setup, and testing costs. Also, given the wide difference between the performance claims of the manufacturer and actual results, to hire a consultant to see if the problem is caused by our installation of the equipment; if not, we recommend not buying from this supplier in the future.

The Lease versus Buy Decision

Once the asset acquisition decision has been made, management still needs to decide if it should buy the asset outright or lease it. In a leasing situation, a lessor buys the asset and then allows the lessee to use it in exchange for a monthly fee. The decision to use a lease may be based on management's unwillingness to use its line of credit or other available sources of financing to buy an asset. Leases can be easier to obtain than a line of credit, since the lease agreement always designates the asset as collateral. Collateral is an asset that a borrower has pledged as security for a loan. The lender has the legal right to seize and sell the asset if the borrower is unable to pay back the loan by an agreed date.

There are a multitude of factors that a lessor includes in the formulation of the monthly rate that it charges, such as the down payment, the residual value of the asset at the end of the lease, and the interest rate, which makes it difficult to break out and examine each element of the lease. Instead, it is much easier to create separate net present value tables for the lease and buy alternatives, and then compare the results of the two tables to see which is the better alternative.

EXAMPLE

Milagro Corporation is contemplating the purchase of an asset for $500,000. It can buy the asset outright, or do so with a lease. Its cost of capital is 8%, and its incremental income tax rate is 35%. The following two tables show the net present values of both options.

Buy Option

Year	Depreciation	Income Tax Savings (35%)	Discount Factor (8%)	Net Present Value
0				-$500,000
1	$100,000	$35,000	0.9259	32,407
2	100,000	35,000	0.8573	30,006
3	100,000	35,000	0.7938	27,783
4	100,000	35,000	0.7350	25,725
5	100,000	35,000	0.6806	23,821
Totals	$500,000	$175,000		$360,258

Lease Option

Year	Pretax Lease Payments	Income Tax Savings (35%)	After-Tax Lease Cost	Discount Factor (8%)	Net Present Value
1	$135,000	47,250	$87,750	0.9259	$81,248
2	135,000	47,250	87,750	0.8573	75,228
3	135,000	47,250	87,750	0.7938	69,656
4	135,000	47,250	87,750	0.7350	64,496
5	135,000	47,250	87,750	0.6806	59,723
Totals	$675,000	$236,250	$438,750		$350,351

Thus, the net purchase cost of the buy option is $360,258, while the net purchase cost of the lease option is $350,351. The lease option involves the lowest cash outflow for Milagro, and so is the better option.

Summary

This chapter addressed a variety of issues to consider when deciding whether to recommend the purchase of a fixed asset. We put less emphasis on net present value analysis, which has been the primary capital budgeting tool in industry for years, because it does not take into consideration the impact on throughput of a company's bottleneck operation. The best capital budgeting analysis process is to give top priority to project proposals that have a strong favorable impact on throughput, and then use net present value to evaluate the impact of any remaining projects on cost reduction.

For a detailed explanation of bottlenecks and throughput, see the author's *Constraint Management* book, which is available on the accountingtools.com website.

Chapter 18
Computer System Selection and Installation

Introduction

The most expensive, prolonged, and risky project that a controller is likely to ever be engaged in is the selection and installation of a new accounting computer system. The selection process involves defining the company's needs for a new system and matching those needs to the offerings of qualified system suppliers. The installation process involves the methodical conversion of existing data to the new system, creating interfaces to link it to other systems within (or outside of) the company, and training employees to use it. In this chapter, we cover how to proceed through the selection and installation minefields.

Controller Responsibilities

The controller is directly responsible for the selection and installation of accounting computer systems. This responsibility is one that most controllers would rather avoid, since a seamless installation is generally ignored by the rest of the company, while a botched installation causes disruptions everywhere and is highly visible. The following responsibilities apply to the controller:

- Select an accounting computer system that meets the expected needs of the business.
- Properly install accounting computer systems, so that the general business of the company is not interrupted.

Computer System Selection

There are many accounting computer systems to choose from, so you need to create a process for defining the requirements of the system and evaluating systems based on those requirements. The steps and inherent time requirements noted in this section for a proper system selection may appear considerable. However, having the proper accounting system can be an important factor in the smooth operation of a business, so the selection team must allocate the time to choose the best system. To do so, shunt aside as many other accounting activities as possible until the selection process has been completed. The key steps in the selection process are noted in the following sub-sections.

Requirements Development

The first step in the system selection process is to develop a set of requirements for what you need. Depending upon how comprehensive you want the system to be, the requirements list will cover some or all of the following functional areas:

- Accounts payable
- Accounts receivable / billing
- Bank reconciliations
- Budgeting
- Employee expense reporting
- Fixed assets
- General ledger
- Inventory
- Order entry
- Purchasing
- Time recording

You could develop this list of requirements yourself, but this is an area in which it makes sense to hire a consultant from an accounting firm. Consultants have a boilerplate set of requirements, which makes it nearly certain that you will at least address every conceivable system requirement. Continue to employ consultants throughout the selection and implementation process, since they have more expertise than the in-house staff.

It is best to expand upon the basic checklist by conducting several forms of investigation to see if the company wants a system based on the current state of affairs, or (better yet) a system that more closely matches where the company's managers want it to be in the near future. You can issue questionnaires to system users to inquire about these changes, but a better approach is to schedule a number of executive interviews, since you can ask follow-up questions to obtain a greater understanding of the company's future requirements. The general areas worth considering during these meetings include:

- What is the opinion of the management group of the current accounting system?
- What are the expectations of the group for a new system?
- Are there going to be changes to the business that should be considered in the selection of the new system?

Tip: If the company plans to embark on a series of acquisitions, this can radically alter your concept of the most appropriate accounting system, since you may then need a much more complex solution that links together multiple locations.

Also conduct a complete walkthrough of the current system, incorporating copies of the forms used to input information into the existing system, to gain a detailed view of exactly how the current system is used. This analysis should include documentation of all interfaces with other systems, control points, and reports generated. It is especially important to estimate the transaction volumes currently running through the system, since there are a reduced number of accounting systems on the market that can handle higher-volume operations.

The final step in developing a proper set of system requirements is to assemble users of the system to review the requirements for each system module. For example, have all users of the accounts payable module discuss the requirements of that specific module, and then have another meeting for users of the general ledger module, and so on. During these meetings, the team should identify every requirement for the system, as well as the level of priority for having it in the new system. Thus, every requirement should be designated as either mandatory or useful but not necessary.

These user meetings are most effective when an initial set of boilerplate requirements can be projected onto a screen for everyone to view, and then interactively adjusted on-screen as the group provides input.

Tip: Use consultants for this requirements development phase, since they have expertise in conducting interviews and facilitating user meetings.

The resulting list of system requirements should be very detailed. The following is an abbreviated example of the system requirements for an accounts payable system:

General Requirements

- Post to expense accounts based on preconfigured settings by supplier
- Accept multiple address records for the same supplier
- Interface with the purchasing module
- Supplier interface accessible through website for payment status inquiries
- Automatic flagging of duplicate invoice numbers

Vendor Master File Contents

- Supplier name
- Supplier number
- Supplier mailing address
- Supplier payment address
- Supplier ABA and bank account number
- Supplier tax identification number
- Form W-9 receipt flag

Reporting Requirements

- Accounts payable aging report
- Cash disbursements register

Search Requirements

- Online record searches based on supplier number, supplier name, and invoice number
- Drill down capability for the current and immediately preceding year

Assemble more detailed requirements for all desired accounting system modules than the example just noted for the accounts payable module.

The Request for Proposals

Once you have completed the list of system requirements, integrate it into a request for proposals (RFP) document, which is then sent to software suppliers. An RFP is a solicitation for bids from suppliers. As such, it must be sufficiently detailed to give suppliers enough information to submit bids. An RFP should include the following:

- *Deadlines*. The deadlines the company plans to follow, such as the date of a bidders conference, when the proposal is due, and when a decision will be made public.
- *Installation dates*. The expected dates for beginning and completing installation of the system.
- *Contact*. The name of and contact information for the person to contact for clarifications of the information in the RFP.
- *Scoring*. The scoring system the company will use to evaluate supplier proposals.
- *General information*. A description of what the company does, the number of people using its existing system, and current transaction volumes.
- *Requirement matrix*. This is a grid that lists each requirement for the new system. Suppliers should state whether or not their system meets each stated requirement, or clarify the changes needed to bring their system into compliance with requirements, or state that their system does not meet the requirement. You may also ask them to cross-reference each answer to their user manual, which provides evidence that the feature exists; however, this greatly increases the response work required of the supplier.
- *Supplier background*. This is a questionnaire to be completed by the supplier, describing its history, size, and financial stability. The intent of this document is to give the company an idea of the reliability of the supplier in supporting its software.
- *Pricing template*. This is a pricing schedule in which the supplier lists the price it is proposing, broken down by software price, hardware price, installation price, ongoing maintenance charges, and other fees.

Bidders Conference

If the accounting software is expected to be an expensive installation that will attract a number of bidders, schedule a bidders conference. This is a meeting in which bidders can ask the company additional questions about its RFP, or to clarify issues that may be unclear. Bidders may attend the conference in person or call in for the meeting.

In a well-run bidders conference, someone designated as the secretary records the meeting, transcribes the recording into a set of meeting minutes, and issues the minutes to those suppliers who have indicated that they intend to submit a bid. By doing so, all bidders have access to the same information regarding the RFP.

Proposal Evaluation

Once the company receives proposals from suppliers, it should go through a detailed evaluation process to determine the winning bid. This involves an examination of not only the specific capabilities of the suppliers' systems, but also an examination of the suppliers themselves. When reviewing suppliers, consider the following factors:

- *Distance*. How far away from the company is the supplier's nearest support office? Some support must be done on-site, and distance from the company impacts the response time of the supplier.
- *Similar installations*. The company does not want to be the first in its industry to install a new accounting system. It is better to be conservative and install a system that is well-proven within the industry.
- *Similar versions*. Is the supplier proposing to install a new version of its software that has not yet been installed elsewhere? Again, it may make sense to be conservative and wait for someone else to install the new version first.
- *Stability*. Has the company been in business long, and do its financial statements indicate that it is likely to be in business for a long time? This is a critical issue. The accounting system is too important to be supported by a supplier that is at risk of failure.
- *Support availability*. Does the supplier offer 24-hour support? This may not be an issue if the company only operates on a single shift.
- *Support staff qualifications*. Get a general idea of not only the qualification level of the support staff that will be working with the company, but also how many of them are available. Service levels could drop if there are only a few support staff.
- *User group*. An active user group can be extremely helpful, since members can swap information about systems. The user group does not have to be local – a robust national group is sufficient.

The supplier-level evaluation is not a minor one. If you determine that some aspect of a supplier's operations, support, or financial condition is suspect, then do not buy its accounting system, irrespective of how excellent the system itself may be.

The responses to the requirements matrix that you issued to suppliers should look something like the following sample, which is based on the requirements for the accounts payable system that were described earlier.

Sample Response to RFP Requirements Matrix

System Requirement	Response Yes	No	Comments
General Requirements			
Post to expense accounts based on preconfigured settings	×		
Accept multiple address records for the same supplier	×		
Interface with the purchasing module	×		
Payment status inquiries accessible through website		×	$10,000 module available
Automatic flagging of duplicate invoice numbers	×		
Vendor Master File Contents			
Supplier name	×		
Supplier number	×		
Supplier mailing address	×		
Supplier payment address	×		
Supplier ABA and bank account number	×		
Supplier tax identification number	×		
Form W-9 flag		×	$500 custom change
Reporting Requirements			
Accounts payable aging report	×		
Cash disbursements register	×		
Search Requirements			
Search based on supplier number, name, invoice number	×		
Drill down capability for the current and preceding year		×	Only for current year

Then aggregate the responses, using your own designations of which items were mandatory and which were useful but not necessary. Then assign a score to the aggregated totals, such as five points for all mandatory items and two points for all useful but not necessary items. The result could look like the following matrix:

Sample Scoring Matrix

Supplier Name	Positive Responses: Mandatory Items	Positive Responses: Useful Items	Total Score
Armand Software	132	48	756
Beatrice Systems	127	63	761
Chancy Brothers	110	29	608
Dolorous Designs	140	56	812

The scoring matrix is useful for comparing the systems proffered by suppliers, but it is even more important to understand exactly *which* capabilities a system does or does not have. Thus, the system provided by Armand Software in the preceding example may actually be a better fit for the company than the one offered by Beatrice Systems, even though Beatrice earned a slightly higher score. The scoring matrix can provide a general indication of which systems *do not* appear to match the company's requirements, which can lead you to drop the lowest-scoring suppliers from consideration. Thus, Chancy Brothers had by far the lowest score in the preceding example, and so could be dropped.

The preceding proposal evaluation steps are designed to introduce some rigor to the system selection process. However, some aspects of the selection are more qualitative than quantitative, such as the distance of the supplier's support staff from the company. Also, the number of points assigned to each positive response in the requirements matrix can skew the results; for example, changing the points assigned to mandatory items from five to ten points could alter the comparative results in the scoring matrix. Consequently, the team assigned to the selection process should take supplier scores into consideration, but can still select a lower-scoring system if there are sufficient judgmental factors in its favor to move it ahead of higher-scoring solutions. The pricing information provided by the suppliers will, of course, also factor into the decision.

At this point, the selection team should reduce the number of supplier solutions under consideration to no more than three systems, and then proceed with an additional round of evaluations, as described next.

Demonstrations and Reference Checks

The selection team should call in those suppliers offering the top accounting system solutions for demonstrations of their systems. These demonstrations should be scheduled by accounting module, so that the relevant user groups can attend each demonstration.

Supplier demonstrations have a strong tendency to be orchestrated in such a manner as to show off the "bells and whistles" of a system, even if those features are not needed by the company. Consequently, it can take a considerable amount of dogged determination to turn the supplier's sales team aside from its usual sales patter and instead show the user groups those features that they actually care about. One way to accomplish this is to have a prepared list of transactions that you ask the supplier's sales team to enter into their demonstration system, so that the users can see exactly how it operates.

Immediately after each supplier presentation, have the attendees complete a form on which they rate various features of the supplier's system. Aggregate the comments on these forms into a summary-level evaluation of each demonstration.

Following demonstrations, the team responsible for making the final selection may choose to drop one or more of the remaining suppliers from consideration, or may elect to proceed with the final steps of the selection process for all of the suppliers that gave demonstrations.

The next step is to obtain references from current users of supplier software. The suppliers will only forward the contact information for their best customers, so keep this in mind when contacting the customers. When you make reference calls, ask a standard set of questions, so that you can more easily compare the results of the calls. Topics to cover during these calls include:

- Level and quality of training provided by the supplier
- Quality of the user group
- Supplier responsiveness to support calls
- System downtime
- System installation issues
- Transaction volumes
- Typical screen response time
- Unexpected fees charged
- Would they buy the system again

Also, ask these references for the names of other users of the supplier's software, and contact these other users with the same questions. By contacting someone not on the supplier's preferred reference list, you may obtain considerably different answers to your questions.

If the selection team is unable to make a decision after evaluating the demonstrations and reference calls, you can also ask the (hopefully) few remaining suppliers to arrange for site visits where their software is in use by an actual customer. The selection team can travel to these locations, watch the systems in use, and make additional queries of users.

At this point, the selection team has a considerable amount of information to call upon in making its selection. By now, there should only be two or three systems left under consideration, with all other supplier proposals having been dropped along the way. Once the team makes its final selection, do not contact the losing suppliers until you are certain that a reasonable contract will be signed with the winning supplier. Occasionally, suppliers attempt to impose such onerous terms in their contracts that it may be better to instead select the second-best supplier.

Tip: The suppliers of accounting systems spend an enormous amount of time responding to requests for proposal, attending bidder conferences, conducting demonstrations, and so forth. For their efforts, the least you can do is inform them promptly if their products have been dropped from consideration. Also, if asked, tell them the reasons why they are no longer being considered; suppliers use this information to improve their products, pricing, and services.

Computer System Installation

The installation of an accounting computer system is an extremely time-consuming process. A large enterprise resources planning system (of which the accounting system is a subset) can require as much as three years to install, while the installation of a smaller system by a local enterprise may only require a few months. Clearly, there are many differences between the smaller and larger installations, so we cannot include a sample implementation sequence that will be broadly applicable. Instead, we include a number of principles to follow in the pursuit of a clean installation. They are:

- *Project manager*. There must be a full-time person in charge of the implementation. This person is responsible for tracking the progress of the various implementation tasks and ensuring that sufficient resources have been assigned to the project.
- *Resources*. A common failing of an accounting system installation is to not provide sufficient staff time or funding to complete it in a timely manner. Instead, employees are asked to fit additional time into their existing work schedules to somehow complete the installation. The inevitable result is a prolonged installation that is at risk of failure.
- *Time duration*. A basic rule of any computer system installation is that the longer it takes to install, the more issues will arise that will cause it to fail. Consequently, it is much better to assign what may appear to be an excessive amount of resources in order to achieve a very fast system installation.
- *Core modules*. If you have a broad-ranging accounting system in place already that has interfaces into many other computer systems throughout the company, it will be extremely difficult to create new interfaces to all of these systems in a timely manner, and then convert everyone to the new system at the same time. Instead, it is easier and less risky (though more time-consuming) to install the core accounting modules first, and create customized interfaces from all the remaining old systems into these new modules, and then gradually roll out the new system with additional modules that will also require interfaces into the decreasing number of old systems.
- *Data conversion*. You never want to manually re-enter information from the old system into the new system, since it is both time-consuming and likely to result in errors. Instead, create a conversion routine that converts the records in every file in the old system into the record format used by the new system. A few standardized data conversion systems are available that convert records from certain popular accounting systems, but this is not the case in most situations.
- *Testing*. When you have converted data into the new record format, test it thoroughly to ensure that information is being placed in the correct fields in the new system. Otherwise, the data in the new system will require extensive cleaning, probably over a number of months.
- *Procedures*. Create procedures that show users how to create transactions in the new system.
- *Training*. Train those employees who will use the new system in how to use it. Do so just before the conversion date to the new system, so that they will still remember their training. Conducting training even a few weeks prior to

the conversion date is too early, since memory retention is greatly reduced even a few days after training.

Without engaging in a detailed discussion of the exact steps required to implement an accounting computer system, be prepared to complete the implementation in roughly the sequence described here:

1. *Configuration.* The software consultants provided by the software supplier will schedule a number of meetings with system users to determine how to configure the system. This may involve several hundred decisions for flags that must be set in the software.
2. *Entities.* The user team must decide upon the number of operational entities for which it wants to collect information. This impacts the chart of accounts.
3. *Chart of accounts.* The user team must create a chart of accounts and account code structure that works best for accumulating data in the new system.
4. *Subledgers.* The user team should determine which subledgers it wants. A subledger accumulates detailed transaction information away from the general ledger, with only summary totals being posted to the general ledger.
5. *Report design.* The software supplier's team will work with users to create a core set of reports that can be printed from the new system. Additional, lesser-used reports will probably be created at a later date.
6. *Data conversion.* The software supplier's team will create data conversion routines that shift the data in the old system's records into the format of the records used by the new system. There may be a large number of files to convert, so this step may require a lengthy period of time.
7. *Data testing.* The combined teams review all data converted from the old system to see if any data is missing or placed in the wrong fields, and revise the data conversion routines to correct any problems found.
8. *Stress testing.* The software supplier's team uses a variety of techniques to stress test the new system, seeing how it reacts to a simulation of large numbers of users simultaneously accessing the system at the same time.
9. *Training.* All frequent users of the old system are trained in the use of those modules they are expected to use in the new system.
10. *Go live.* Officially shut down access to the old system and have employees start using the new system. Have the entire installation team on hand for the first few days of operations with the new system, to ensure that problems are dealt with promptly.
11. *Repeat.* If the initial installation was only for a few system modules, then reiterate the process for each module added at a later date.

Tip: Do not attempt an excessive amount of reconfiguration of the new system to match your existing process flow. Doing so will lengthen the installation period, and may also render the new system so ineffective that it no longer operates as planned. In short, if the supplier's project manager recommends against a proposed modification, it is best to follow his or her advice.

If you are installing a larger accounting system, this will almost certainly call for the services of an implementation team provided by the software supplier. You should ensure that the company provides sufficient staff to complete all tasks assigned to it by the supplier. Otherwise, the implementation process will extend beyond the supplier's original time estimate, which may result in the supplier charging more fees for the extra hours worked by its implementation team.

Summary

This chapter has made it clear that an accounting system selection and installation is a massive and prolonged undertaking. Because of the cost and effort required to successfully complete an installation, think long and hard about acquiring a new system at all. In many cases, it may become apparent that there is a significant risk to the company of making such a large investment. Instead, you may want to consider engaging in a variety of other improvement projects first that have better returns on investment, and delaying the acquisition of an accounting computer system until a later date. In short, if you were to categorize the cost and benefit of the various improvement projects available to the accounting department, the cost of this system may force it well down in the rankings.

If you elect to proceed with the acquisition of a new accounting system, buy one that is more than the company currently needs. By doing so, the new system will be able to service its needs for a number of years, making it less likely that the new system will, in turn, have to be replaced in the near future. In short, you want to install new accounting systems as infrequently as possible, so buy an unusually robust system.

Glossary

A

Accelerated filer. A company having an aggregate market value owned by investors who are not affiliated with the company of less than $700 million, but more than $75 million.

ACH. ACH is an electronic network for the processing of both debit and credit transactions within the United States and Canada.

Allowance for doubtful accounts. A reserve for bad debts that offsets the accounts receivable balance on the balance sheet.

B

Balance sheet. A report that summarizes all of an entity's assets, liabilities, and equity accounts as of a given point in time. It is also known as the statement of financial position.

Bank reconciliation. A comparison of the cash position recorded on an entity's books and the position noted on the records of its bank, usually resulting in some changes to the entity's book balance to account for transactions that are recorded on the bank's records but not the entity's.

Bill of materials. A record of the materials used to construct a product. It can include raw materials, sub-assemblies, and supplies, as well as an estimate of the amount of scrap that will be created during the manufacture of the product.

Borrowing base. The ending balance of a company's accounts receivable and inventory, multiplied by the allowable percentage of each one against which the business is allowed to borrow by its lender.

Bottleneck analysis. A capital proposal evaluation technique that is based on the impact on throughput of a fixed asset acquisition.

C

Capital expenditure. A payment made to acquire or upgrade an asset. It is recorded as a fixed asset, rather than being charged at once to expense.

Cash equivalent. A short-term, very liquid investment that is easily convertible into a known amount of cash, and which is so near its maturity that it presents an insignificant risk of a change in value because of changes in interest rates.

Chart of accounts. A listing of all the accounts used in the general ledger, usually listed in order by account number.

Chief operating decision maker. A person who is responsible for making decisions about resource allocations to the segments of a business, and for evaluating those segments.

Collateral. An asset that a borrower has pledged as security for a loan. The lender has the legal right to seize the asset if the borrower is unable to pay back the loan by an agreed date.

Collection effectiveness index. A comparison of the amount of receivables collected to the amount of receivables available for collection. This metric reveals the ability of the collections staff to collect overdue receivables.

Common size balance sheet. A balance sheet that includes a column noting the financial information as a percentage of the total assets (for asset line items) or as a percentage of total liabilities and shareholders' equity (for liability or shareholders' equity line items).

Comparative balance sheet. A balance sheet that presents side-by-side information about an entity's assets, liabilities, and shareholders' equity as of multiple points in time.

Condensed income statement. An income statement with many of the usual line items condensed down into a few lines.

Contribution margin income statement. An income statement in which all variable expenses are deducted from sales to arrive at a contribution margin, from which all fixed expenses are then subtracted to arrive at the net profit or loss for the period.

Cost pool. A grouping of individual costs, typically by department or service center. Cost allocations are then made from the cost pool. For example, the cost of a maintenance department is accumulated in a cost pool and then allocated to those departments using its services.

Credit risk. The risk of loss by a business that has extended credit to another party, if that other party does not pay the specified amount within the appointed time period.

Cycle counting. The process of counting a small proportion of the total inventory on a daily basis, adjusting the inventory records for errors found, and investigating the causes of those errors.

D

Days sales outstanding. The number of days required to collect the average account receivable. This is calculated as average accounts receivable divided by the average sales per day.

Deposit in transit. Cash and/or checks that have been received and recorded by an entity, but which have not yet been recorded in the records of the bank where the entity deposits the funds.

Depreciation. The gradual and systematic charging to expense of a fixed asset's cost over its expected useful life.

Direct costs. Costs that can be clearly associated with specific activities or products.

Direct method. A method of presentation for the statement of cash flows that presents specific cash flows associated with items that affect cash flow.

Direct write off method. The practice of only charging customer invoices to bad debt expense when specific invoices are identified as unlikely to be paid.

Discount rate. The interest rate used to discount a stream of cash flows to their present value. It may, for example, be based on a company's cost of capital or the current market rate.

Discrete view. The assumption that the results reported for a specific interim period are not associated with the revenues and expenses arising during other reporting periods within a fiscal year.

E

Earnings per share. A company's net income divided by the weighted-average number of shares outstanding. This calculation is subject to a number of additional factors involving preferred shares, convertible instruments, and dividends.

F

First in, first out method. A method of inventory valuation that operates under the assumption that the first goods purchased are also the first goods sold.

FOB destination. A contraction of the term "Free on Board Destination." It means that the buyer takes delivery of the goods being shipped to it by a supplier once the goods arrive at the buyer's receiving dock.

FOB shipping point. A contraction of the term "Free on Board Shipping Point." It means that the buyer takes delivery of goods being shipped to it by a supplier once the goods leave the supplier's shipping dock.

Form 10-K. A document that a publicly-held company must file with the Securities and Exchange Commission once a year, detailing its financial results for the preceding year.

Form 10-Q. A document that a publicly-held company must file with the Securities and Exchange Commission every quarter, detailing its financial results for the preceding quarter and the year-to-date.

G

General ledger. The master set of accounts that summarize all transactions occurring within an entity.

Generally Accepted Accounting Principles. A set of authoritative accounting standards issued by several standard-setting bodies, which entities should follow in preparing their financial statements.

Gross margin. Revenues less the cost of goods sold.

I

Indirect method. A method of presentation for the statement of cash flows that begins with net income or loss, and then adds or subtracts non-cash revenue and expense items to derive cash flows.

Income statement. A financial report that summarizes an entity's revenue, cost of goods sold, gross margin, other expenses, taxes, and net income or loss. The income statement shows an entity's financial results over a specific time period, usually a month, quarter, or year.

Intangible asset. A non-physical asset having a useful life greater than one year. Examples of intangible assets are trademarks, patents, and non-competition agreements.

Integral view. The concept that results reported in interim financial statements are an integral part of the full-year financial results.

Interest capitalization. The inclusion of any interest expense directly related to the construction of a fixed asset in the cost of that fixed asset.

International Financial Reporting Standards. A set of authoritative standards set by the International Accounting Standards Board, which an entity must comply with if it wishes to create financial statements that are accepted in those countries mandating the use of IFRS.

Item master. A record that lists the name, description, unit of measure, weight, dimensions, ordering quantity, and other key information for a component part.

L

Large accelerated filer. A company having an aggregate market value owned by investors who are not affiliated with the company of a minimum of $700 million.

Last in, first out method. A method of inventory valuation that operates under the assumption that the last goods purchased are the first goods sold.

Lifting fee. The transaction fee charged to the recipient of a wire transfer, which the recipient's bank imposes for handling the transaction. The term also applies to foreign bank processing fees, which may be applied to a variety of other financial transactions besides a wire transfer.

Lockbox. A bank-operated mailbox to which customers send payments, and from which the bank processes and deposits payments on behalf of the company.

Lower of cost or market. A rule requiring you to record the cost of inventory at the lower of its cost or the current market price.

M

Matching principle. The concept of recording the expenses related to revenue in the same accounting period when you record the revenue.

Multi-period income statement. An income statement that presents the financial results of a business for several periods in a side-by-side format.

Multi-step income statement. An income statement that uses multiple subtotals to aggregate such information as the gross margin, operating expenses, and other income.

N

Net operating loss carryforward. A loss experienced in an earlier period that could not be completely offset against prior-period profits. This residual loss can be carried forward for up to 20 years, during which time it can be offset against any reported taxable income.

Net present value analysis. A capital analysis proposal that is based on the discounted cash flows associated with a fixed asset purchase proposal.

Nexus. The concept that a business is subject to local government taxation if it has a place of business in a location, or uses its own vehicles to transport goods to customers there, or has employees situated or living there.

Non-trade receivables. Amounts due for payment that are not related to the normal customer invoices for merchandise shipped or services performed.

Not sufficient funds. Refers to a check that was not honored by the bank of the entity issuing the check, on the grounds that the entity's bank account does not contain sufficient funds.

O

Other comprehensive income. A statement that contains all changes not permitted in the main part of the income statement. These items include unrealized gains and losses on available-for-sale securities, cash flow hedge gains and losses, and foreign currency translation adjustments.

Outstanding check. A check payment that has been recorded by the issuing entity, but which has not yet cleared its bank account as a deduction from cash.

P

Payback method. A capital budgeting evaluation proposal that is based on the speed of repayment of the initial investment.

Payment factory. A centralized and highly automated accounts payable processing group.

Payroll cycle. The length of time between payrolls. Thus, if a business pays its employees every Friday, that is a one-week payroll cycle.

Periodic inventory system. An inventory calculation method under which you only update the ending inventory balance when you conduct a physical inventory count.

Perpetual inventory system. The continual updating of inventory records to account for additions to and subtractions from inventory.

Petty cash. A small amount of cash kept on hand in a business to pay for incidental expenses.

Posting. The process of copying either summary-level or detailed entries in an accounting journal into the general ledger. Posting is needed in order to have a complete record of all accounting transactions in the general ledger.

Procurement card. A credit card used by employees to make purchases that are the liability of their employer.

R

Remote deposit capture. The use of a check scanner to deposit checks from a remote location.

Retail inventory method. An inventory valuation method used by retailers to estimate their ending inventory balances. It is based on the relationship between the cost of merchandise and its retail price.

Reversing entry. A journal entry made at the beginning of an accounting period, which reverses selected entries made in the immediately preceding accounting period. A reversing entry is typically used in situations when either revenue or expenses were accrued in the preceding period, and you do not want the accruals to remain in the accounting system for another period.

S

Segment reporting. A requirement to report the results of the operating segments of a publicly-held company.

Single-step income statement. An income statement format that contains a single subtotal for all revenue line items and a single subtotal for all expense line items.

Standard costing. An inventory valuation method that assigns a standard cost to each item in stock, and then tracks any variances between standard and actual costs.

Statement of cash flows. An element of the financial statements that contains information about the flows of cash into and out of a company.

Statement of retained earnings. An element of the financial statements that reconciles changes in the equity accounts of a business.

Step cost. A cost that does not change steadily, but rather at discrete points. Thus, it is a fixed cost within certain boundaries, outside of which it will change.

Suspense account. An account in the general ledger that is used to temporarily store any transactions for which there is some uncertainty about the account in which they should be recorded.

T

Three-way matching. The verification of a supplier invoice by comparing it to an authorizing purchase order and evidence of receipt.

Throughput. Revenues minus totally variable expenses. Totally variable expenses are usually just the cost of materials, since direct labor does not typically vary directly with sales.

Trade receivables. Amounts billed by a business to its customers when it delivers goods or services to them in the ordinary course of business. These billings are typically documented on formal invoices.

Trial balance. A report listing the ending debit and credit balances in all accounts as of the date of the report.

U

Use tax. The same as sales tax, except that the party remitting the tax to the applicable government entity is the buyer of taxable goods or services, rather than the seller.

W

Weighted average method. A method of valuing ending inventory and the cost of goods sold, based on the average cost of materials in inventory.

Index

Made in the USA
Monee, IL
09 August 2020